Sable Island Shipwrecks

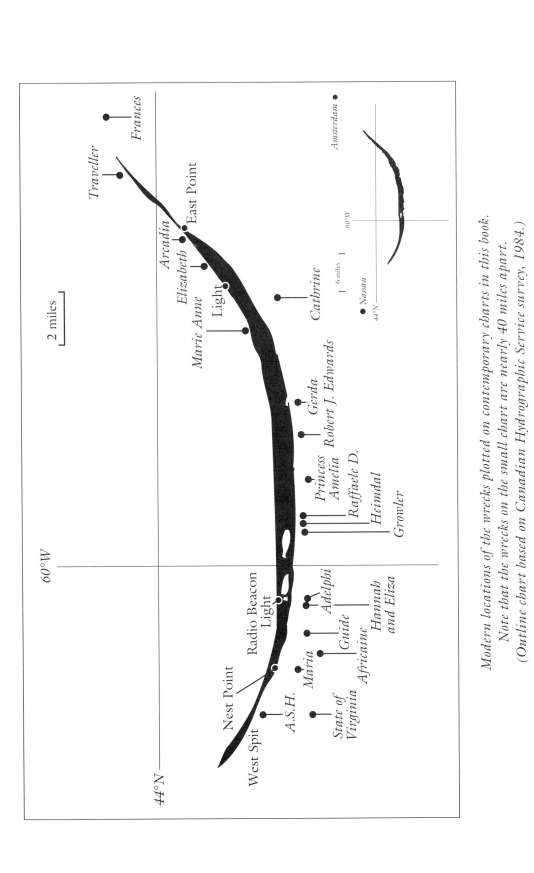

2 miles

60°W

44°N

West Spit
A.S.H.
Nest Point
Radio Beacon
Light
Maria
State of
Virginia
Guide
Adelphi
Africaine
Hannah
and Eliza
Princess
Amelia
Raffaele D.
Heimdal
Growler
Gerda
Robert J. Edwards
Marie Anne
Light
Elizabeth
Arcadia
East Point
Cathrine
Traveller
Frances

6 miles
60°W
44°N
Nassau
Amsterdam

Modern locations of the wrecks plotted on contemporary charts in this book.
Note that the wrecks on the small chart are nearly 40 miles apart.
(Outline chart based on Canadian Hydrographic Service survey, 1984.)

Sable Island Shipwrecks

Disaster and Survival at the North Atlantic Graveyard

Lyall Campbell

NIMBUS
PUBLISHING

Nimbus Publishing Limited
PO Box 9166
Halifax, NS B3K 5M8
(902) 455-4286

Design: Arthur B. Carter, Halifax
Printed and bound in Canada

Canadian Cataloguing in Publication Data
Campbell, Lyall.
Sable Island shipwrecks
Includes bibliographical references.
ISBN 1-55109-096-1

1. Shipwrecks—Nova Scotia—Sable Island—History.
2. Sable Island (N.S.)—History. I. Title.
FC2345.S23Z68 1994   917.16'99   C94-950199-9
F1039.S13C36 1994

In the quotations, the original spellings (and misspellings) and other textual oddities have been retained for authenticity. A notable exception is the tailed S of manuscripts, which was printed as an f with only half the crossbar.

Credits
Title page, pp. 92, 109, 113, 114, 157 and 158 *Harpers Monthly, Shribner's Magazine* and *Century Magazine*
p.vii *Voyages of Elizabethan Seaman to America* (Clarendon Press), second edition (Oxford, 1900)
p.5 Peter J. French, *John Dee, The World of an Elizabethan Magus*, (Routledge & Kegan Paul), (London, 1972)
p.8 Hakluytus Posthumus or Purchas His Pilgrimes (Hakluyt Society Publications, Extra Series), vol. xiii (Glasgow, 1906)
pp.16, 48, 51, 83, 146, I55, 161, 167 Public Archives of Nova Scotia
p.43 Nova Scotia Leglislative Library
pp.54 and 62 Public Archives of Canada
p.86 Dr. Willard Goff
pp.108 and 142 Thomas E. Appleton, *Usque ad Mare. A History of the Canadian Coast Guard and Marine Services* (Ottawa: Department of Transport, 1968)
pp.104, 111, 144, 147, 168, and 169 Maritime Museum of the Atlantic
p. 152 *Canadian Geographic Journal* 1932

Contents

Preface

This book is by no means a history of Sable Island shipwrecks or of the Sable lifesaving service. It is a collection of accounts of selected wrecks in the context of the evolution of Sable Island. The wrecks have been chosen, from a documented compilation of nearly three hundred lost vessels, for their historical import and for the inherent appeal of their stories. Also a factor, as with all written history, was the amount of information available. A caution for the reader: while this selection of shipwrecks typifies losses at the old Graveyard of the Atlantic, it magnifies the number of castaways and of deaths in the average known Sable disaster.

The writing aims to appeal to the general reader rather than the scholar, but every fact or judgement may be documented. From the most gruesome disaster to the weather, the descriptions derive from contemporary accounts, usually eyewitness reports. The tragedy, drama, heroism, mystery are a natural part of Sable Island's past. The style of the book eschews the overkill of fictional techniques like invented dialogue and other unfounded imaginings that mar so much Sable writing. On the other hand, actual documentation has been kept to a minimum and is presented as unobtrusively as possible. It represents a compromise between conflicting demands: of readers who find the trappings of scholarship annoying (all those raised numbers in the text!); of readers who want to know the sources of knowledge; and of authors who look for deserved credit for the use of their works.

The sketch maps showing the different locations of Sable Island and its shipwrecks through time are based on the author's own interpretation of the data. They differ in some details, presumably on the side of greater accuracy, from all previous maps of the kind.

Some readers may see the whole book as an extended statement of the value of resident lifesavers at Sable Island. Some, those perceptive souls who divine an author's secret hopes, will reflect upon what they have read. They will perhaps conclude that the unique "Sable Island Establishment" and the people who laboured in its service have been denied their rightful place in history.

*Sir Humphrey Gilbert, the man responsible for the first
known shipwreck at Sable Island.*

Chapter One

A Rash Nobleman, A Cool Pirate, and an Unsolved Mystery

For the English-speaking, or English-reading, public the printed work of Richard Hakluyt led to the discovery of Sable Island. Sable emerged from the mists of the unknown as a figure in a tragic tale of an Elizabethan nobleman, the last voyage of Sir Humphrey Gilbert. The way Hakluyt presented the story gave no hint that he foresaw how Sable Island would overshadow his great man in the history of the New World. Yet hindsight suggests that Hakluyt unwittingly began what was to become the Sable Island mystique. And today the Hakluyt version gives rise to a genuine historical mystery.

Richard Hakluyt was the greatest authority on exploration and discovery of the Elizabethan Age. He compiled an unrivalled collection of accounts of voyages and skilfully selected and edited the most inspiring for publication. He also played an active part in the planning of some ventures. One such was the 1583 voyage of Sir Humphrey Gilbert.

Gilbert was both literally and figuratively a Renaissance man. He was well educated and a courtier, soldier, sailor, author—a man of wide interests and large ambition. He was also arrogant and given to blind rages. Although some might see these traits as flaws in a leader, Gilbert himself had no doubts about his capacity. He sought out the greatest challenges, and in 1583 the challenge that appealed to him most was the founding of a settlement in North America.

Gilbert set his sights on the more northerly part of the New World. He developed an elaborate plan for its conquest. He would cross the North Atlantic in command of a force large enough to take possession of the territory for England. He would sail all the way down the coast from Newfoundland to the River of Norumbega (Narragansett Bay, Rhode Island); here he would found a settlement, unless he sighted a location along the way that was too attractive to resist.

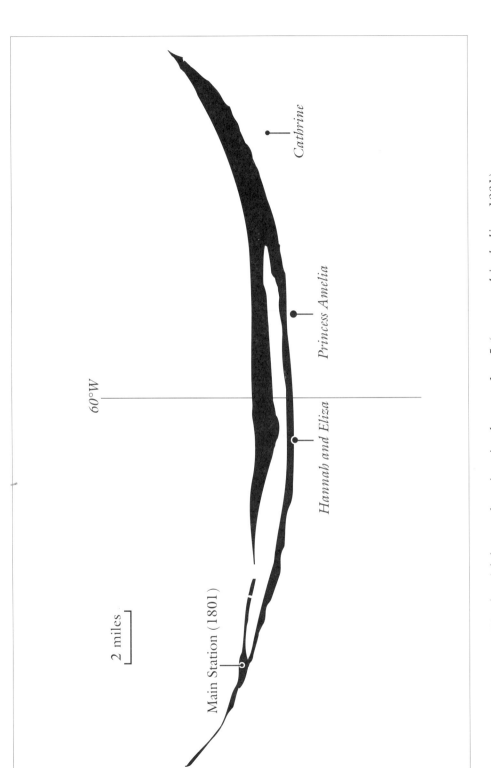

2 miles

Main Station (1801)

60°W

Hannah and Eliza

Princess Amelia

Cathrine

Wrecks with known locations in chapters 1 to 5 (up to and including 1801).
(Outline chart based on Des Barres survey, 1766–67.)

Critics might say that Sir Humphrey was a less than ideal choice to lead such an expedition. A first class mariner he was not; and his volatile nature might transform courage and confidence into reckless presumption. Gilbert, however, had more than enough support to override any naysayers. His backers included his brother Sir John Gilbert and other noble cronies, and his young half-brother Walter Raleigh, destined for fame in his own right. As a publicity agent for his venture, Gilbert had Hakluyt. Another expert on the geography of the New World, Dr. John Dee, provided an authoritative map that "assembled all the knowledge at that time available to Englishmen." As useful as was all of this support, it was of little value without the one thing needful: the favour of the queen. Queen Elizabeth looked on both Gilbert and his voyage with approval, but she showed concern about the two in combination. When the expedition was nearly ready to depart, she asked Gilbert to stay behind because he was "a man noted of not good happ by sea." This may have been a polite way of saying that she had doubts about his seamanship. Whatever her concerns, she relented and allowed Sir Humphrey to sail.

He departed from Plymouth with a fleet of five vessels. Before they cleared the Channel, the largest, the 200-ton bark *Raleigh*, commanded by Gilbert's half-brother, developed problems that forced it to turn back. The fleet was reduced to four: the *Delight*, 120 tons, Capt. William Winter, who was also part-owner along with Sir John Gilbert; the *Golden Hind*, 40 tons, owned and commanded by Edward Hayes; the *Swallow*, 40 tons, Capt. Maurice Browne; and the frigate *Squirrel*, 8 or 10 tons, Capt. William Andrewes, owned by Sir Humphrey. The *Delight* was the flagship or "Admirall," and so carried Gilbert, "General" of the expedition.

One of the *Swallow*'s company was an unlikely passenger called Stephanus Parmenius, a young Hungarian poet. He had joined the voyage as a result of his friendship with Richard Hakluyt. Parmenius had helped Hakluyt at Oxford with research and translations of his book, and Hakluyt had introduced him to Gilbert. Sir Humphrey accepted Parmenius for the voyage only as a last-minute replacement for Hakluyt, who had actually contemplated sailing with Gilbert. A diplomatic appointment in France with the chance to further his geographical knowledge tempted Hakluyt back to his true calling.

If Hakluyt had joined Gilbert's company of adventurers, he might have written an eyewitness account of the voyage. On the other hand, he is more likely to have met the fate of Parmenius or Gilbert. By staying behind when Sir Humphrey sailed, Hakluyt survived to publish his great *Principal Navigations*. In it he included his edited version of the description of the voyage by Capt. Edward Hayes. This account is both the chief authority for Sir Humphrey Gilbert's last great adventure and a recognized classic of the genre.

After Gilbert's four ships left the Channel, the ill luck that Queen Elizabeth feared dogged the voyage. North Atlantic storms and contrary winds prolonged the crossing, and as the squadron approached Newfoundland, fog dispersed the ships. The seamen in the *Swallow* used this time on their own to nasty advantage.

The long passage had used up most of the provisions on board the *Swallow*. Sighting a bark homeward bound from the Newfoundland fishery, the crew asked Captain Browne to allow them to board it to obtain food and clothing. Browne granted the request, charging his men "to deale favorably." The captain himself, according to Hayes, was "very honest and religious." Most of his crew, however, were men of a different stamp, "such as had bene by us surprised upon the narrow seas of England, being pirats." On boarding the bark, they reverted to type. They simply took what they wanted: food, clothing, sails, and other ship's materials. In search of hidden riches, they resorted to torture. In the end, they left the bark's crew destitute, some seven hundred leagues from home. The *Swallow* sailed onward to St. John's, where it joined the rest of Gilbert's fleet.

Two days later, on 5 August 1583, Sir Humphrey Gilbert took possession of Newfoundland, plus the land 200 leagues to north and south, in the name of Queen Elizabeth. He imposed his authority on the merchants and fishermen then in harbour. He was less effective in controlling his own men.

The privations of the seven-week journey from England had taken their toll. Many men had died, others were too sick to go on, and some simply wanted out of the expedition. Deserters hid in the woods to wait for a chance to board one of the ships that were frequently departing for home. Gilbert decided to send the *Swallow* back to England with the sick. The fleet was now reduced to three.

In dispatching the *Swallow*, Gilbert did not get rid of the crew. He appointed Maurice Browne captain of the flagship *Delight* and transferred Browne's former crew along with him. Among the men already in the *Delight* was the master Richard Clarke (or Clerke), who was the chief navigator for the expedition. Like the incoming crew, Clarke had piracy in his past. The changes boded ill for the future. Gilbert's most fateful decision, however, was more fundamental: he changed the plan of the voyage.

When Sir Humphrey left England, he had intended to carry out his grand scheme. He would follow the well-known track of the Newfoundland fishing fleet to the Banks, then sail to Cape Breton and on down the coast to what is now New England; here he would carve up the territory as grants to wealthy Englishmen for large estates.

According to Hayes, a providential meeting in St. John's changed Gilbert's mind. Among the fishermen was a Portuguese who claimed to have been at Sable Island thirty years earlier when his people landed cattle and pigs, which had since multiplied. He recommended that Gilbert visit the

John Dee, the intellectual promoter of Elizabethan exploration, who made a map for Sir Humphrey Gilbert that showed the location of Sable Island.

island and stock up on fresh meat. The best modern authorities have concluded that Gilbert still felt duty-bound to go to New England to claim land for his backers but that he decided to sail to Sable Island first. From St. John's he would follow a course that the obliging Portuguese had worked out.

∽∽∽

On 22 August 1583 Gilbert and his remaining adventurers left Newfoundland and headed for Sable Island. The subsequent courses published by Hakluyt have led to conflicting conclusions about their route. Hayes says that by Tuesday 27 August the ships were at 44°N. Gilbert's vessel, the *Squirrel*, took soundings and found white sand at thirty-five fathoms. From this point, the ships followed a steady course to south and west until Wednesday night, when "the wind came South." An argument then arose as to their future course. Both William Cox, master or navigator on Hayes's *Golden Hind*, and Clarke on the *Delight* disagreed with Gilbert. Naturally Sir Humphrey's opinion prevailed; he insisted on a change of course to westnorthwest. The three ships sailed in this direction all night, the *Delight* in the lead. At first the weather was fair but with signs of an approaching storm, which struck before daylight: "the wind rose, and blew vehemently at South and by East, bringing withal raine, and thicke mist, so that we could not see a cable length before us."

On the *Golden Hind* Cox cried out that he saw land. Soundings taken at once revealed "shoale and deepe in every three or foure shippes length." Nobody else saw land, and Hayes later concluded that Cox had mistaken the sea breaking white for white cliffs. The ships were nonetheless in peril. Most threatened was the *Delight*, being largest and farthest into the danger zone. Hayes signalled for it to cast about to seaward, but he was too late. The flagship crew knew nothing of their danger until they felt the vessel strike. Hayes witnessed the destruction, "her sterne and hinder partes beaten in pieces."

The *Golden Hind* and *Squirrel* turned tail and ran. They headed eastsoutheast bearing to the south "even for our lives into the windes eye, because that way caried us to the seaward." All the while, the *Hind* sounded desperately: seven fathoms, five, four and less; then deeper, and again four, three—the whole time "the sea going mightily and high." At last both ships made it "in some despaire, to sea roome enough." While fleeing, the crews tried to spot survivors of the wreck. Afterward they beat up and down, crisscrossing the sea, "as neere unto the wracke as was possible for us." But their rescue efforts were "all in vaine, sith God had determined their ruine," says Hayes. A more pragmatic explanation concerns the weather and the caution of the would-be rescuers. Because of poor visibility and high winds, they kept well clear of the wreck site. It lay to the north, their lee side, in an area that they now knew to be "full of flats and dangers." They feared a sudden increase in the south winds to gale force or stronger that would drive them to the same doom as their lost comrades.

For a brief time they thought the weather might clear and reveal land, which they assumed was nearby because of the soundings: between fifty and forty fathoms "and lesse." At last they faced the more likely prospect that, as time went on this late in the season, the weather would only worsen.

In truth, the loss of the *Delight* had demoralized the survivors. Aside from the deaths "to the number almost of a hundreth soules," the disaster cost them their supply ship, and already "provisions waxed scant." The seamen in the tiny *Squirrel* were on short allowance, and their clothing was thin and ragged. They signalled their plight by gestures to their mates on the *Hind*, who at first sympathized, then joined in their pleas to head for home. Sir Humphrey himself discerned in the Jack Tars "no want of good will, but of meanes fit to performe." For reasons of his own he, too, was ready to give up the voyage. He had lost the desire to explore the region farther west and southward. Against the preference of Hayes and Cox, two days after the shipwreck Gilbert granted the men's wishes and turned the vessels homeward.

The mariners had hardly changed course for England when they sighted a strange apparition. Between them and the assumed land passed "a very lion to our seeming." It was not swimming like a fish, not leaping out and diving under the water like the dolphin and porpoise or moving like a beast that paddled with its feet,

> but rather sliding upon the water with his whole body (excepting the legs) in sight,...confidently shewing himselfe above water without hiding: Norwithstanding, we presented our selves in open view and gesture to amase him, as all creatures will be commonly at a sudden gaze and sight of men. Thus he passed along turning his head to and fro, yawning and gaping wide, with ougly demonstration of long teeth, and glaring eies, and to bidde us a farewell (comming right against the Hinde) he sent forth a horrible voyce, roaring or bellowing as doeth a lion.

All wondered at this phenomenon, "to see a lion in the Ocean sea, or fish in shape of a lion."

A high wind made for rough seas, but it was also fair for the return passage. In two days the two vessels covered the same distance as they had in a week or more on the outward journey and were within sight of Cape Race. The rest of the voyage was remarkable for one of the best-known incidents in the history of exploration. Sir Humphrey Gilbert ignored Hayes's warning that the *Squirrel* was over-gunned and unsafe. He remained aboard the tiny frigate until it foundered in heavy seas north of the Azores, where Gilbert met a hero's death. His last words as recorded by Hayes were: "We are as neere to heaven by sea as by land." Edward Hayes sailed on to Falmouth, arriving on 22 September, the only captain to complete the luckless voyage to Sable Island.

*A walrus, or morse, as pictured for the British public
in the early seventeenth century.*

When Capt. Hayes reported the loss of the *Delight*, he said that all hands went down with the ship. (Hakluyt's version, not published until 1589, includes a story of survivors that Hayes could not have known until months afterward.) Hayes reported in good faith but he was wrong. The man who gave the lie to Hayes was Richard Clarke. Clarke's version of the incident reveals that he was the unlikely hero of Gilbert's Sable Island misadventure.

By 1583 Clarke had much in common with men like Drake and Hawkins, seadogs of the romanticized Elizabethan Age. As captain of a vessel, he had raided foreign shipping during the years of undeclared war on England's rivals. Only the year before, he had attacked Portuguese fishermen in Newfoundland, plundered ships and assaulted men, stopping just short of murder. Clarke claimed to have a royal commission justifying his conduct. Since he did not, he and his crew were in law pirates. As we know, a technicality like that did not make him unfit for service with Sir Humphrey Gilbert. On

8

the contrary, his known experience in Newfoundland waters and his navigational skill qualified him for chief navigator of the expedition.

That Gilbert would make use of Clarke's expertise did not mean that he would always accede to it. The loss of the *Delight* is a case in point. According to Clarke, in the discussion about the course to be sailed on that fatal night, he favoured an opposite course to Gilbert's. Westnorthwest was the path of danger, he said, for Sable Island lay only fifteen leagues away, the wind was south, and night near at hand. The "Generall" said Clarke's reckoning was wrong and, invoking the name of the queen, overruled him. The *Delight* held to Gilbert's chosen course until about 7:00 A.M. when it struck bottom. What followed was a triumph of irony.

As the sands gripped the hull and the seas poured over the decks, smashing all in their path, luck—and his reputation—saved Richard Clarke. His good fortune stemmed from an incident the day before. A soldier on the *Delight* had shot some wildfowl, and some of the ship's company hoisted out a boat to recover the game. When the seamen returned to the ship, the weather being calm, they neglected to hoist the boat aboard. With typical carelessness, they left it trailing in the ship's wake. The one-and-a-half-ton boat was still in the water when the *Delight* struck the sandbar. As the ship broke up, some of the crew who could swim recovered it. Amid the turmoil, they hauled as many shipmates as possible from the water. Meanwhile they kept an eye out for the captain or the master, whose expertise and leadership might prove the means of their survival. Spotting Clarke, they rescued him.

Sixteen men escaped from the wreck; in the boat with them was "one oare and nothing els." For two days and nights the survivors, in Clarke's words, "looked every moment of an houre when the Sea would eate them up, the boate being so little and so many men in her, and so foule weather." They used the single oar as best they could to maintain the boat's balance and direct the bow but in general "went even as the Sea would drive us." Then they faced the classic lifeboat problem: Since it seemed likely that all in the overladen boat might die, should some be sacrificed to give the others a better chance? One man suggested that they draw lots and cast overboard those who drew the four shortest. Clarke, as an officer and their navigator, would be exempted from the draw. In his role of leader, Clarke replied to the suggestion, "saying, no, we will live and die together."

Clarke told the others that he knew where in the sea they were and that he hoped to reach land—shrewdly unspecified—in two or three days. Three days later, with no land in sight, two men died, one the man who had suggested drawing lots. The rest were fading fast. Their only sustenance for five days had been "the weedes that swamme in the Sea, and salt water to drinke," including their own urine. The weather was "so foule" that they only saw the sun once and the stars only one night. The next day, weak in body and spirit, the men were ready to welcome death. Clarke promised they would reach land on the morrow, the seventh day since the wreck. The following day, they made a landfall and in the afternoon set foot on the south coast of Newfoundland. Clarke knew how lucky they were, for the wind blew from the southward for a week. "If the wind had in the meane time shifted upon any other point, wee had never come to land."

Living off the land, the castaways made their way westward. At last they found what they sought: a French Basque whaler homeward bound from its annual voyage to the Gulf of St. Lawrence. The French captain agreed to take them to Europe. From the continent Clarke and his thirteen comrades made their way back home "toward the end of the year." Only then did England learn that not all on the *Delight* had perished and, nearly four months after the return of Hayes, hear Clarke's version of the disaster.

The diligent Hakluyt carefully preserved Clarke's narrative of the wreck and its aftermath and published it along with Hayes's account of Gilbert's voyage. all subsequent descriptions of the loss of the *Delight* have been based directly or indirectly on Hakluyt's work. The oft-repeated tale has led to questions, and some answers, perhaps not enough of either, especially in regard to Sable Island.

The most important question concerns the location of the wreck. Hayes provided two logs of the courses from Newfoundland to the scene of the disaster, one by navigator Cox, the other by Cox's assistant John Paul. These courses, laid down by dead reckoning, are imprecise; they also contradict one another. As a result, experts have held different opinions about the *Delight*'s final stop, some doubting that the ship ever reached Sable Island. The best modern opinions favour Sable.

The leading authority on English voyages of that era, David Quinn, concluded with his usual caution that the *Delight* probably passed north of the island and struck "the shoal (the West Bar) which stretches out to the west behind the island." The American expert on European voyages of discovery, Samuel Eliot Morison, himself an experienced navigator, was more emphatic:

> There can be no doubt that the *Delight* came to grief on Sable
> Island. Hayes prints her log from Cape Race, kept by her master's
> mate John Paul and which, laid down on a chart, leads directly to
> the north end of Sable Island.

Since the east end of Sable Island stretches much farther north than the west, Morison presumably meant that the ship struck the northeast bar.

Other evidence supports the Sable location. One salient item has been disregarded, probably because of its strangeness: the incident of the lion in the sea. That neither Hayes nor Hakluyt understood it, only adds to its weight as evidence. The ocean lion Hayes saw was not, as we might guess, one of the eared seals that later became known as sea lions. No sea lions lived at Sable Island. What did live there at that time was a colony of walrus. In the summer season, walrus by the hundreds frequented the bars and offshore waters. To Hayes and his comrades the animal in the water seemed aggressive and fearless, and to Renaissance Englishmen one of the most "fearful" animals was the lion. In England the walrus was as yet unknown. Allowing for the emotional colouring of Hayes's description, his ugly animal with glaring eyes, roaring mouth, and long teeth seems the very picture of a walrus.

Another point in favour of Sable Island is the description of the escape route followed after the loss of the *Delight*. The course given by Hayes would work for either end of Sable Island. The same might be said of the course logged by John Paul for the last two days of the approach to Sable. Given the inexactness of dead reckoning, it could lead to either of the Sable bars. In a general way, however, its beginning and its end seem certain: it traces an indirect path from Banquereau to Sable Island.

Banquereau stretches eastward from 60°W. to 57°15'W., nearly one hundred and forty miles. The largest sandbank south of Cape Breton and east of Sable Island, it lies just above 44° latitude, with depths of sixteen to fifty fathoms, many in the thirties. Many points on Banquereau would fit Hayes's description of about 44°N., sandy bottom, depth of thirty-five fathoms. From this point, the courses laid down by both Cox and John Paul agree as to broad pattern while differing in detail: the squadron sailed down to a low point in the south, then back up to where the wreck occurred. In both logs, the journey south is longer than the return. The site of the wreck, then, was below the starting point which, if on Banquereau, was some miles above 44°N. Both Cox and John Paul place the wreck site less than fifty miles north of where they turned around. This fact brings to mind Clarke's claim that he opposed Gilbert's orders to change direction to westnorthwest because he knew that Sable Island was only fifty miles away.

∞

If the Where of the loss of the *Delight* has been settled as Sable Island, the larger question of Why remains a mystery. Why was the squadron at Sable at that particular time, and why did it blunder into disaster? The standard explanation follows Hayes: Gilbert was motivated by the Portuguese fisherman's tale and relied on the foreigner's route to the island. But this explanation will not hold water; it is full of holes.

Hayes recorded the "intelligence we had of a Portugal" and commented on it.

> This seemed unto us very happy tidings, to have in an Island lying
> so neere unto the maine, which we intended to plant upon, such
> store of cattell, whereby we might at all times conveniently be
> relieved of victuall, and served of store for breed.

He certainly makes it sound like hot news.

What nobody seems to have considered is that this information was not news to knowledgeable Englishmen. An existing document associated with Gilbert's plans but predating his voyage reveals how much they already knew about Sable Island. The paper comprised instructions to the navigator of an earlier voyage (which in the event was aborted). It offered detailed advice on how "to finde the Isle of Sablon which is very full of cattell and swyne which may supplye your wantes with greate gaine." The attempt to discover the island was to be made on the homeward passage, "when you have perfectly discovered all the coste then in your retorne as you put of from Cape Briton."

The instructions spelled out the technique for searching:

And for the more certaine finding of the sayd Isle of Sablon direct your course from Cape Briton with one of your shippes south & by west./
And another Shippe to go Sowthe
And another shippe to go Sowthe and by East.
And sett of from the foresayd cape a watche before day./

If one of the ships discovered the island in daylight, it was to signal the others.

And yf you discover not the Island by day then att night to Sommon & speake with the admyrall uppon newe conference for farther search thereof./

Clearly English geographers and explorers knew everything that Hayes reported later except his stated distance of Sable from "Cape Briton": about twenty-five leagues (which was too short). They had a general idea of its latitude and longitude, though they were vague about its shape and size.

The wonder would have been if Sir Humphrey Gilbert was so ignorant of Sable Island that he had to learn about it from a fisherman. After all, Sable had been discovered more than sixty years before 1583, and it had since appeared on numerous maps, albeit under various names. The name "I. de Sablon," Isle of Sand, appeared as early as 1546, and the French name has persisted, eventually anglacized to Sable Island. The map John Dee provided for Gilbert's voyage included Sable clearly marked south of Cape Breton and near 44°N. latitude. Exact location hardly signified when an error of up to 2° of latitude, nearly one hundred and forty miles, was possible in observations taken at sea. What did matter on this voyage was the reckless approach to the island.

Hayes blamed the loss of the *Delight* on the carelessness and lack of discipline of the crew. Clarke charged Gilbert with wilful neglect of his warning about the fatal course. Hayes let the reader conclude that Clarke was responsible for the course, while absolving his own navigator by saying that Cox disagreed with it. The biases of the witnesses make it difficult to know what really happened. But the instructions for finding Sable Island quoted earlier raise new questions and evoke speculation.

Hayes's criticism of the *Delight* seamen for keeping a poor lookout has been played up too much. The far greater crime was to be sailing toward Sable Island at night. The instructions for finding the island virtually stated that it should be approached only during daylight. Common sense would seem to dictate as much. Gilbert, as leader of the expedition, must be faulted for allowing the ships to so heedlessly run with the wind. This bravado was the conduct of an impatient man, which Sir Humphrey was known to be.

The question here is, What was he impatient about? At the petty personal level, it is likely that he was annoyed at his chief navigator for having missed Sable Island on the way down and, from excess of caution, now counselling further delay. If the island was to their north, Gilbert may have reasoned, then they should hurry back to the right latitude and find it. Gilbert's impulse to speed up the operation may, however, have been based on a recent change in his thinking. Perhaps he was impatient to return to England.

It has generally been assumed, following Hayes/Hakluyt, that the loss of the *Delight* caused Gilbert's decision to abandon his project, that prior to this disaster he had every intention of sailing onward to the coast of America. Nobody, to the best of my knowledge, has suggested that Gilbert seized on the Sable disaster as a good excuse for returning to England, which had been his real intention ever since his stopover in St. John's. Yet a body of evidence supports this conclusion.

The instructions for the navigator of the earlier voyage that was aborted clearly intended the search for Sable Island to be left until the homeward passage. This search was to begin at Cape Breton. Gilbert's squadron, said Hayes, tried to sail to Cape Breton from Newfoundland before heading seaward for Sable Island.

Newfoundland had impressed Sir Humphrey Gilbert. Not the least of its virtues in his eyes was a store of rich minerals, a heavy cargo of which had been loaded into the *Delight* for transport to England. Besides finding this illusory treasure, in St. John's Gilbert had achieved another of his goals: he had staked a claim for Queen Elizabeth in North America. If Sir Humphrey was intending to use Newfoundland for his future settlement, the livestock resources of Sable Island would be a greater boon for it than for the distant Norumbega, his reputed goal. A trip to Sable was in order before heading home. In "discovering" Sable Island, the only known source of fresh beef and pork in the northern New World, he could fulfil one of the aims of English exploration and at the same time replenish his provisions for the long transatlantic passage.

The vain and ambitious Sir Humphrey, keen to reap the accolades for his success, may have found his obligation to his backers to establish estates in Norumbega a reluctant burden. He was arrogant enough to abandon the project regardless, but the loss of the *Delight* gave him a legitimate excuse. The accident at Sable Island, followed soon afterward by his heroic death, helped save Gilbert's reputation.

Captain Hayes protected his own good name by saying he wanted to continue the original voyage even after the Sable shipwreck. At the same time, though he hinted that Gilbert's satisfaction with Newfoundland was a factor, he said that Sir Humphrey was moved to truncate the expedition by compassion for the survivors. Hakluyt gave Hayes's interpretation to the world. It included the fortuitous nature of the Sable trip—its origin in the chance revelations of an anonymous Portuguese. Yet Hakluyt, if not Hayes, must have known that such an explanation was unconvincing. It was good enough, however, for his purpose.

Hakluyt wished to inspire Englishmen to emulate heroic deeds of exploration and discovery. He had no desire to asperse Gilbert as a man who had abandoned his great scheme of colonization in favour of what he mistakenly thought was a source of quick riches and from impatience for fame. Far better to present Sir Humphrey as ready to follow any lead that might benefit England and as the victim of bad luck at Sable Island that prevented him from completing his voyage. The story of Sir Humphrey Gilbert's expedition could then proceed dramatically to its tragic climax in the death of the hero.

Vital to this story is the legend of the Portuguese fisherman, which may be the first in a long line of Sable Island myths. Nobody has ever explained why a native of Portugal, especially a fisherman, should be helpful to the English. In 1583 Portugal belonged to Spain, Elizabethan England's mortal enemy. In recent years Portuguese fishermen at Newfoundland had suffered at the hands of Englishmen. One of the chief officers in this very expedition, Richard Clarke, had commanded a piratical raid on them only the year before. Under the circumstances, if an anonymous Portuguese offered to draw up a course for Sable Island, Gilbert would surely have been a fool to rely on it.

Yet it must be admitted that the story of Sir Humphrey Gilbert, the *Delight*, and Sable Island reads much better with the Portuguese connection. Like the best fiction, it embodies a larger truth. The Portuguese did discover Sable Island and put it on the map, and they did stock it with domestic animals. The English did learn about Sable from them, directly or indirectly, and that knowledge lured the *Delight* to its doom.

If Hakluyt's publicizing of this story failed to illuminate the reality of Sable Island, it created an impact that would last for centuries. It imbued Sable with an air of mystery and danger. The unforgettable scenes of the shipwreck and its aftermath had an impact on the imagination.

Hakluyt made a point that quickly gained international recognition. Sable Island soon became a place "having a bad repute for shipwrecks."

Chapter Two

Destroyer of Ships and Haven of Wild Horses

By the second quarter of the eighteenth century Sable Island had gained notoriety in the ports of eastern North America and among the European powers that ruled the colonial world. Sable had seen the losses of English, French, and colonial vessels, and of fishermen, sailors in the navy, soldiers, and passengers and seamen on merchant ships. The chief cause of so many shipwrecks was recognized as Sable's location. The island lay near the main shipping lanes between Europe and North America and even closer to many colonial seapaths, as well as in the midst of the offshore fishing banks. Whatever a vessel's mission, peaceful or warlike, Sable spelled danger and perhaps death.

The point was well illustrated by two unfortunate vessels of this period, the *Cathrine* and the *Légère*. The stories of these shipwrecks and the aftermath added to the Sable Island lore of tragedy and survival, with a touch of mystery.

The details of the stranding of the *Cathrine* in 1737 were better known and more widely publicized than any Sable loss since Sir Humphrey Gilbert's *Delight*. They were also more appalling. A description of the disaster was published in the Boston *Weekly News-Letter* in August.

The *Cathrine*, about 110 tons "burthen," of Workington, Ireland, had sailed from the homeland for Boston "having on board Two Hundred and Two Persons, Men, Women and Children." All was well on board the windjammer until it drew near Sable Island on Sunday 17 July, then

> they had very thick hasy Weather, the wind blowing very hard at
> S.S.E., and a very high Sea beating over them; their Tiller being
> lash'd close down was broke in Two by the Force of the Sea
> against the Rudder, and by Distress of Weather in the Night, the
> Vessel was drove upon a Reef of Sand, about a Mile distant from
> the High Land at the East End of the said Island.

J. F. W. DesBarres' impression (about 1766) of the area of Sable Island where the survivors of the wreck Cathrine *came ashore.*

The wind forced the stranded vessel over the bar, then combined with the strong currents to drive it right on shore,

> where the Sea with a vast Force bea[t] against her and broke over her, and first carrying away her Main Mast, in a few Minutes after stove her in Pieces, and left the whole Company to the Mercy of the Waves and the broken Pieces of the Wreck; Very pitiful were the Crys of the poor People for Mercy, In that distressing Moment.

The surf washed many of the ship's company up on the beach, "some being much bruis'd by the Waves and Pieces of the Vessel and others much spent by the Fatigue." Three or four of these survivors later died on shore. In the wreck, ninety-eight persons drowned.

At daylight the morning after the wreck, the castaways began to face up to their plight. Their first concern was shelter. The place where they had come ashore, on the south side a few miles east of the lake, offered a natural windbreak of sorts: the so-called Naked Sand Hills. Occasional breaches or gulches between the hills led upward and inland from the beach. Through one of these, a castaway might reach the inner island or at least climb to a lookout. The view from the highest vantage point would reveal a central east-west valley bounded on north and south by protective palisades of sand. At this season of the year, the prevailing colour was green. The different shades revealed the most varied vegetation on the island, with blueberry and cranberry bushes forming darker patches among the light but ubiquitous island grasses. A castaway might understandably not be entranced by the beauty of the scene. The pattern of the landscape, with shadowy ravines winding among rolling hills, concealed more than it revealed, and the strangeness spelled intimidation. For the moment the shipwreck survivors chose the lee side of a nearby hill as the place to build instant shelter.

In the absence of trees, materials for construction were scarce. The builders did the best they could with the flotsam cast upon the beach. From the ship's mainsail they made a tent of sorts on the side of the hill. For warmth they cut open a great number of feather beds "and with the Tick cover'd themselves." They also took the time to perform a grimmer task. Among the debris washed ashore were the bodies of many of their dead comrades. The survivors buried them—the first known burial of shipwreck victims on Sable Island.

While some of the castaways strove to insure survival on the island, others tried to devise a means of getting off it. With the aid of "sundry Tools providentially drove ashore in the Carpenter's Chest," and "Pieces of Boards and Staves, with some Canvas" they repaired a damaged longboat. When all the leaks were patched up, some of the ship's crew opted to once again trust their lives to the fortunes of the sea. Three days after the wreck the captain, mate, and seven other seamen set off for Canso about one hundred miles away.

The adventurers reached their destination in two days. Luck aside, this trip shows how seamen's knowledge of the area had increased in one and a half centuries. The nearby mainland, on the other hand, remained largely undeveloped. Canso was little more than a fisherman's port of call presided over by a military garrison. The commander of the troops was Alexander Cosby, a self-important man of whom historians say little good. But on this occasion, except for giving the castaways the impression that he was governor of the province, Cosby seems to have behaved well. Perhaps as a fellow Irishman he was more able to empathize with the refugees. At any rate, he and some "Gentlemen" companions welcomed the seamen "and very readily administred to their Relief."

The mission of the longboat was a resounding success. On Sunday 24 July a schooner sailed from Canso for Sable Island. It anchored off the island on Monday within sight of the castaways, "to the great Joy of those poor Creatures." The marooned people, in total about ninety, boarded the schooner at once and sailed for Canso. All arrived safely, "tho' some remaining weak, and others much wounded, were put under the Doctor's Care."

Most of the immigrants remained at Canso for two or three weeks, then proceeded to their various destinations. Three or four reached Boston by 12 August; no doubt they were the source of the newspaper report of the disaster.

The final paragraph of the published story assured a notoriety for this shipwreck well beyond the ordinary. It said the *Cathrine* was "accounted the richest Vessel that ever sail'd from the North of *Ireland.*" The report had stated earlier that two of the noteworthy people drowned in the wreck were "wealthy Cloth Merchants" on the way to Boston to set up in cloth manufacturing. Now it added that several persons and families on board were bringing most if not all of their "Estates" with them. The silver and gold in plate and specie on the *Cathrine* were said to amount, by a conservative estimate, to more than three thousand pounds sterling.

The story of the loss of the *Cathrine* was the answer to a journalist's prayers. It included poor immigrants, women and children, mass deaths, heroic deliverance, and lost treasure. Thanks to the *News-Letter*, in Boston this tragedy was bound to be the talk of the town.

In the spring following the wreck of the *Cathrine*, the minister of the French Protestant Church in Boston petitioned the Nova Scotia government. Calling himself a naturalized Englishman, Andrew LeMercier sought approval of a proposal about Sable Island. He knew that Sable, as part of Nova Scotia, had become permanently British by the Treaty of Utrecht in 1713.

LeMercier, then in his mid-forties, had been a Boston resident for more than twenty years. Although he was on very friendly terms with his colleagues in the English-speaking churches, LeMercier was far from the stereotype of a Boston Puritan minister. One historian coined for him the happy euphemism "enterprising character." His enterprise focused mainly on acquiring land, the symbol in his day of both wealth and prestige. His ambitious pursuit of real estate was hampered by a lack of money but not of ideas. Like many Massachusetts entrepreneurs of the time, LeMercier looked to Nova Scotia to fulfil his dreams.

About a decade earlier this clergyman had developed a scheme for settling French Protestants in Nova Scotia. It was an ingenious plan. The government was to provide free transportation and start-up funds for the settlers, while LeMercier and his associates would receive 5,000 acres of land for their trouble and expenses, which would be minimal. The Board of Trade in England, the recognized authority on the colonies, rejected the proposal, and that was the end of it. A modern authority on the subject, however, has praised LeMercier for his insight into the needs of a successful settlement in Nova Scotia.

LeMercier's 1738 proposal imitated his earlier scheme. The land he sought belonged to Nova Scotia. It was unoccupied and in need of settlers. The capital investment required from him and his partners was minimal, and they were likely to realize a quick return of their expenses. LeMercier's new plan also showed that he had learned from his previous experience: it contained a gimmick.

The proposal aimed to convince the Board of Trade that to grant land to LeMercier and his colleagues free of charge was in the public interest. Hence the location: Sable Island. The recent tragedy of the *Cathrine* had shown that a settlement on Sable Island, by its mere existence, would be performing a public service. So we find Lieutenant Governor Armstrong and the Nova Scotia Council on 1 April 1738 considering the following petition from Andrew LeMercier and some unnamed associates.

> ...Whereas it might be a great service to his Majesty's Subjects who have the Unhappiness to Make Shipwreck upon or near the Isle of Sables; if the said Island was settled and a sufficient stock of cattle kept in it to support the Lives of the Persons who after a Shipwreck may get ashore, And whereas your Humble Petitioners with some Associates has bought a Schooner and has transported thither at several times already horn Cattle swine & sheep with a Considerable Charge and has built a house and maintain now upon the said Island several men to look after their stock. Your Petitioner in his own behalf and in the behalf of his associates Prays your Honour and the Honourable Council to give them leave to settle the Isle of Sables and to forbid any of His Majestys Subjects within your Government to Disturb the said settlement by killing their Cattle or any other way Discouraging their good Intentions and to Secure unto them as much as lyes in your power the Property of said Island, Cattle, &c. as according to your Wisdom and goodness you shall think fit.

To make a long story short, LeMercier and his colleagues never secured a grant of Sable Island. What they did achieve in relation to it was *de jure* control. Lieutenant Governor Armstrong took LeMercier at his word. (If LeMercier had indeed sent men and livestock to Sable, he must have done so after August 1737, for the survivors from the *Cathrine* reported no people or domestic animals on the island.) The lieutenant governor issued a proclamation by which all under his authority were "forbidden to harm, molest or interfere in any way with A. le Mercier and his associates in settling and stocking the island." He also ordered Alexander Cosby, still in command at Canso, to give all assistance to the enterprise.

After Armstrong's death in December 1739, Paul Mascarene, an army officer with close ties to Boston, succeeded to his authority, though not to his official title. Mascarene reinforced LeMercier's Sable rights and even upgraded his claim. According to Mascarene, Armstrong had allowed LeMercier to keep livestock and people on the island in order to carry on a fishery, which LeMercier still intended to do. The fishery referred to was mainly the so-called seal fishery, the hunting of seals for their oil and skins.

Mascarene said that the cattle raised on the island were to be used both for the relief of castaways and for the "advantage" of the owners. In effect, Mascarene granted LeMercier the exclusive right to exploit Sable resources. This support for his Sable settlement was justified on the grounds that shipwreck at the island was something "which yearly happens." In Nova Scotia, Sable Island was already a notorious ship-killer.

Official proclamations and moral support were one thing, Sable reality another. LeMercier learned over time that the banks fishermen and others who frequented the waters around Sable Island had their own code of behaviour to suit their own priorities. Six years after his original petition, he published a notice in the paper complaining about fishermen at Sable. He said,

> they have sundry Times Stole our Cattle and our Goods, regarding neither the Laws of God or of Man, neither Justice to me, or Humanity to shipwreck'd Men.

Taking matters into his own hands, LeMercier offered a reward to anybody who should identify the maurauders so that they might be brought to justice and convicted. He also guaranteed amnesty to any offender who would inform on his accomplices. Informers might report to LeMercier himself or to Capt. John Gorham of Casco Bay, Maine. The name of one of LeMercier's silent partners was here made public. It was a name calculated to give this notice clout.

∽∾

John Gorham belonged to a well-known Massachusetts fighting family. For generations they had produced military officers, and in 1744 John, who had just turned thirty-four, held the rank of captain in the Massachusetts army. He was also a captain in his own right. From his birth in Barnstable, Cape Cod, he was close to salt water and ships, and for his first career he had turned to the sea. He commanded his own vessel in the Newfoundland trade, a route that regularly took him past—perhaps on occasion, to—Sable Island. At the time of LeMercier's notice, Gorham was living on his land grant near the present Gorham, Maine, but he would soon be moving his family to Boston. This move was the first step in the pursuit of a wider ambition.

Gorham may have come to a sudden decision at the outbreak of war with France in March. From his wife's point of view, the timing of the move could have been better. She gave birth to one of her fifteen children aboard the vessel taking her to Cape Cod in July. Combining realism and poetry, the parents named the baby Sea Deliverance.

The baby's father was soon off again, headed for Nova Scotia on orders from Massachusetts Governor Shirley. Gorham commanded a company of fifty men, mostly full-blooded Mohawks, who would become famous as Gorham's Rangers. The Rangers were Shirley's response to a request from Paul Mascarene for aid against the natives besieging his garrison at Annapolis

Royal. This mission began John Gorham's successful military career in Nova Scotia, which lasted to his death. But Gorham had more than warfare on his mind.

In the autumn of 1744 John Gorham presented a memorial to Mascarene and his council requesting a grant of Sable Island. Mascarene forwarded it to London with his government's recommendation for acceptance. From then on, its fate rested with the bureaucracy that ran the British Empire.

Gorham made his request on behalf of himself and associates, one of whom was LeMercier. His memorial differed from LeMercier's, however, in two important respects: one was the leadership role of Gorham himself; the other was an expressed intention to build lighthouses, the first known suggestion to build a lighthouse at Sable Island. The Board of Trade responded favourably to Gorham's leadership, to the idea of settling Sable Island under his auspices—but it turned thumbs down on lighthouses. It doubted that lights would be of any value at Sable. On 8 August 1745 the Board notified Mascarene that it had passed Gorham's memorial on to the Privy Council along with the Board's opinions. Mascarene and Gorham were left to wait on the Privy Council's decision. (And wait they did—it never came.)

In the meantime, Gorham and LeMercier acted as though they held the rights to Sable Island. They continued their Sable activities. Those activities, according to the partners' recent claims, had already included the saving and supporting of two hundred and fifty people from nine or ten shipwrecks. No argument against this assertion resulted from the Board of Trade inquiry into Gorham's memorial. The lifesaving service was neither proved nor disproved.

Gorham and LeMercier undoubtedly conducted operations at Sable Island over a period of years. Although LeMercier is unlikely to have visited the island, he knew more about it than most of his contemporaries. His information could only have come from people who lived on Sable, for it was not available in any known published or official source. In fact, LeMercier himself published the most accurate description of Sable Island to his time. It gave the best idea of Sable as a place to live prior to its permanent settlement in the nineteenth century.

Andrew LeMercier's Sable Island was twenty-eight miles long by one wide, "a total of about 10,000 Acres of Land." LeMercier meant "land" to be taken literally. His total acreage omitted the area of the lake in the centre of the island. This lake, which was about fifteen miles long and at most four fifths of a mile wide, covered some eight thousand acres. The actual width of Sable Island at its widest point, including the lake, was about one and a half miles. The climate, said LeMercier, was temperate: in winter snow seldom lasted more than three days, and in summer the days were never "extream hot." The air was "healthy," being cleared by high winds; it was also thick with "Fowls," especially black ducks. No trees but many bushes grew on the island; the sandy soil contained not a single stone. It produced "wild or Beach Pease" in abundance and many kinds of wild berries. The lake abounded with flounders and eels, the beach with sand eels and clams. Sable was home to "no venomous Creatures" and hardly any flies. Although the island lacked rivers, brooks, or open fresh water, you could find "fresh clear Water" everywhere by digging about three feet in the sand. (Actually, fresh water ponds did exist, but the water in them often became brackish.) When LeMercier "took Possession" of Sable, it contained no "four-footed Creatures" except a few red and black foxes, some of which still remained. Since then, he had added domestic livestock, which now roamed the island.

LeMercier's picture of the Sable environment is supported by the later testimony of expert surveyors such as DesBarres. The most convincing statements in this published description, however, relate to the life of Sable settlers. They ring true in the light of subsequent experience.

LeMercier revealed that the sandy soil supported all sorts of cultivated roots, especially turnips, which were uncommonly sweet and large. The plentiful natural grass, tall and thick, was sweet and nourishing for livestock. Sable Island contained enough to feed about one thousand cattle. The kinds of livestock that could be raised to best advantage were sheep, horn-cattle, and horses. The best of the best were the horses.

> Horses breed and grow there without Care or Trouble; there is all
> Winter long grass enough or near enough for them, so that they
> eat but little of the Hay which is made for them in the Summer or
> the Fall.

The round of activities of the settlers made for variety.

> The Care of Gardens and Cattle take up our People's Time in
> Summer, in Winter they go to kill Seils and boil their Fat into Oyl,
> as well as that of Whales, which now and then are cast away dead
> upon the Beach. The Island finds them in Turf and the Sea brings
> them Wood; so they are not deprived of the Necessaries of Life,
> nor without Profits of several Sorts; besides their having the
> pleasure of saving many Men's Lives, according to the motto of
> the Island, viz- *Destruo & Salvo*.

LeMercier himself no doubt coined the decidedly theological Sable Island motto, "I destroy and I save."

LeMercier and John Gorham had little time to develop their plans for Sable Island because Gorham's military role in Nova Scotia kept him busy. Even when Gorham came to Boston in January 1745, an upcoming military expedition soon became his prime concern. He was recruited for the invasion of Louisbourg. Appointed lieutenant-colonel in the 7th Massachusetts Regiment, he took an active part in what has been called "one of the greatest upsets in military history." After the capture of Louisbourg, he remained there until April 1746. But Gorham did not forget Sable Island, as a quarrel with Brig.-Gen. Samuel Waldo shows.

The quarrel related to the use of a schooner in Louisbourg Harbour for the war effort. Waldo accused Gorham of refusing to give it up because he planned to use it to bring livestock off Sable Island. Waldo was probably right about Gorham's intention. At any rate, his accusation—which we may note in passing supports LeMercier's statements about Sable livestock—shows that some contemporaries knew about Gorham's Sable interest. John Gorham would soon pursue that interest across the Atlantic Ocean and in international negotiations.

∽⌣∾

The loss of the great fortress of Louisbourg shocked France but also served as a catalyst for revenge. By June 1746 the avenging force was ready. A great armada commanded by Jean-Baptiste-Louis-Frédéric de la Rochefoucauld de Roye, Duc d'Anville, departed from France for Nova Scotia and sailed right into disaster. Hampered by alternate calms and contrary winds, d'Anville's squadron took nearly three months to cross the Atlantic. On finally reaching coastal waters in September, it ran into a violent gale that scattered the ships and sowed destruction. One of the victims of wind and sea plus Sable Island was the corvette *Légère*, commanded by twenty-four-year-old, Quebec-born Charles-François Guillimin.

The *Légère* was driven away on 13 September; by noon of the fourteenth it was in danger of foundering. Guillimin threw six guns overboard to lighten his vessel but was forced to sail before the wind. Heading eastnortheast and northeast, Captain Guillimin thought he would pass well east of Sable Island. Too late, he discovered his error. Noting the amount of sand in the waves crashing over his vessel, he realized that he must already be at Sable.

At 10 or 11 o'clock that night, the *Légère* ran aground. Like the *Delight* and *Cathrine*, it struck from the southward. And like the *Cathrine* but not the *Delight*, it had the good fortune to strand off the south side of the island rather than on the end bar. As the waves battered the trapped vessel through the hours of darkness, the ship's company held tight. In the morning, Captain Guillimin ordered the mainmast cut down to lighten the ship. That afternoon at low water, he gave the order to abandon ship.

All on board reached shore safely about 3:00 P.M. In the opinion of one of the survivors, the high seas that had driven the *Légère* to its doom also saved the men. The waves had tossed the small warship to within three hundred feet of the beach, almost on it at low water.

During the next few days the castaways worked like so many Robinson Crusoes, as one of their comrades in arms later put it, to salvage what they could to help them survive the winter. All they managed to save was some powder and shot for hunting and some sails for making tents. Then help arrived from an unexpected source.

The French seamen were working on the beach when they sighted a man with a dog looking at them from high up on a distant sandhill. Their first thought was that he was another unfortunate like themselves. They picked up their weapons and headed for him; he anticipated them and met them halfway. The man spoke to them in English, and seeing that they could not understand, made signs for them to follow him. He led them inland to a little dwelling somewhat sheltered in a valley. Here he introduced two companions who also spoke only English. He showed the Frenchmen a small supply of goods and some domesticated livestock, which by means of signs he offered to share with them. This man also provided valuable information, such as where to find the best fresh water. Guillimin called him "Sr. Sincht," which is probably a French phonetic rendering and may be wide of the mark.

Captain Guillimin and his men—a total of eighteen—now had a better chance of lasting through the winter, but nobody's survival was guaranteed. On 28 September one man died of scurvy, a victim of the long voyage from France rather than of Sable Island. During the night of 29 January the ship's carpenter froze to death in his hut. Described as a Dutchman, he apparently chose to live alone, perhaps in quarters built by himself, and his isolation contributed to his death.

A third man, a ship's cooper, had died in December, more clearly a victim of his chosen way of life. He was an alcoholic, and even on desolate Sable Island he was able to find the means of catering to his appetite. This man, according to his shipmates, had lived a wild life, and excessive drinking had affected his mind. He refused to heed the warnings of the ship's surgeon and others, and when some wine and brandy floated ashore, he went missing for twenty-four hours. An extensive search discovered his body on the beach. The surgeon, acting as coroner, examined it. His verdict stated that there was not a mark on the body to indicate any cause of death other than that the man had been dead drunk and then, from exposure to the cold, just dead.

These three deaths were the only ones to result from the loss of the *Légère*. Captain Guillimin and the other castaways survived for nine months until help arrived to take them off Sable Island. Six fishing schooners from New England came on 13 June and, according to Guillimin's official report, took him and his companions to Boston. No longer a prisoner on Sable Island, Guillimin became a prisoner of war. In Boston he was treated very civilly right up to his August departure with his crew as part of a prisoner exchange. He arrived home in Quebec via Louisbourg in September, about a year after his shipwreck. The delivery of his report in Quebec was for Captain Guillimin the final act of the adventure that began at Sable Island. But it was not the end of the story.

Where Sable Island is concerned, every story seems to contain some paradox or contradiction, or some unknown that adds an element of mystery. In Guillimin's case, the mystery relates to a nineteenth man: the pilot of the *Légère*. He did not die, and he did not spend the winter on Sable Island. In fact, he escaped from Sable soon after coming ashore.

Captain Guillimin reported that the pilot had left the island on the fifth day after the wreck. An "English" schooner happened to be passing the island, so Guillimin put his pilot aboard it to seek help in any port at which the schooner would eventually call. Guillimin seems to have had no curiosity as to the fate of this man. Fortunately for those of us who do, this pilot—unlike most of the anonymous characters in the Sable story—did not simply vanish without having his say.

The anonymous pilot's version of his adventure is preserved at second hand in a journal kept by a soldier in the ill-fated d'Anville expedition. This soldier was a captive on the mainland after part of the squadron had staggered into Chebucto (Halifax) Harbour where it was decimated by disease. He was at Chebucto in October when the pilot arrived from Louisbourg as part of a prisoner exchange. The pilot said that he had been aboard a transport ship that stranded at Sable Island on 14 September. His description of the wreck matches Guillimin's, with minor differences of detail. His description of his departure from Sable Island, however, contradicts Guillimin.

The way the pilot told it, his escape from Sable Island resulted entirely from his own initiative. He was walking along a beach near the spot where the *Légère* lay stranded when he saw a fishing vessel come to anchor offshore. As he watched, the fishermen lowered a boat into the sea. Feeling certain that these men were coming ashore to inspect the wreck, the pilot ran to it and hid. The boat thumped on the beach nearby, and the fishermen pulled it up free of the surf. They tramped through the loose, dry sand to the hulk. As they came on board, the pilot jumped out and scrambled along the beach to their boat. The fishermen followed in hot pursuit. Recognizing the pilot as a Frenchman and fearing the arrival of others, they pushed off the beach, piled into their boat, and pulled seaward. They boarded their schooner without delay and set sail for Louisbourg taking the pilot with them. The French pilot became a prisoner of war at Louisbourg until he was exchanged under a flag of truce in Chebucto Harbour.

The pilot's story may be suspect because of the way it differs from Guillimin's. It tends to make the teller the hero of the tale. On the other hand, it does explain how he alone got off the island, and it links up with later events. The pilot did not say why no help was sent to his still-stranded shipmates. He implied that the fishermen saw nobody else on the island, but he failed to account for his apparent inaction after he arrived at Louisbourg, where he could have made a report to the English authorities.

Guillimin's version leaves even more unanswered questions. He does not explain how he arranged the pilot's removal with the English-speaking fishermen. He remained unaware that the fishermen's destination was

Louisbourg. And he fails to tell why, if the fishermen had spoken with him, they did not inform somebody so that the castaways might be rescued. We might go a step further and ask why, once the fishermen knew about the men stranded on Sable Island, Guillimin would feel any need to send the pilot with them.

If the pilot for some reason did not notify the English authorities at Louisbourg, he certainly spread news of the wreck among the French at the prisoner exchange in October. Why, then, did nobody send help to the *Légère* castaways before the arrival of winter?

The mixed messages and strange lack of communication about the shipwreck gave rise to confusion about the rescue of Guillimin and his men. An argument developed as to who deserved the credit, and the chief claimant was a familiar figure in Sable Island affairs: John Gorham.

Long after the loss of the *Légère*, John Gorham made claims upon France for expenses incurred in saving the survivors of the wreck. Gorham cited two activities as the basis of his claim: 1. sending a schooner to Sable Island; 2. preserving the lives of the castaways. While some of Gorham's statements might be questioned, he seems to have truly believed that he deserved credit for service on behalf of the *Légère*. Some evidence exists to support this belief but not enough to prove Gorham's case.

The focus of Gorham's appeal to France was Jacques-Pierre de Taffenel de la Jonquière. The Marquis de la Jonquière was the officer who took command of the remnants of d'Anville's invaders after the death of their leader in Chebucto. He was in charge when the *Légère*'s pilot arrived in the prisoner exchange. According to John Gorham, when Jonquière learned of the Sable wreck, he wrote to Charles Knowles, the English governor of Cape Breton, requesting that the French sailors marooned on the island be rescued. Knowles sent the request on to Boston, and Gorham responded to it. He sent a schooner to Sable Island, but on arrival it found only one Frenchman still there.

Aside from the inexplicable abandoning of one man by his comrades, Gorham's story presents problems. When Knowles was questioned on the subject, he said that he had sent a schooner to Sable in the spring of 1747 with orders to carry all the castaways straight to France. Perhaps Knowles simply expressed himself carelessly; he may have meant that these were the orders he sent to Boston. Gorham was in Boston early in 1747, but he departed for England in late April or early May. If Gorham had sent a schooner to Sable before leaving Boston, it would have found Guillimin and his men there, since they remained on the island until after the middle of June. The case for Gorham's rescue attempt seems weak.

The other aspect of Gorham's claim was costs of food and other support for the shipwrecked sailors. Since Gorham himself admitted that he did not transport them from Sable Island and they were government prisoners in Boston, the goods must have been supplied prior to their rescue. The only known source of such support was the mysterious Sr. Sincht. The logical conclusion is that Sincht, his two companions, and all their equipment and supplies, including livestock, belonged to the Gorham/LeMercier operation at Sable Island.

Gorham implied as much in his request to France for reimbursement. He argued that stocking Sable Island with provisions served the general good of all nations. He declared that if France paid him for the used supplies, he would then be able to succour other unfortunates cast ashore at Sable Island, as he had done in the past. This line of reasoning is believable, the facts likely, though specific documentation is lacking. Such documentation was exactly what the French authorities demanded in the case of the *Légère*. Although Gorham continued to write to La Jonquière seeking support for his claim, he never received the compensation he said was due him.

For Gorham, LeMercier, and their associates in the Sable Island venture, the wreck of the *Légère* was a dead loss. It even failed to provide them with good publicity. A contemporary history of the British settlements in North America said of Sable Island: "The property is loudly (that is in the publick news-papers) claimed by some private persons; I shall not inquire into the merit of the affair." The author, who was shrewdly correct in his skepticism as to the ownership of Sable Island, penned this section of his manuscript during the winter of 1747–48. He was William Douglass, a Scot who had settled in Boston thirty years earlier and had since developed a large medical practice. Dr. Douglass said that his information about Sable Island came from "people who were shipwrec'd there, and lived some months upon the island."

Among the most recent Sable castaways were Captain Guillimin and his men. They arrived in Boston in the summer of 1747 and may well have gone to Dr. Douglass for medical treatment after a winter of deprivation at Sable.

Given the likelihood that they were Douglass's informants, the wreck of the *Légère* may deserve a footnote in Sable history as the indirect source of Douglass's admirably succinct description of the island:

[I]t is a low land, with small rising knowles of sand called downs, in form of an elbow, the bite to the northward, about 20 miles in length, and narrow; by reason of shoales of sand, small tides 5 or 6 feet, and a great surf; it is inaccessible, excepting in the bite, where boats may land.

The loss of the *Cathrine*, though, if it was the inspiration of Andrew LeMercier's Sable activities, had the greatest effect on Sable reality. It may even have helped save the lives of the *Légère*'s crew. This influence died with the passing of LeMercier and his colleagues, except in one regard:

some of the livestock survived to provide a source of food for future castaways, and one herd became a permanent feature of Sable Island.

Speaking from long experience, LeMercier said that horses needed no human assistance to breed and grow on Sable Island. Time has proven him right. The feral horses of Sable Island increased in numbers and evolved into a distinct breed. While not fugitives from a shipwreck, as some have called them, they were nonetheless the paradoxical children of catastrophe, for disasters like the wreck of the *Cathrine* fostered their race.

Chapter Three

Meeting Spot of Privateers, Fishermen, and Unfortunate Others

The paradoxical Seven Years' War—which lasted nine years in North America—produced some notable Sable Island anomalies. The years that saw the last of the fighting between the forces of France and England in the Western colonies produced the first known conflicts between French and English at Sable. And soldiers on the island suffered most after virtually all the fighting was finished. In one notable respect, however, the events of this period maintained Sable Island tradition: all the trouble arose from shipwrecks.

At the previous peace, England had returned Louisbourg to France. In the new war, the great fortress served as a nest of privateers. In December 1756 a Boston newspaper published a warning on this score. A former captain of a brigantine had just arrived in Boston as a released prisoner of war. His vessel had been captured by a privateer and taken to Louisbourg. While a prisoner there, he had seen other privateers in port. Five of them, he said, had recently fitted out for a cruise. The captain knew whereof he spoke. During the next several months, French privateers took a heavy toll on shipping in colonial waters.

In the spring of 1757 reports of another kind began to reach Boston. Fishermen returning home to the outports said that they had seen a ship ashore at Sable Island. Soon news from another source confirmed these reports; it also added a new twist to the tale of a Sable shipwreck.

The new source, cited in the Boston *Weekly News-Letter* of 12 May, was a certain "Mr. Kirke." This man was among another batch of prisoners released from Louisbourg, seventy-three in number, which had arrived at Marblehead, Massachusetts, in a vessel flying a flag of truce the day before. Kirke had come on from Marblehead to Boston, where he reported his news to the colonial government. The Massachusetts council passed his information on to Lord Loudoun, Commander in Chief of the British forces in America, the only central authority in the American colonies at that time.

> One of our Vessells inward bound discoverg a Vessell ashore about 3 weeks ago on the Isle of Sables went to their Relief: it proved to be an Eng: prize Ship fr. Portugal having 13 Hands aboard which the French had taken off Virginia; the French Man secured the Vessell & her Crew which came to their Releif, and proceeded therewith for Louisbourgh, in their way thither they took another small Vessell, and having more English men aboard than they chose to trust themselves with, they put most of them aboard the last mentioned Vessell, which is since arrived at Cape Ann, but we have seen none of the People.

The newspaper story expanded slightly on this information. The prize ship was being sent to Louisbourg—which means that it was manned by only part of the privateer's crew. Having wrecked their prize on Sable Island, the privateers hoisted its English colours to entice the schooner crew ashore. The actual takeover of the New England schooner resulted from "some Difference arising," which the *News-Letter* did not explain. The privateers had arrived at Louisbourg in the captured schooner "with some of the Ship's Sails, Rigging and Stores, which they saved she being left a Wreck," just before the flag of truce vessel departed.

A month later, the newspaper published a follow-up story, based on eyewitness accounts by the captain and crew of the captured English ship.

> A fishing Schooner which arrived last Week at Newbury, brot in capt. Lawrence with his Company, belonging to the Ship that Capt. Comrin and others saw ashore on the Isle of Sables (as formerly mentioned); she was bound from Gibraltar for Virginia, but taken by the French; who after they were ashore, upon having some Difference, fired upon Capt. Lawrence's Men and wounded two of them, and after taking out some of her Effects, proceeded in a Schooner to Louisbourg, leaving all the English on the Island.

While this item provides a different perspective, it does little to clarify what happened. It implies that the quarrel was between only the crew of the English ship and the French, but it still fails to explain who started the fight. It says nothing of the crew of the New England schooner. Captain Lawrence apparently took it for granted that they were all carried to Louisbourg while he and his men, "all the English," were abandoned at Sable Island.

A modern researcher, Robert F. Marx, has identified the lost ship as the "English merchantman *Buchanan*, Captain Lawrence." Marx dates its shipwreck on Sable Island as some time after 22 April, the day it was captured by the privateer. If we assume that Marx discovered or verified this information by his research at Lloyd's of London, we may accept his identification of the ship. Use of the name *Buchanan* helps clarify the following retelling of the Sable Island story.

An unnamed privateer was going about its business when it captured the *Buchanan*. The purpose of that business was to take advantage of a state of war to make money for the owners and operators of the privateer. If the French seamen on this privateer had wished to harm Englishmen, the time to do it was at the moment of capture. The privateer's crew at that time greatly outnumbered the merchant seamen on the *Buchanan*. Captain Lawrence never charged his captors with any such aggression. The French privateers simply followed the usual custom of putting some of their own men aboard the captured ship to sail it to their home port. In this case, the home port was Louisbourg, and the French seamen took their English prisoners along for delivery to the proper authorities.

Unfortunately for all concerned, the seamanship of the skeleton crew on board the *Buchanan* proved unequal to their task. They ended up on the beach at Sable Island. Here they and their English prisoners came into conflict. The chances are at least fifty-fifty that the English seamen started the fight. The certainty is that the French privateers finished it. Still they did not kill anybody. They concentrated on getting off the island.

Sighting a New England fishing schooner offshore, the French seamen used the ruse of hoisting the colours on the *Buchanan* to appeal to the assumed patriotic sympathies of the fishermen. The ruse worked. When the fishermen came ashore, the privateers overpowered them and took possession of their schooner. The French then sailed for Louisbourg, taking the New England fishermen as prisoners in place of the *Buchanan*'s crew, which they abandoned on Sable Island.

On the passage to Louisbourg, the captured schooner met up with another New England schooner, which the privateers also took. At this point, the French were forced to make a choice. They could either divide their numbers further and sail both schooners home or stay together and give up one of the captured vessels. For safety's sake they chose to put most of the captives on their latest prize and leave them to their own devices. The privateers no doubt kept some prisoners as hostages—and to avoid giving the other schooner too much manpower. When the exchange was completed, the privateers sailed for Louisbourg and the fishermen for Cape Ann. Naturally the French, being so close to home, reached port first.

In Louisbourg a flag of truce ship was just about to sail when the captive fishermen arrived. They told their story to fellow prisoners, who included "Mr. Kirke," and they may have sailed on the flag of truce with him. Kirke acted as the spokesman in Boston for both the prisoners and the fishermen in the other schooner when he made the initial report of the Sable Island incident.

Meanwhile the marooned *Buchanan* seamen waited at Sable to be rescued. At last another fishing schooner took the chance of coming to the aid of Sable Island castaways and picked them up. Captain Lawrence and his crew reached port in Massachusetts around the first of June.

The way these events were reported in Boston reveals no animosity on the part of the privateers toward the New England fishermen. The French privateers were simply plying their trade, which did not exempt fishermen. If fishing schooners made poor prizes, they were also easy prey. While the taking of the first New England schooner may be justified on grounds of necessity, the same excuse does not apply to the second; and the release of the second schooner was an act of self-interest, not charity. The only true acts of charity in this entire episode were the efforts of the fishermen to relieve castaways. Yet the fact remains that the privateers committed none of the acts of carnage that some writers would have us believe were then the norm at Sable Island.

Another incident about a year later strengthens the impression that the privateers from Louisbourg were motivated by policy rather than by murderous impulses or nationalistic fervour. The *News-Letter* of Thursday 20 April 1758 reported the latest Sable incident:

> Last Monday Morning a fishing Vessel belonging to Capt. Coles of Marblehead, arriv'd there from the Banks; which Vessel, with a Schooner belonging to Mr. Samuel Selman, having put in at the Isle of Sable about a Week before to get wood, were taken by a Number of Men, which belong'd to a French Privateer Sloop that had been cast away on that Island: The last mention'd Schooner they kept Possession of; and in the other sent all the Men home.

In this case, the privateer itself had suffered shipwreck at Sable Island. Assuming that the full fighting crew was aboard and that most of the men survived the wreck, plenty of seamen were available for duty. The expression "a Number of Men" implies more than a few. The privateers, then, were capable of sailing off with both of the captured vessels and leaving the fishermen stranded. That they did not, argues a concern only to escape from the island. They showed no desire to harm the fishermen or force them to endure their own recent experience. The record does not reveal how long the French sailors had been marooned on Sable, whether for months or days, but even in April life would be hard enough without proper shelter and provisions.

A sequel to this story appeared in the *News-Letter* three weeks later. The paper told how three fishing schooners had returned to Cape Ann from the Banks and "brought with them from Isle-Sable, the Cannon of the French Privateer Sloop, that was cast away there, the Crew of which had taken a Marblehead Schooner and gone off." The salvaging of the "cannon"—no doubt used in the collective sense, as a plural—was well worth reporting. It would help boost the morale of the fishing community faced with the usual high losses during wartime, mostly to privateers.

From a long-range perspective, it adds a nice touch of irony. Over the years the Sable Island story has been filled with unfounded statements about wreckers, pirates, and murderers. Here the fishermen on the three schooners were wreckers trying to turn a profit from the misfortune of a privateer that ran afoul of Sable Island. The whole episode is about the fortunes of war, with none of the protagonists deserving to be ranked as villains.

These incidents in 1757–58 support the notion that the most frequent willing visitors to Sable Island in this era were fishermen. When privateers and their ilk who preyed on ships at sea ended up on Sable Island, they were most likely to be there by accident, as victims of a shipwreck. On the available evidence, if privateers and pirates were a menace at Sable Island, the prime cause was that Sable was a menace to them.

The climactic battle of the Seven Years' War, as every Canadian schoolchild presumably knows, took place on the Plains of Abraham in 1759. From then on, the British forces engaged in a series of mop-up operations. One of the officers engaged in these operations was Robert Elliot of the 43rd Regiment, who was then about forty-five years old. Elliot, though only a major, had led his regiment into the great battle, where it served well in the centre of the British line. The following summer the 43rd took part in the successful attack on Montreal. The regiment then moved to winter quarters at Quebec. Major Elliot and his wife, who was accompanying him after the custom of the time, might look forward to months of relief from campaigning. But in the latter part of September, Elliot received a special assignment. He was to take a detachment of men to Restigouche on Chaleur Bay. There he would receive the formal surrender of the French commander, then continue on to New York for the winter.

Taking his wife with him, Elliot sailed down the St. Lawrence and carried out his mission in Chaleur Bay. He embarked the French troops in a flag of truce, gave the military provisions to the civilian Acadian population, and made a ceremonial gift of some blankets and provisions to the leaders of a Micmac village nearby. On 5 November Major Elliot again set sail with his squadron to complete his journey.

Before the vessels cleared the Gulf of St. Lawrence, Elliot's schooner became separated from its companions and never sighted them again. Soon afterward, as it sailed through the Gut of Canso toward the open Atlantic, the schooner ran into a storm at night. The storm lasted three days, during which the vessel was forced to lie to. Facing into the wind with shortened sail, it was unknowingly travelling seaward, carried along by the currents. On the morning of 14 November the weather cleared for a moment and the people on the schooner saw land, but they did not know where they were or where they were going.

Although Elliot was the commanding officer, on board ship he was dependent on the captain for control of the vessel. On the night of the fifteenth, in thick weather, the captain ran the schooner aground. Major Elliot and his companions were stranded on the northeast bar of Sable Island.

For four hours the schooner thumped on the bar, while more than sixty people, including women and children, waited anxiously on board. They expected it at any moment to go to pieces. The wonder is that it did not. Anchored by the grip of Sable sands, the vessel had no give, no capacity to roll away from the pounding waves. It survived long enough to be lifted off the sand at about two o'clock in the morning. Tide and current carried it across the bar. The schooner was by then taking in so much water that it barely remained afloat. All hands strained for hours to manoeuvre it toward land. On the following afternoon, it struck again and stuck fast in the shallows on the south side of the island. The ship's company saw that they were now at the mercy of the Sable surf, "the sea being so very high."

High sea or not, with the beach only eighty yards away, Major Elliot and others saw a chance for survival. If a rope could be stretched between schooner and shore, the people on board might be drawn safely to the beach. The problem was to get the rope ashore, obviously a job for seamen. Some of the schooner crew accepted the challenge. They took the vessel's only boat and rowed through the surf with the rope, landing a man to secure the end on solid ground. On the return trip, their luck ran out. The surf upset the boat and it was lost, along with two of the brave Jack Tars.

This loss was a devastating blow for Robert Elliot and the others who watched from the deck of the stranded schooner. But rather than give up hope, they combatted despair with action. They focused on a single goal: "tossing over board such provisions as we could come at, for our future sustenance, in case we were any of us lucky enough to get on shore." Even so, terrorized by the crashing waves that threatened to demolish the schooner at any moment, they endured a night of hell. The next morning, although the sea continued high, they realized that they must abandon ship. The schooner's hold was nearly full of water and sand. It must soon be overwhelmed.

Thanks to the anonymous drowned sailors, the means of survival was at hand: the rope attached to the shore. Some of the men rigged up a method for pulling an empty cask back and forth between schooner and beach. The cask became a life car, as all the castaways "one by one, were drawn through a very great surf." Not a single person of Elliot's party was lost.

> Providence was pleased even to preserve two little infants that were on board, the one brought on shore upon the father's back, and the other on its mother's.

All were once again on solid ground, but their sufferings were far from over.

Major Elliot and his people spent their first forty-eight hours on Sable Island in wet clothes while searching out enough sails to form a temporary shelter. On the third day they discovered his officer's tent washed up on the beach. For provisions they gathered up the bundles and casks they had jettisoned from the schooner, a surprising quantity of which had reached shore with their contents in edible condition. Elliot rationed these provisions to last until May because he did not expect to see any vessel until the fishermen arrived on their usual spring voyage. This thinking may have been based on information from some other castaways. They were the crew of a fishing schooner from Ipswich, Massachusetts, which stranded at Sable shortly after Elliot's party landed. Elliot included them in the rationing. Each adult was allowed four or five ounces of flour and one gill (four ounces) of rum or wine a day; each group of six would receive four pounds of pork for seven days.

Elliot had hardly finished his calculations when some of the castaways roaming the island made a discovery that relieved them from "this pinching allowance." They came upon a herd of wild horses. The shipwrecked people shot some of the herd and gladly ate horsemeat. Later they saw some "horned cattle," which they also hunted, no doubt by preference.

The reluctant Sable settlers set about constructing some buildings. Their need for shelter was more urgent than that of the victims of the wrecks *Cathrine* and *Légère* because Elliot's party were stranded so late in the year. At that season Sable Island was no stranger to freezing temperatures or to the harshest storms with winds of near-hurricane force and snow or freezing rain. Death from exposure was a very real threat. So the people collected more sails plus yards from the schooner "and Erected ourselves Barracks & a Store house." Each structure was topped by a thatched roof made of Sable marsh grass, or as Elliot called it, "a long sedge that grows there."

Sheltered in these primitive quarters and in no danger of starving, the people endured. But Elliot the army officer did not stoically accept the dictates of fate. Although he was prepared to spend the whole winter on Sable Island, he kept alert for any chance to get off. Every time a vessel was sighted, the castaways made signals to call attention to their plight. Some of the vessels saw the signals but sailed blithely past, filling Elliot with frustration. In his most tolerant moods he showed understanding: "it was too dangerous for them to attempt any thing for our preservation." At other times, he was more inclined to curse their indifference: "none had Charity enough to Come to our relief." Finally on 31 December a schooner appeared offshore and did not go away. It hung around the island for a week sizing up the situation. At last on 7 January 1761 it sent a boat ashore. Deliverance was at hand! But not for everybody; not yet for Major Elliot.

The castaways began embarking the next day. The boat took off a sergeant and seventeen men of Elliot's regiment, the master and sailors from his schooner, and the fishermen from the sloop wrecked after Elliot. In all, less than half the people marooned on the island. Then the weather took a turn for the worse, and the captain of the rescue vessel, a small schooner from Marblehead, opted for departure. Elliot "dispatched" him to Halifax and stayed on Sable Island with his wife and the remainder of his group. Ten days later the schooner was back. It picked up everybody and delivered them to Halifax. Elliot's only complaint, a mild one, was that he was forced to abandon what remained of the salvaged stores.

On the whole, Maj. Robert Elliot was fortunate at Sable Island, but the aftermath of his ordeal shows that his Sable experience was costly. In a personal letter from Halifax, he said that he and all the other survivors arrived there "as naked as beggars." Both he and his never-named wife had lost all the personal belongings they had with them. Elliot delayed reporting to his commanding officer in New York on the grounds that he was "in no very good condition for a Voyage." Later that year he suffered a long bout of illness that may have been generated by the strain and deprivation of his time at Sable Island.

In his official report of this episode, Elliot singled out two men for special mention. One was Lieutenant Dalton, who had also lost everything; the other was Sgt. Maj. Thomas Bell. Bell appears to have played a heroic role: "Bell Exerted himself upon this occasion very much, which he has likewise done upon many others." Elliot provided no details, however, in recommending that General Amherst give Bell his due.

Without detracting from the credit due Bell, and Elliot himself, another candidate comes to mind as the hero of this story: the master of the anonymous rescue schooner. To learn about his role we need to shift perspective to Massachusetts. At the same time, looking at events from a different point of view will help fill out Elliot's story and, if we are lucky, support it.

∽∽∽

A memorial to the Governor and Council of Massachusetts in 1762 by "a Number of the Inhabitants of the Town of Marblehead" made no mention of Elliot, but it certainly referred to his Sable Island misadventure.

> A Fishing Vessel belonging to this Town being missing in December 1760 and Two Signals being Perceived on the Isle Sables, by a Vessell returning from the Banks, & Apprehending said Vessell might have been Cast away on said Island, and the People saved, one Mr. Archabald Selman of this Town, made an Offer of himself and his Schooner, to go in Quest of said People.

A group of Marblehead citizens accepted Selman's offer, agreeing to pay him $100 (£30 Massachusetts money) and provide him hands and provisions for the voyage. Without delay Captain Selman sailed for Sable Island.

When Selman reached Sable waters, stormy weather and the dangerous onshore surf prevented him from landing. But he saw signals "hung out" and thought they might be from the missing Marblehead schooner. Selman therefore resolved to keep within range of Sable Island, awaiting an opportunity to go ashore. After riding out several gales, he tried to land a boat. Some of his men reached the beach despite "the Sea Running high"; others, with Selman, were compelled to pull the boat off and head back to the schooner. The next day Captain Selman tried again, with success. His satisfaction was, however, short lived.

Selman found no Marblehead men on Sable Island. He had no choice but to take off some of the people he did find. He and his crew rescued twenty-five men "belonging mostly to his Majesty's Regulars" before conditions again became too dangerous. Rather than hang about waiting on the weather, Selman sailed to Halifax. There he delivered his load of castaways and reported the Sable wreck.

Thinking that he had done his duty, Captain Selman prepared to return to Massachusetts with the Ipswich fishermen. Much to his chagrin, the authorities in Halifax had other ideas. "Lord Colvil and the Governor of Hallifax Engaged, and forced" Selman to sail back to Sable Island. On this second voyage he brought off forty-six more people, "being all the Persons then Living on said Island." After transporting all of his passengers to Halifax, Captain Selman then "brought home Eight of them belonging to Ipswich."

On the whole Selman's story and Elliot's are in agreement; the differences are minor. By Selman's count, the total number of castaways was seventy-one; in an informal letter, Elliot said seventy. Elliot's group, then, numbered sixty-two or sixty-three persons. This total included women and children, who remained on the island until the second trip, according to both men. Neither explains why. A probable cause is the violent surf during the first rescue mission. The Marblehead memorial implies that Selman did not take off the Ipswich fishermen in the first load, but Elliot lists them among the departing castaways. Elliot is undoubtedly right, since Captain Selman intended to sail home from Halifax.

Selman's first loyalty was to the Cape Ann fishermen. Perhaps more to the point, his self-interest gave them priority. Selman's ideas on this score conflicted with those of the men in charge at Halifax: Alexander Colvill, commander-in-chief of the British naval forces, and Jonathan Belcher, the administrator of the civil government who was soon to become Lieutenant Governor of Nova Scotia. Their priority was the rescue of the remainder of Major Elliot's party. Apparently they made no offer to pay for Selman's service but coerced him into making an unpaid contribution to the war effort.

That was the point of the Marblehead memorial. It stated that Captain Selman had been rewarded for his service to the Ipswich men but "he has not been Rewarded for his first adventure." Since none of the rescued people belonged to Marblehead, the petitioners thought it "hard to be Chargeable" for Selman's claim. The committee of the Massachusetts legislature that considered the memorial agreed. It deducted about eight pounds from Selman's expense account, and the House of Representatives and Council authorized a payment of seventy-six pounds and change. (One of Selman's expenses that might have been reduced or disallowed was £4/5/4 for thirty-two gallons of rum.) Incidentally, this Captain Selman was not the same man who owned the schooner lost to the privateer at Sable in 1758, but he was probably a relative.

∽∾∾

Another person also had a valid claim to credit for the survival of the Elliot castaways: Andrew LeMercier. While his associates deserve a share of his honours, as the initiator of the whole operation LeMercier must be given first place. His name was the first officially connected with the Sable Island project and the last publicly, spanning a period of fifteen years. The minister's most active partner during that time was John Gorham, and his most silent one was Thomas Hancock. Hancock, one of the wealthiest men in the colonies, was a source of money and influence. No proof has ever been offered that he expended much of either on behalf of Sable Island. Because of his high profile—the famous John Hancock was his nephew and heir—Thomas has often been credited with founding the herds of Sable livestock. But if Hancock paid the costs of shipping any domestic animals to the island, which is quite likely, he did so only as part of Andrew LeMercier's grand scheme.

By 1760 the active involvement of LeMercier and his people with Sable Island was a thing of the past. LeMercier had given notice of his decision to abandon Sable Island when he offered it for sale in February 1753. Word of the death of John Gorham, a victim of smallpox in London, had reached Boston in 1752—surely no coincidence. In 1753 LeMercier still had people on the island looking after livestock. Among the livestock were "20 or 30 Horses including Colts, Stallions and breeding Mares, about 30 or 40 Cows tame and Wild." Nobody bought the island, which is just as well, since LeMercier did not own it. He probably could not afford to pay the cost of rounding up and shipping off all his animals, and Hancock was unlikely to help out a man who was laying claim to an island that he desired for himself. LeMercier's Sable project was not destroyed by the attacks of privateers or renegade fishermen. It just petered out, ending not with a bang but a whimper.

No residents and few comforts existed on Sable in Elliot's day, as his dismal description of the island in winter makes clear:

an island barren and uninhabited, with neither a stick of wood upon it, a stone, or a spot of earth, but one intire bank of sand.

(The reference to wood is not meant literally; it refers to the lack of trees not of wreckage.)

Yet Elliot confirms the presence of free-ranging horses and cattle that common sense dictates were some of the animals referred to by LeMercier or else their progeny. No contemporary document denies that Andrew LeMercier began the herds of Sable livestock. Between 1737 and the time of Elliot's shipwreck, nobody independent of LeMercier professed to have shipped livestock to Sable Island. Elliot's record of the killing of horses and cattle documents for the first time the slaughter of LeMercier livestock for

38

the benefit of castaways. The Guillimin episode almost certainly saw the same use made of some of Sr. Sincht's domestic animals, but the known records do not say so.

The aid to shipwrecked people at Sable Island in 1760–61, then, came from Massachusetts. LeMercier's horses and cattle served a good purpose, though there is no proof that he left them for that reason. The rescue effort by Captain Selman resulted from an attempt by the fishing community of Marblehead to look after its own. Nevertheless, the efforts of the Massachusetts entrepreneurs clearly had a potential for good. In Selman's case, the action of the Massachusetts legislature—which sported a codfish symbol in its House of Representatives—showed a recognition of the value of attempts to aid fishermen who ran afoul of Sable Island.

The action of the Nova Scotia authorities, on the other hand, contained a negative potential. However justified Lord Colvill might have been to insist on the English policy that colonials like Selman should contribute to the war effort, his attitude was short-sighted. It was also too contemptuous of Sable Island. Nothing was more certain than that Sable would continue to take a toll of shipping, and the most likely rescuers of Sable castaways were the banks fishermen. The best possible lifesaving service for Sable Island, given its unoccupied state, was encouragement of their charity. Whatever the cost of such encouragement, which would in fact have been minimal, it was cheap at the price.

And yet, the only guarantee of aid to Sable castaways was a settlement on the island all year round. Eventually, somebody in a position of authority was going to be forced to face up to this reality.

Chapter Four

The Impact of Sinking Ships and Mounting Tragedy

By the last decade of the eighteenth century, Nova Scotia was becoming more aware of Sable Island as a serious threat. Halifax had gained importance as a British port with the loss of the American colonies, and the conflict with Napoleon assured its continuing value as a military base. As traffic increased in the sea lanes from Britain to Halifax, more vessels sailed close to Sable Island. Some came too close. In the last years of the century, several of these ships ended their voyages at the island. With each loss, public interest grew, and newspapers both catered to it and aroused greater concern. The published reports were on the whole objective and accurate, but over time factual accounts gave way to rumour and innuendo. Two of the last reported wrecks of the century caused a great deal of excitement at the time, and confusion then and since.

In early January 1798 a message reached Sir John Wentworth, Lieutenant Governor of Nova Scotia, in Halifax. It was a written note from one Thomas Cunningham, master of the American schooner *Hero*, which had staggered into a mainland outport near the end of December. At that time Captain Cunningham and his crew were "in the greatest distress." They were almost out of provisions and water and had suffered greatly from a succession of storms and "the severest Cold." A poor family took the destitute seamen into their cottage and cared for them until they recovered. Cunningham wrote his note in the cottage, for delivery as soon as weather permitted. He left it there when he and his crew departed to complete their voyage. Cunningham's note reported

> that upon the 14th of December, he saw a Number of Men, upon Sable Island making Signals, but the Weather being tempestuous, and he, not in any Situation to relieve them, availed himself of the first opportunity of communicating the melancholy Information.

Lieutenant Governor Wentworth immediately arranged a rescue mission to Sable Island. He hired the Liverpool schooner *Black Snake*, commanded by Thomas Parker, which was fitted out to accommodate passengers. He loaded it with provisions obtained from government stores "thro' the benevolent Orders of Lieutenant General His Royal Highness Prince Edward" plus blankets and warm clothing "by a Loan from a number of the liberal Inhabitants." Wentworth also provided the schooner with an experienced pilot from the government armed brig *Earl of Moira*. On 12 January the *Black Snake* departed for Sable Island.

At Sable Island in the weeks since Captain Cunningham sailed right past, the shipwrecked people had concluded that nobody was coming to their aid. If they were to be rescued before the end of winter, or before winter ended them, they must take action on their own behalf. They decided to send a party to the mainland for help.

Having salvaged the ship's longboat, they decked it with canvas and otherwise did their best to fit it for ocean passage. When the boat was ready, they hauled it to the north beach for launching. Captain Wyatt and four of the hands from the lost vessel, plus a passenger, Lieutenant Cochran of the 7th or Royal Fusiliers Regiment, climbed in and set sail for the mainland.

Another passenger, a merchant named Robert Williams, volunteered to remain on the island. Williams lacked the skills, and probably the physical fitness, to be of use in the boat. Rather than be a hindrance aboard, he hoped to be a help ashore, thinking "that he might encourage and keep up the spirits of his fellow sufferers."

Williams and his companions had hardly settled down to await the outcome of Captain Wyatt's mission when the *Black Snake* hove in sight. But their patience was yet to be tested further; so was Captain Parker's. The always dangerous Sable surf was high. For several days Parker was forced to beat about, encountering "the greatest dangers and severest Weather" before he could send a boat ashore. He was unable to sail his schooner right to the island because Sable lacked both natural harbour and constructed pier. At last a boat crew rowed in to the beach, quickly took the castaways aboard, and rowed them off to the schooner. The *Black Snake* delivered them safely to Halifax on 28 January.

Meanwhile, Captain Wyatt and his longboat crew had reached one of the eastern harbours, where the captain hired a pilot to take them on to Halifax. Their arrival was eagerly and hourly expected when the newspaper account of the wreck was published.

Soon the whole town knew that the lost vessel was the brig *Princess Amelia* on the passage from London to Halifax. The drama of the story was heightened by the local connection. Both the civilian and the military populations were represented among the passengers. The Robert Williams who remained at Sable Island to encourage others was coming to visit his brother, a Halifax resident. The 7th Regiment, whose Lieutenant Cochran had braved the seas in a small boat, was garrisoned in town.

The commanding officer of the 7th also commanded all the forces in Nova Scotia and New Brunswick. He was the previously mentioned Lieutenant General His Royal Highness Prince Edward, fourth son of King George III. Though unpopular among his troops because of his strict military discipline, Edward was more than welcome in Halifax society. Haligonians were English enough to love a lord, not to mention royalty, and North American enough to appreciate his value to the local economy. (His good works in Halifax included a contribution toward the construction of St. George's Round Church.) The prince's friendship with Lieutenant Governor Wentworth added cachet to Wentworth's authority, and his participation in the rescue mission to Sable Island guaranteed the support of local merchants and all with any claim to respectability. Edward's own interest in the wreck could only be increased by its name: Princess Amelia was his youngest sister. This coincidence of names may explain a confusion that arose later. In local annals the *Princess Amelia* became identified with a later wreck of far more personal concern to the prince, one that had much greater impact on the history of Sable Island.

For the record, the interest aroused by the loss of the *Amelia* resulted in a rather half-hearted attempt to provide ongoing aid to victims of shipwreck at Sable Island. On 9 February 1798 Lieutenant Governor Wentworth issued a commission to two Halifax "mariners," Andrew and William Miller.

> Whereas The preservation of the Lives of all such unfortunate persons as may be Shipwrecked on the Island of Sable as well as the saving all such property as may from time to time be cast on shore on the s^d Is^d or the Banks & Soals adjacent thereto are measures which I have thought proper to promote & Encourage as much as in me lieth and having confidence in your fidelity & Zeal I do therefore by Virtue of the Power & Authority to me Granted for that purpose Constitute & appoint you the said A. & W. Miller Keepers of the said Island of Sable for & during pleasure Giving & granting to you by these presents full power & Authority to take all Lawful ways & means in your power to prevent any trespass being committed on the said Island & to Secure & preserve all the Horses & Stock of Cattle which now are or hereafter may be on the s^d Is^d.

The commission continues with more detail and much repetition, but this passage makes its intent clear enough. It marks the first grant of power over Sable Island solely for humane purposes. The Millers received no land rights, no right to exploit Sable resources. On the other hand, they were expected only to keep an eye on the island by occasional visits, not to take up residence. This arrangement was haphazard at best, almost a token reaction to the excitement caused locally by the recent wreck of the

The Duke of Kent (Prince Edward). The prince's residence in Halifax and his intimate friendship with Sir John Wentworth were influential in the founding of the Sable Island Establishment.

Princess Amelia. It lacked any real commitment to solving the problem of Sable shipwrecks.

The *Amelia* incident attracted attention, but something was missing. This shipwreck failed to qualify as the catalyst for a truly historic event. While the story contained dramatic elements, as a motivator it was somehow flawed. Hindsight identifies the flaw as the happy ending. The appeal of a happy ending outweighed concern about the suffering of the castaways and the disastrous loss of property. The destruction of the *Princess Amelia* lacked the high drama of tragedy. The tragic Sable shipwreck of the era was yet to come.

∾∾

Prince Edward sailed for England in October 1798 to convalesce from an injury suffered in a fall from a horse. The following April he became Duke of Kent and Strathearn, and in May commander-in-chief of all British forces in North America. He returned to Halifax in September 1799 an even grander figure than during his previous residence. In keeping with his station, the duke arranged for a magnificent equipage to be shipped to him as soon as possible. The vessel carrying his possessions departed from England in October—and vanished.

By May 1800 the fate of the transport seemed to be sealed. In Halifax concern was all the greater when news arrived that the ship, named *Frances*, was carrying a number of passengers for that port. Many a tall ship of the Age of Sail was posted missing and never heard of again, but in this case Sir John Wentworth decided to check out one possible source of disaster on the North Atlantic run: Sable Island. He arranged for the island to be visited by a small naval vessel bound for Newfoundland. The cutter *Trepassey*, commanded by Lieutenant Scambler, would stop off at Sable and find out whether the *Frances*, or any other vessel, had been wrecked there during the winter.

Scambler arrived at Sable Island on the morning of 13 May and went ashore while the schooner landed some livestock, "the Ewe, goat, Sow, and two Pigs" sent by Wentworth. The lieutenant looked around for about an hour without discovering anybody ashore. Then he noticed a schooner anchored some distance away off the north side. He immediately reboarded the cutter and tried to beat up to the other vessel, but a strong contrary current foiled his efforts. About four o'clock, seeing the schooner under sail, he at once weighed anchor, made sail, and put to sea. He soon came within hailing distance of the schooner and spoke it, like a present-day traffic patrol ordering a motorist to pull over.

On boarding the schooner, Scambler learned that it was the *Dolphin* of Barrington, Nova Scotia, commanded by a Captain Reynolds. At first glance, the schooner seemed to be laden with fish, seal skins, and seal oil. But it also carried some other items of far more interest to Lieutenant Scambler.

She had several Trunks very much damaged on board, and appeared to have been Washed on shore—one trunk was directed, *His Royal Highness Prince Edward No. 2.* Another trunk directed, *Captain Sterling of the 7th Regiment foot*, both empty.—Also a trunk containing two Great Coats, the livery worn by the Servants of His Royal Highness.

Scambler naturally asked how Captain Reynolds happened to be in possession of these articles, which obviously came from the missing *Frances.* Reynolds said that two of his men had spent the winter at Sable Island "on the sealing concern." They had lived in a hut they built at the east end. The two men were on board the schooner, so Scambler questioned them.

The professed sealers told the lieutenant that about the twenty-second of the previous December, "after a very severe gale of wind from the S.e., a woman was found, washed on shore on the south side of the Island." Other flotsam that ended up on the Sable beaches included the trunks found on board the schooner, parts of three boats, papers and letters, and the bodies of twelve shod horses, a few cattle, and a couple of sheep. Captain Reynolds gave Scambler some papers that he had saved. Scambler sent them along with his report of all the other details, which was delivered in Halifax by the man from the *Earl of Moira* who had piloted the *Trepassey* to Sable Island.

The pilot told his own more circumstantial tale. His avowed source was also the two men who had wintered on Sable Island. They told him that they had actually seen the *Frances*, or at least "a large Snow," heading to its doom. (A snow was the largest two-masted ship of the time, rigged as a brig, with square sails on both masts, plus a trysail with a boom set on a small trysail mast behind the mainmast.) When they sighted the snow, it was already close to the northeast bar. "The weather was remarkably fine for a Winter's day, but the Wind was extremely light and baffling." All day long the windjammer tried to beat off the bar, without success. As night was falling, the weather began to thicken, and soon a tremendous gale struck from the southeast. It continued all night. In the morning, no sign of the vessel could be seen. The men and the pilot concluded the obvious: the *Frances* "must have been driven on the Sands, and in the course of the night, have gone to pieces."

Up to this point, the pilot's version was a fairly standard account of a shipwreck. Then, knowingly or otherwise, he added a detail that was bound to give rise to controversy. He referred to the corpse of the woman that came ashore after the storm, which Scambler had mentioned, but the pilot added his own embellishment. "She had a ring on her finger, but not being able to get it off, the men declared they had buried it with her."

The story of the wreck published in the Halifax *Royal Gazette* stated as fact that the corpse was "a woman, with a ring on her finger." The newspaper listed nineteen passengers lost in the wreck including Captain Holland of the 44th Regiment, Captain Sterling and Lieutenant Roebuck of the 7th, Lieutenant Mercer of the Royal Artillery, and "Dr. COPELAND, Surgeon of the Royal Fusiliers, his Lady and family, consisting of five persons." Although the paper did not say so, one of the five in the "family" was a female servant. The only other female in the list was "a woman coming out as housekeeper to Lady WENTWORTH." Of the three women, the only one likely to be wearing a ring of any value was Mrs. Copeland. She and her husband were well known and respected members of Halifax society. The doctor received the only separate epitaph in the article:

> The death of Dr. COPELAND, from an intimate knowledge of his character and worth, having long resided here, is greatly to be lamented, as his manners were amiable, and in every point of view, was by his acquaintance, deservedly considered an ornament to his profession and society, and whilst we deplore his loss, we mingle the tears of sympathy and of condolance, with the surviving relatives and friends of the other unfortunate victims.

The personal connection with the Copelands brought the tragedy home to many. The vision of a wrecker bending over Mrs. Copeland's body to pull a ring off her finger added horror to the tragedy. Speculation and rumour became the order of the day.

The power of the subsequent story of the *Frances* disaster depended on logic rather than facts. It illustrates the danger of ignoring the hidden biases in "common sense." The solid basis of the story was Lieutenant Scambler's report. It revealed that two men living on Sable Island at the time of the wreck had found the corpse of a woman passenger. A hearsay report said that she was wearing a ring and that the men tried to take it off. This statement made the two men into confessed wreckers. At this point, all bets were off, so to speak. The same hearsay report said that the men claimed to have buried the ring with the body. But who would believe a wrecker? If the ring would not come off, a wrecker would hardly have scruples about cutting off the finger. By this reasoning, the next step cast doubt on the drowning of the woman: What if she came ashore alive? In the pursuit of plunder at isolated Sable Island, a wrecker might even resort to murder.

We might be inclined to think that these provocative suspicions were the purview of ignorant and uneducated minds. Such was not the case. These beliefs were sanctioned at the highest official level; for example, in a report written for the lieutenant governor by John Howe, who was soon to become the King's Printer and publisher of the *Royal Gazette*. Howe, whose son Joseph would later achieve greatness, was one of the most respected men of his day. In his "Statement of Facts" about Sable Island, Howe referred to "lawless, unfeeling persons who have chose to winter there." He pointed out how difficult it was for the authorities to discover what property these people might salvage at Sable.

> To prevent such discovery, there is reason to fear that some who
> have escaped shipwreck, have been deprived of their lives by beings
> more merciless than the Waves.

Howe wrote this report shortly after the news of the *Frances* reached town,
and he undoubtedly intended his remarks to apply to it.

What really happened in the shipwreck of the *Frances* and its aftermath
has remained largely a mystery. The attempts to explain the unknown, the
search for a comforting legend, as it were, culminated in a ghost story. The
authoritative version of this legend, titled simply "A Sable Island Ghost
Story," appeared a generation later in *Sam Slick's Wise Saws and Modern
Instances* by another famous Nova Scotian, Thomas Chandler Haliburton.
In this tale, wreckers at Sable Island are suspected of murdering survivors
from a lost ship for their possessions. Prince Edward sends a military officer to the island to investigate. In his hut on Sable one night, the officer
sees the ghost of one of the victims:

> a lady sitting on one side of the fire, with long, dripping hair
> hanging over her shoulders, her face pale as death, and having no
> clothes on but a loose, soiled white dress, wet as if it had come out
> of the sea and with sand sticking to it.

Mutely the woman holds up her hand, and the officer sees that one of the
fingers has been cut off. The wound is still bleeding. He recognizes the
spectre as Mrs. Copeland and realizes that her ring has been stolen. He
swears a vow to the pale lady that he will recover her ring. She smiles,
waves, and runs off. On returning to the mainland, the officer keeps his
word. He tracks down the family of one of the wreckers, recovers the ring,
and sends it to Mrs. Copeland's friends in England.

This curt summary, which hardly does justice to Haliburton's story, is
not intended to denigrate a literary work. Its purpose is to show the lasting
fascination with the *Frances* disaster. Nearly a century after the wreck, in an
addendum to his history of Sable Island, George Patterson tried to analyse
Haliburton's story to get at the underlying facts. Patterson pointed out
many examples of conflict between Haliburton's statements and the historical evidence—including his mistaking the *Princess Amelia* for the
Frances—which showed that they could not be relied on as history. Yet
Patterson himself reached a number of conclusions that were unsupported
by valid historical evidence.

Patterson said wrongly that Lieutenant Scambler's report, rather than
the anonymous pilot via Howe, was the source of the story of Mrs.
Copeland's ring. He stated as fact that her body came ashore with the
finger so swollen that the ring could not be removed. Then he questioned
the credibility of the only possible primary sources of this information.
"The story of the finders that they buried it with her is quite incredible."
At this point, Patterson resorted to innuendo:

This scene by DesBarres based on his visits to Sable in 1766–67, encouraged the belief that wreckers had long inhabited the island. The wild horses on the right, however, were not figments of the artist's imagination but progeny of animals sent by Andrew LeMercier.

> tradition…tells that she was cast upon the shore not dead but only
> in a state of insensibility, and that when the wretch began cutting
> off her finger to get the ring she rose to confront him.

So "there were those who believed that the robber had added murder to his other crimes." Tradition also said that the ring was recovered, and Patterson had "not the least doubt" about that. Haliburton said that the robber would not go out at night, and a widespread story depicted the man as suffering all the anguish and terrors of a guilty conscience. Some alleged that the man saw a continuous vision of his victim pointing her mutilated finger at him. Patterson concluded with a passage intended to be taken as fact, suited to the biases of his educated audience.

> The case was one fitted to excite the superstitions of the fishermen.
> So that we need not be surprised to learn, that in the weird shapes,
> which the mists and vapours assume amid the gray sandhills, they
> believed they saw the shade of the pale lady in her long white robe,
> her hair floating to the wind, and her hand stretched out as in the
> act of reclaiming her ring.

That a respected historian would take these traditions seriously so long after the event, accepting without question the hearsay report on which they were based is a sign of the mythic power of the catastrophe of the

Frances. Patterson's instincts told him that what actually happened might not be as important as what people thought happened. In this context, both he and Haliburton said that rumours of piracy after the wreck led to government action. In other words, concern about what might have happened in the past led to concern about what might happen in the future. The dangerous potential of Sable Island took on a new immediacy. The *Frances* remains a symbol for this heightened awareness, which was to have long-lasting results.

∞∞

By coincidence the Lady Wentworth whose prospective housekeeper had died in the recent shipwreck was named Frances. And her husband happened to be Sir John Wentworth, Lieutenant Governor of Nova Scotia, who became the leader of the effort to change the status of Sable Island.

On several previous occasions Sir John had taken steps to alleviate suffering at Sable: by sending aid to known shipwrecks, by putting domesticated animals ashore, and by appointing keepers of the island. The *Frances* catastrophe seemed to make nonsense of those attempts. Aside from the content of the rumours that floated freely about the port of Halifax, their very existence made a crucial point. In the words of John Howe,

> even where Vessels and their Crews are totally lost, as in the case of the Francis, how great would be the satisfaction to ascertain to a certainty the fate that had awaited them.

There was only one way to achieve such certainty. Sable Island must be permanently populated, and the settlers must be in government service. The term adopted to embody this idea was "an establishment on Sable Island."

Wentworth knew that the time was ripe for such a proposal. The climate of opinion in Nova Scotia favoured some measure to combat Sable terrors. He also knew the limitations of local support. In Nova Scotia generally, concern for safety at sea rated a far lower priority than concern for the development of roads inland. When the crunch came, inflamed emotions were not likely to overrule local self-interest. Although the people's representatives in the House of Assembly would support a plan for Sable settlement, they would keep the costs down. The support of Wentworth's cronies in the Council, selected by himself, and the power of his patronage over ambitious men could take him only so far. But in the betwixt and between role of a lieutenant governor of a colony in the British Empire, Wentworth had another string to his bow. He could turn to the Home government for sponsorship of his plan. To tap the vast imperial resources, all he had to do was sell his scheme to the Colonial Office. In view of the far greater potential, financially speaking, of English support, Wentworth tried London first.

In the summer of 1800 he dispatched a package to Whitehall. Included in it were a copy of Scambler's report, John Howe's "Statement of Facts," and his own "Observations," which expounded his concept of the required establishment. The theme of this package was the value of a Sable Island Establishment to international shipping. Howe adopted a journalistic approach, striving for maximum effect rather than strict accuracy, but on the whole his picture of the destructiveness of Sable Island was valid. He described a series of past wrecks at the island, ending with a detailed report of the *Frances*. His message was clear:

> Every year adds to the calamities occasioned by this dreadful
> Island, and points out the necessity of some establishment under
> the sanction of the government.

Wentworth's plan for that "establishment" insisted on certain points. The first step must be to induce families, not just male workers, to reside on the island by the offer of pay and provisions. The settlers would be subject to the control of a "Commandant," who would be "a Gentleman of respectability and character." In other words, the "Families in the lower classes of Life," the only kind who would be attracted by the available wages, would be kept in line by a man from the upper classes hired to take charge of them. This man would be directly responsible to the lieutenant governor and would have six men under his command. Wentworth expected the total number of families to be the same as the number of men employed, presumably including the Commandant's.

With regard to costs Wentworth was ambiguous. He said that the start-up cost would be about fifteen hundred pounds, and annual expenses about nine hundred pounds plus the cost of provisions, i.e., well over one thousand pounds a year. He thought that in the long run these costs might be largely offset by salvaging aided by the exploitation of Sable Island resources. At the same time, Wentworth hinted at the need for financial support from elsewhere. He said that the commercial and military interests of Great Britain "suggest that this Establishment should be under the Control of, and made and Maintained by Great Britain," though he went on to say that it must be "furnished, supplied, supported and Governed" from Nova Scotia. He added that since it would benefit the eastern states of America, they would probably willingly contribute toward its expense.

The secretary of state in charge of the colonies ignored Wentworth's hints and adopted a policy of delay. In an October dispatch, he commented that Wentworth's proposal required "mature consideration." He advised that the first thing to do was to survey the island and look for a good spot for a lighthouse. Wentworth had already said that current opinion doubted that a lighthouse would prevent many of the wrecks at Sable Island and that only future observation and experience could settle the matter. The secretary of state was therefore wilfully avoiding the immediate needs at Sable Island as revealed in the package Wentworth had sent him.

Those needs had more force in Nova Scotia, where the calamity of the *Frances* was not forgotten. In early June 1801 another Sable wreck was

*Sir John Wentworth, originator of the Sable Island Establishment,
the forerunner of Canada's coastguard service.*

reported in Halifax, and the lieutenant governor dispatched a vessel to its assistance. Meanwhile the House of Assembly took more decisive action. On 15 June it appointed a committee to devise a plan for settling some families of good character on Sable Island for the preservation of lives and property wrecked there. The committee decided on a total of three families, and the House agreed to grant up to £600 "which the House conceive will be sufficient for attaining the Object in View." In July Wentworth appointed a five-man joint committee, two from the Council and three from the Assembly, who received £600 from the provincial treasurer to carry out the Assembly's plan.

This committee constituted Commissioners for Sable Island, though they were not immediately known by that title. They carried out their mission of settling the island, but the arrangements they made differed from what the Assembly had envisioned. The Assembly plan called for three houses to be built, one for each family of unpaid settlers. The Commissioners later explained that they were unable to find fit persons willing to settle permanently on Sable Island without government assistance. So the Commissioners were "compelled to agree with persons on terms of Wages and Support for eight or nine months, or to abandon the Undertaking entirely!" They also found that £600 was not enough for three houses plus the other necessary supplies and equipment for the Establishment. They therefore built only one, plus a smaller building to serve as shelter until the house was finished. For staff they hired "three men and a boy" to accompany the man in charge, who would come to be called the Superintendent of Sable Island. The Commissioners' choice for Superintendent was James Morris, who was recommended as possessing "activity, resolution, and a considerable degree of resource," and was "also known to be humane and friendly."

The prospective settlers left Halifax for Sable Island in early October 1801. By the fourteenth all the people and supplies had been landed, and the two vessels that delivered them had departed. Nearly two years after the destruction of the *Frances* on the northeast bar, the Sable Island Establishment was beginning.

Chapter Five

The Loss and Gain of the
Hannah and Eliza

In December 1801 a full-rigged ship was nearing home on the last leg of a transatlantic voyage, her hold filled with salt from Lisbon. A salt cargo in a windjammer in the North Atlantic carrying trade signalled a good tight vessel. Rated A1 at Lloyd's, the 231-ton *Hannah and Eliza* was indeed a quality ship. By the general rule, the captain and crew would match their vessel in merit. But good ships and good men guaranteed no immunity from the hazards of the sea, or Sable Island.

The *Hanna and Eliza* was clawing a passage against contrary winds and currents. It had reefs taken in the topsails to offer less resistance to the strong winds. Even so, as the square-rigger tacked to make progress westward, the wind was forcing it north. The ship's captain, William Burrows, thought that he was well past Sable Island and to the south of it. He expected soon to strike soundings on Brown's Bank off the southwest end of Nova Scotia. His reckoning was off by some 5° of longitude, about two hundred and fifty miles, as well as about 1° of latitude. This error doomed his ship. On 16 December the *Hannah and Eliza* sailed blindly into the south side of Sable Island.

The grasping sands paralysed the ship's legs, while the waves began to pound the body to death. The December gale bent the sails and masts to the sea. The same forces that had given the ship life on the open sea now became a deadly threat to all on board.

Recovering from the shock of their stranding, the ship's crew did what had to be done. They cut down all three masts, which fell overboard in a mess of spars and rigging. Then they abandoned ship. They launched two boats, jumped into them and, by a combination of luck and skill, rowed through the lethal breakers to shore.

All thirteen of the ship's company landed safely on the beach. Wet, cold, at the mercy of the piercing wind, they now faced death by exposure.

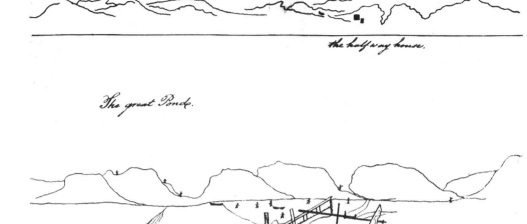

the half way house.

The great Pond.

The wreck Hannah and Eliza *as sketched by Superintendent Morris.*
This is the earliest known picture of a Sable wreck by an eyewitness.

Struggling through the drifts of sand piled up like snow, they searched along the wall of low but steep hills for an easy route inland. They headed eastward to keep the wind at their backs. After trudging a short distance down the beach, they spotted a breach in the natural barrier, climbed through, and found themselves in a small valley. It was the most sheltered location around.

The shipwrecked seamen returned to the beach to recover what they could from their lost vessel. With the ingenuity of their kind, they used salvaged materials to build themselves a den. It was a makeshift tent formed from a sail, the sides held down and barricaded by casks of bread and other heavy articles. When the Jack Tars finished it, they crawled inside to spend the night. They were safe from freezing for now, but their future prospects looked grim.

The next morning brought snow and cold westnorthwest winds with violent squalls. The castaways huddled in their den to wait for a change of weather. Late in the morning, they heard a noise outside. Peering out they saw, to their surprise, a man on horseback. The seamen rushed out and discovered that their visitor was James Morris, Superintendent of the Sable Island Establishment. All at once their survival was certain, their future prospects bright.

Captain Burrows deferred to Superintendent Morris in making plans for the treatment of the castaways and the handling of the wreck. Morris directed two of his men to help the seamen move across the lake to a building called the halfway house, located about midway between the ends of the lake. It was a cabin made of plank, about twenty-four by eighteen feet, built by some unknown Sable dweller of the past. It had everything needed for a comfortable residence except that it was in poor repair.

While two of Morris's men helped collect firewood for the halfway house and grass for bedding, Captain Burrows accompanied Morris to the Main Station, where he and his servant were to live among the Establishment people.

Burrows discovered that the islanders were a mixed lot. Seven were his housemates: Superintendent Morris and his wife, their female servant, Morris's boy apprentice John Myers, and three Sable hands named Adam Moore, David Ross, and James McLaughlan. Only the males received wages from the Sable Island Commissioners. The women were of course expected to perform the usual household duties and also attend to the needs of castaways when required. They would treat Captain Burrows, for example, as a special guest.

The only other Sable residents, bringing the total number to twelve, were the King family. They lived apart from the official house but nearby, in their own little shack. The Kings were squatters whose Sable settlement predated the founding of the Establishment. When the government settlers arrived, the father of the family had been compelled to make a deal with Superintendent Morris. To prevent himself, his wife, and their three children from being deported, Patrick King signed an agreement to serve under Morris without pay or provisions.

The little settlement that made up the lifesaving station included Morris's two-storey house, a storehouse, and a barn for the few livestock. Situated just west of the lake, it was about five and a half miles from the west end of the island. About eight miles to the eastward, on the north side of the lake, stood the halfway house. With its eleven castaways it was now the only other occupied building on the island. From the halfway house to the east end, a distance of about sixteen miles, Sable was deserted. The only shelters in the eastern half of the island were a few small and rundown huts of unknown origin.

For the first few days after the wreck, Captain Burrows and his crew worked with Morris and his men to salvage as much as possible from their ship. They used their den for temporary shelter near the work site. Their first priority, being mindful of the long winter ahead, was to salvage their personal baggage plus provisions from the ship's stores. When the sea fell, they boarded the wreck and brought ashore boatload after boatload of goods. With weather and seas so uncertain, they hurried to land all available property. Then with the help of Morris's horse, Jolly, the only domesticated horse on the island, they hauled it overland to the lake. Here they again loaded it into boats for the crossing to the halfway house.

On 21 December Captain Burrows walked down with Morris to pay a visit to his men in their new quarters. The two commanders found all well "except one man taken with the cramp in the water, being wet and cold so long." They also witnessed the arrival of a boatload of goods from across the lake: "the appearance of the men, and the confused order of the things saved from the wreck (being all wet and in sand and snow) was truly lamentable."

Feeling sorry for the *Hannah and Eliza* men, Burrows and Morris worked together to make their living quarters more comfortable. The self-appointed handymen covered the roof with sails and caulked the sides to keep the wet and wind out and the heat in. They cut more grass for bedding and made a storeroom for the provisions. With these improvements, and a good supply of firewood, the halfway house promised to be a warm residence for the winter. (The castaways in fact made such good use of their fireplace that the Superintendent would soon find it necessary to supply them with fifteen sheets of tin for the back of their chimney for safety.)

By Christmas Day all the castaways were settled into their new quarters. The men had sorted out their chests and bags and dried out their clothes and other things. Captain Burrows did the same with his baggage, though he had help from others in Morris's house. Burrows and Morris had calculated a schedule of rations from the available provisions for the seamen living on their own, to which "All cheerfully agreed." The weather remained cold and frosty with heavy gusts of wind, but Burrows and his shipwrecked company had good reason to echo Morris's Christmas sentiment that "Hallelujahs should be sung."

The good fortune of their survival did not alter the fact that the *Hannah and Eliza* seamen found themselves in an odd position. Most, if not all, of them belonged to the first generation of Americans. Some may have fought against the British during the Revolution. Now they found themselves stranded indefinitely on a desolate island under the control of a British governor of ill-defined powers. They had reason to be grateful to Superintendent Morris, but gratitude did not dictate unqualified acceptance of his authority in their everyday lives at Sable Island. Under the circumstances, the Jack Tars looked to their captain for leadership.

The odds seemed to be that Captain Burrows would come into conflict with Superintendent Morris. Aside from the difference of nationality, there were other potential sources of rivalry. Burrows was a merchant seaman, while Morris had spent fourteen years in the Royal Navy. Burrows was still an active mariner, commanding his own ship, whereas Morris had retired from the sea. And Burrows had lost his ship under circumstances that might have invited comment from a person with a critical bent.

In the event, Burrows learned that he and Morris had a lot in common. Both had roots in Massachusetts. Morris's mother and father lived for years in or near Boston, Burrows's hometown. Morris himself had been born near Boston, in Hopkinton, where he lived as a child. His family had moved to Nova Scotia long before the Revolution; they were not United Empire Loyalists. The connection between the Nova Scotia Morrises and family members in the United States was still strong. Both Burrows and Morris were veteran mariners, and the captain's role on board ship was comparable to that of the Superintendent of Sable Island. Each man was the only social equal of the other among the men at Sable. While the two had good reason, then, to treat one another with respect, a closer relationship would depend on the mysteries of personality. In this regard, we do not know whether the deciding factor was what they had in common or what we call an attraction of opposites. We can only know the result.

Captain Burrows gave Morris his personal support, both moral and practical. He also encouraged the *Hannah and Eliza* crew to follow his lead. Burrows extended his influence to the halfway house through his ship's officers, the two mates living there. They were well situated to exert control over their shipmates and to extend a line of communication between the halfway house and the Main Station.

For the most part, the seamen lived independently at Sable. On their own behalf, they collected and cut up firewood—an endless task in winter—and hunted game, mostly ducks, to supplement their supply of food. But they also contributed to the Sable coastguard service.

Merely by living at the halfway house, the *Hannah and Eliza* sailors provided a second manned outpost well down-island. In their wanderings, they extended the patrols for signs of wrecks. And their very presence tripled the available manpower on the island. The value of these extra hands in case of an emergency was incalculable. The expanded workforce was also a huge advantage for any large project or heavy work of the Establishment. The only question was the willingness of the Jack Tars to contribute to such work. Thanks largely to the example set by Captain Burrows, the answer to that question was positive.

The first labours of the castaway hands were in their own interest: saving provisions and personal baggage from the wreck. Next they extended their efforts to salvaging the ship's materials: sails, rigging, spars, cables, anchors, "camboos" (ship's stove). Working with the government salvagers, they were able to pick up most of the sails and rigging when a southeast gale drove them onto the beach "in a miserable grope [group]." Another storm turned the stranded hull sideways, parallel to the beach, and drove it in as well, enabling the men to walk on board dry. In the following days, they made short work of taking off everything removable, including three anchors. By this time the sand was almost up to the deck. A fine tall ship had become nothing but a good source of firewood.

The next contribution by the seamen arose from a grand project conceived by Superintendent Morris. He had decided to build an ocean-going vessel to take them and some of the salvaged goods to the mainland. The foundation of this vessel would be the ship's longboat, which Morris intended to lengthen and deck over. The first step in the project was to bring the longboat to a convenient work site, near the Main Station. Even with a large workforce, this job would be difficult, and not without danger.

All hands laboured in wind and rain to drag the longboat from the south beach into the lake, then take it across to the north side. Here they left it until better weather would allow them to drag it across "our hawling place," an overland passage between lake and sea. They planned to launch the boat from the north beach and take it by sea up to the Main Station. The *Hannah and Eliza* men, who might have favoured Morris's idea out of self-interest, worked with a will. It was Establishment hands who showed a lack of enthusiasm. Superintendent Morris was dissatisfied with David Ross's half-hearted effort. He also noted that Adam Moore complained about injuring himself in a fall in the longboat. Although both incidents were trivial at the time, afterward Superintendent Morris began to view his own crew with a jaundiced eye. For support he looked more and more to Captain Burrows and the other officers and men of the wrecked *Hanna and Eliza*.

Early in the new year 1802 all hands laboured to bring the ship's longboat the rest of the way to the construction site. This stage of the journey was the most dangerous, with the Sable surf an ever-present threat. As they were launching the longboat from the north beach, a sudden heave of the sea threw some men under it. This time luck was with them: all escaped serious injury.

With the longboat hauled up close to home, the Sable crew prepared tools and collected materials for renovating it. They sharpened adze and ax, both crosscut and whip saws. They travelled down to the wreck and cannibalized it, taking timber, spars, iron—whatever might prove useful. Back at the station they sawed the salvaged wood into lumber suitable for the planned vessel.

Meanwhile, Morris and Burrows began work on the longboat itself. They would perform most of the skilled labour on the project. Morris was a talented boat builder, and he recognized Burrows as "a handy man at the business." They knew that the longboat would serve as a good foundation for a sloop or schooner because it was both new and strongly built. So the first thing they did was saw it in two across the middle! Then they restructured the entire vessel from the bottom up. They added a six-foot keel and put in the "Garboard streaks," or strakes, the planks whose sides were rabbeted into the keel, running from stem to sternpost. The island crew helped with the heavy labour, as the Superintendent and captain laid the kelson, or inner keel, and attached the frame timbers to form the skeleton of the new vessel. The purpose of this remodelling was twofold: to increase the size of the original boat and to strengthen the whole structure. Morris and Burrows attached the planks on the bottom and sides to complete the outer shell of the hull. Meanwhile the men picked oakum or old rope to make caulking for filling in the cracks between the planks.

In the dead of winter progress was slow, for the boat builders were working outside. The weather allowed only four workdays in one three-week stretch. By mid-February the builders had added the top timbers to the ribs and completed the frame at stem and stern. From then on, Morris and Burrows were able to work fairly steadily. They laid the main deck, caulked the seams and waterproofed them by covering the oakum with hot pitch, then added a layer of canvas. On top of this deck they built a quarterdeck, "done in the same manner." By 19 March the masts and bowsprit were in, the rudder was hung, and Captain Burrows was adding the finishing touches to his paint job.

The original open boat, nineteen by seven feet, had been transformed into a decked vessel twenty-seven feet long and eight feet nine inches wide. The new two-masted sailing vessel was completely fitted, right down to the anchor made from the rudder irons of the *Hannah and Eliza*. The name on the stern bespoke the purpose for which it was built: *Hazard*.

Morris and Burrows were justifiably pleased with their handiwork. Captain Burrows had additional cause to be satisfied. The *Hazard* was his ticket to the mainland. It symbolized freedom for himself and his marooned crew. And yet, in the event, not all of the castaways would escape Sable Island when the *Hazard* sailed. No explanation was offered for the failure of five of the ship's crew to depart with Captain Burrows. A possible explanation may be found in other happenings during this period.

∽⌇∼

While Superintendent Morris and Captain Burrows were enjoying the exercise of their craftsmanship, and other seamen were living peacefully at the halfway house, some of the Sable Island crew were not happy in their work. The trouble seems to have begun over horsemeat. On 23 January Superintendent Morris sent his men to the east end "with Snares to catch a wild horse for beef." The men returned empty-handed. Their failure in the hunt and their general behaviour afterward signalled a strong distaste for the very idea of killing and eating Sable Island horses.

On the way home the hunters had stopped off at the halfway house, where one of them gave voice to a litany of complaints. The list included standard items in such conflicts: too much hard work for too little pay, inadequate provisions (including in this case a dearth of rum), and flaws of the man in charge. Captain Burrows either witnessed or was told about this performance. He loyally reported the incident to Superintendent Morris.

The Superintendent viewed such talk as dangerous: it might "poison the minds" of others. He saw a need to deliver a message to warn off potential troublemakers. Since the only man in Morris's own house who was reasonably certain to back him up was Captain Burrows, Morris chose not to confront the real issue head-on. Without naming the Sable hand who had done all the talking, he decided to make an example of Patrick King.

The Superintendent's rationale for choosing King to act against was that King had embezzled a quantity of cotton from a wreck before the founding of the Sable Establishment. The truth is that King, for whatever reasons, had failed to find favour with Morris and he was a safe target. A conflict with him would likely have fewer repercussions than one with a man living under the same roof. So on a frosty February morning Superintendent Morris led a group of men through ten inches of recent snow to the door of King's house. At Morris's side was Captain Burrows. In short order, the men seized all of King's cotton and returned it to the station.

It soon became clear that the indirect approach would not work. The Superintendent and his crew were heading for a confrontation. When Morris sent the men down to the *Hannah and Eliza* to spend a few days breaking up the wreck, they hardly made a dent in it. The weather had turned bitterly cold, but Morris did not offer this as an excuse. Twice he sent them to dig up an anchor from an earlier wreck that lay buried in the sand and nearly covered with water. Both times they failed. On the second occasion, in early March, two of the men gave vent to their frustrations. This time Morris named the culprits: "Moore and Ross, shews bad dispositions." The next day he sent the crew after a boat that had been left down the lake past the wreck. They came back and reported it frozen in the ice. Doubting their word, Morris turned to the *Hanna and Eliza* seamen for assistance.

He sent his apprentice boy with a letter to the halfway house. The letter requested the sailors to check the eastern part of the lake for ice and as soon as possible bring up a boatload of plank. The boy returned about four o'clock and told Morris that east of their quarters the seamen found the lake clear. This report confirmed Morris's suspicion that his crew had lied about the boat being iced in. The time had come to confront them about their bad attitude.

> I took a copy of their Articles of agreement – and nailed it on the partition in their room, as by their conduct, I had reason to suppose they were ignorant of their duty – but when I left the house with Cap:t Burrowes, to work at the long boat – Mr. Moore and Ross by force took down the paper and divided it between them – my wife in the interim begged of them not to do it - but they did it in defiance of my authority – Thus the public are insulted.

This act of defiance brought the conflict between Morris and his men to a head.

The Superintendent took steps to resolve what he now viewed as a crisis. With the support of Captain Burrows, he turned again to the halfway house for help. The day after the outburst by Moore and Ross, on Saturday 6 March, Morris paid a visit to the seamen in their quarters. He arranged with the mates for the *Hannah and Eliza* crew to come to the Main Station after the weekend and help bring Moore to book and separate him and Ross.

At 10:00 A.M. on Monday, eight men arrived from the halfway house to take Moore away. One of the seamen had agreed to remain as a replacement. Faced with a showdown, Moore gave in. In front of the whole company, he promised "that he would conduct better in future." So Superintendent Morris relented and let him stay. The sailors returned home without Moore, but they had served their purpose. The open rebellion of the Establishment hands was over. The Sable staff might still complain and gripe on occasion, but so long as the marooned sailors stood behind Superintendent Morris, the outnumbered malcontents posed no threat.

∽∾∽

On 3 April 1802 the schooner *Hazard*, ballasted with bags of Sable Island sand, was launched from the north beach for its trip to the mainland. The crew comprised Capt. William Burrows with his servant John Baptisto; first mate J.T. Clarke; seamen Thomas Thomas, Stephen Davis, Daniel Row, and Amos Atwill; and cook Samuel Britton. Besides the men's chests and bedding, it carried enough wood, water, and food for fifteen days. Captain Burrows also carried a letter from Superintendent Morris for the Sable Island Commissioners in Halifax.

Five men from the *Hannah and Eliza* remained on the island: second mate Robinson and four seamen. Whether they stayed by Superintendent Morris's request is unknown, but they undoubtedly favoured him by their presence. With their backing, Superintendent Morris could still outnumber any agitators among the Establishment hands.

The number of the reputed culprits—and of the coastguard crew—was in fact reduced by one on the day the *Hazard* departed. The boat taking off the last load of chests to the schooner was caught by the surf, just as the longboat had been in January. This time all did not escape unharmed. A wave threw Patrick King under the boat, which might have proved fatal if Morris had not quickly hauled him out, "for the next Sea would have crushed him, but one of his legs was shockingly wounded." This accident was hardly a good omen for the people who must remain on the island and wait for relief.

Despite the approach of spring, the weather remained generally cold, and occasional warmings brought fog that blotted out the sun. The cold killed the newborn lambs. The supply of provisions was fast running low,

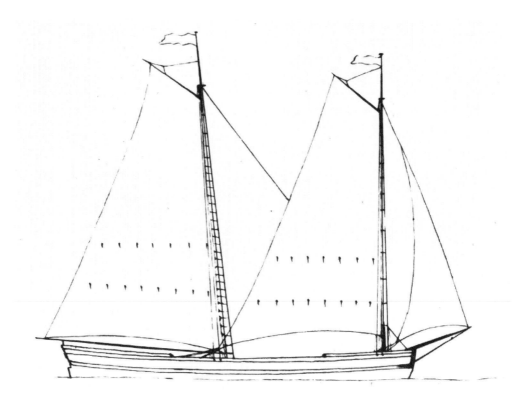

Superintendent Morris's schooner Hazard. *Though far from being the first sailing vessel built at Sable Island, the* Hazard *is the earliest of which we have a visual record and the first built at the Sable Island Establishment.*

and none of it was fresh. One likely food source, fishing from the island, was prevented by the dangers of the surf and the distance offshore of the schools of fish. The first fresh fish received at the Main Station was by way of a gift. Of slight value in itself, its worth to the Establishment can hardly be exaggerated.

What happened was that Superintendent Morris invited mate Robinson to come live at his house to replace Captain Burrows, and Robinson did not come empty-handed. He brought "a large Codfish – gave him yesterday by a fisherman – which landed abreast of the wreck in a Schooner, ten days from Boston." This mundane gift to Morris by a castaway from a Boston vessel, himself probably a New Englander, exudes symbolism. Robinson's codfish represented the beginning of friendly contact between the fleet of American fishermen and the Sable Island of the Establishment era. Robinson would later serve as a go-between for Morris and the New England fishermen.

In the meantime, Superintendent Morris deemed the threat of scurvy serious enough to warrant the slaughter of a ram. The people had begun to complain of pain and dizziness, which he diagnosed as symptoms of a more serious illness than malnutrition.

A few days afterward four schooners hove in sight off the north side when the sea was relatively smooth. Superintendent Morris took advantage of the favourable conditions to sail off to them, accompanied by Robinson. He and Robinson boarded a fine new schooner from Chatham, Cape Cod, only twelve days out from Boston.

The captain and crew greeted them hospitably and offered Superintendent Morris provisions or anything else he needed. But the fishermen refused to take any payment. Morris therefore felt constrained by his official orders, which forbade the taking of gifts, to refuse their offer. The solution to this farcical dilemma was second mate Robinson. Not being a member of the Sable Island Establishment, he was free to accept gifts. So he did. The fishermen loaded him up with supplies: a gallon of molasses, a bushel of potatoes, a bottle of spirits, "some fish, tobacco, &c." Robinson would naturally share his good fortune with his shipmates and the people he lived with in Morris's house. Protocol was satisfied—and for the moment, so were the people's stomachs.

Morris would still have preferred to catch his own fish. But the prevailing conditions were against him: "the wind never ceases to blow, and a continual sea on shore, that at the smoothest time, it is dangerous to launch the boat." At last a calm day in April permitted a boat to be launched and rowed nearly ten miles out to sea. Aided by mate Robinson, the Sable crew caught twelve cod, a haddock, and a pollock. On this trip, Superintendent Morris discovered that, even under the best conditions, seamanship was not his crew's métier. He said bluntly that Robinson was the only good oarsman. So Morris decided to try the lake instead; the fishermen had told him that a few years ago it contained plenty of haddock. The trip down the lake produced no fish, but it led to an eventful discovery.

On the way home, the Sable fishermen stopped off at the halfway house, where four of the castaways were still living on their own. The day before, being out of provisions, the Jack Tars had gone hunting. Two of them had bagged a pair of ducks and an owl when they suddenly came face to face with a herd of wild horses. Horses and men were both startled. The master stallion recovered first and charged the sailors. One man fled behind a sandhill; the other stood his ground and fired. The musket shot struck the horse in the upper chest, killing him. The practical seamen skinned and quartered the carcass for meat. According to Morris, they found the horsemeat "excellent venison, and very fat."

Superintendent Morris here saw more than a gift horse; it was a heaven-sent opportunity. He decided to move the four seamen to his house, with their baggage and their game. By this move, he acquired not only a good boat crew but also the first Sable Island horsemeat for the Establishment menu. He cut up and salted a barrel of the meat and served some fresh. He also announced a horsemeat policy: "They may eat of it who has a mind, I shall neither ask or desire any to eat." To set an example, Morris and Robinson ate the "Horse beef" daily; so did Morris's apprentice boy and the family maid, neither of whom had much choice in the matter. The seamen said they liked it, but the Establishment hands steadfastly rejected it though little else remained for them to eat.

As April turned to May, with the dearth of provisions and a return of cold, squally weather, everybody's patience was wearing thin. The people complained at the lack of bread; the only ground meal available was sour and musty. They said they liked seal meat, so Morris sent the men to the northwest bar on a hunt. They came back empty-handed—seals were scarce, but Morris blamed their failure on "Inactivity." Robinson and his ship-mates took on the duty of fishing for the Establishment. They made a few forays out to sea, also without success. On one occasion, the weather shut down just as they were leaving the beach, and they dared not go offshore in thick fog. On another, an equally calm day but clearer, they tested numerous spots between three and fifteen miles from shore but caught nothing—this time Morris blamed poor bait. The only successful pursuit of game was the occasional bagging of wild ducks. Morris and his men had recourse to some odd food items. On their return from one failed seal hunt, the Sable hands brought two halibut heads found on the beach. Once, Morris used a piece of despised horsemeat as bait and shot four seagulls. By mid-May the grumbling had become general.

Finally Superintendent Morris decided that the state of privation justified the slaughter of more livestock. He killed the boar early in the morning on 17 May. A few hours later, the relief vessel from Halifax arrived.

Fueled by fresh provisions, all hands spent several days landing supplies for the Establishment and shipping off salvage. Boatload after boatload travelled between vessel and beach without serious incident. On 22 May the last of the *Hannah and Eliza* castaways sailed for the mainland along with Superintendent Morris and most of his people.

∽∾∽

The loss of the *Hannah and Eliza* was a historic event. This ship was the subject of the first lifesaving and salvage operation by the Sable Island Establishment. The ship's crew, like others before them, might have been able to survive through their own unaided efforts, but they would certainly have suffered more. Captain Burrows made no bones about his appreciation of what Superintendent Morris and his people had done for him and his men. The Sable Establishment not only guaranteed their survival but also enabled most of them to return to civilization much earlier than would otherwise have been the case. As captain, Burrows could also appreciate the salvage operation, though the sale of saved *Hannah and Eliza* property realized only a few hundred pounds. His cargo was worthless, since the salt was destroyed in the wreck. If Burrows had been carrying a less fragile cargo of greater value, the efforts of the Sable salvagers would have been worth considerably more. Captain Burrows also realized that the Sable settlement by its very existence prevented the loss of stranded property to random wreckers, including those operating more or less within the law.

On the other side of the coin, the *Hannah and Eliza* castaways demonstrated how a shipwreck might be to the advantage of the coastguard service. They made a valuable contribution to the fledgling Sable Island Establishment. Almost from the moment they landed on the Sable beach, officers and men alike expanded the potential of the island station.

By vastly increasing the population and by their highly cooperative attitude, they made the tiny group of settlers more secure. Above all, led by Captain Burrows and later by mate Robinson, they bolstered the authority of Superintendent Morris and insured that the first season of the Sable Establishment did not end in a debacle. They behaved as though they believed in the goals of the Establishment and truly wished it well. The stranded Jack Tars also clearly put in a good word with their fellow Americans on the fishing schooners, helping Superintendent Morris to get off on the right foot with them. Robinson and the four others in the final five adapted particularly well to Sable necessity. They did their part to overcome the prejudice against horsemeat that was one cause of the Sable crew's opposition to Superintendent Morris. When it came to setting an example, the castaways outshone most of the men in the government service.

In Halifax, the survivors from the first Establishment shipwreck helped to advertise a new positive image of Sable Island. Captain Burrows brought the first news of the Establishment to Halifax after the winter. On the whole, in contrast to the horror stories of the past, the news was good. With obvious sincerity, Burrows spoke of Superintendent Morris "in terms of the warmest gratitude & thankfulness." When Robinson and his four shipmates reached the mainland, they did not dwell of the privation they had experienced at Sable.

If the Sable Island Establishment was a godsend for the crew of the *Hannah and Eliza*, the loss of the *Hannah and Eliza* was a gain for the Sable Island Establishment.

Chapter Six

A Plethora of Shipwrecks

The tally of ships lost at Sable Island continued to mount at a rate of slightly more than one a year. Then, following a shipwreck in the first part of 1824, a period of fourteen months passed without any disasters. This period was like the calm before the storm for the Sable Island Establishment. In the next nine months, the Superintendent would see as many wrecks as he had witnessed in the preceding nine years.

This Superintendent was Edward Hodgson, the man who had served as second-in-command under James Morris from 1804 until Morris's death in the fall of 1809. After Hodgson succeeded Morris in office, he continued the good work of the Sable Island Establishment. And the Nova Scotia government continued to support the Sable service just as it had in Morris's day—which was both a boon and a curse. The government grant remained static at £400 a year, enough to allow the lifesaving service to exist, too little to let it expand. So Hodgson's Establishment resembled that of the earliest days, the time of the *Hannah and Eliza*, before he and his family had moved to Sable Island.

In 1825 the only inhabited dwelling on the whole island was the Superintendent's house, the station occupied by the coastguard crew. Its chief difference from Morris's Main Station or headquarters was its location: near the site of the former halfway house. Superintendent Hodgson had been forced to relocate because the sea was washing away the west end of the island at an alarming rate. The new station was about nine miles from the west end and midway between the lake and the north beach.

Two other dwellings, both uninhabited and little more than shacks, were maintained for the use of castaways, each stocked with provisions, tinder box matches, and other supplies. One was four miles from the west end, on the north side of the lake. The other was midway between the east end and the Superintendent's house—about nine miles from each—near

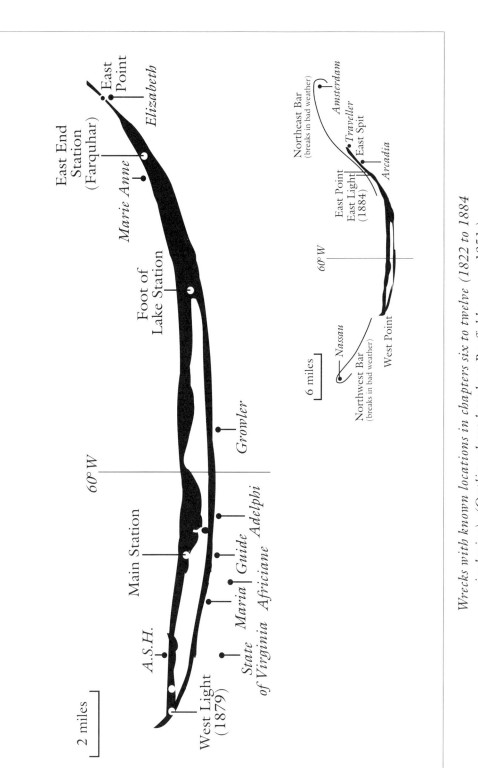

West Light (1879)

A.S.H.

Main Station

East End Station (Farquhar)

60° W

East Point

Elizabeth

Marie Anne

Foot of Lake Station

Growler

State Maria Guide Adelphi
of Virginia Africiane

2 miles

Northeast Bar
(breaks in bad weather)

Amsterdam

Traveller

East Spit

East Point
East Light (1884)

Arcadia

60° W

Nassau

Northwest Bar
(breaks in bad weather)

West Point

6 miles

Wrecks with known locations in chapters six to twelve (1822 to 1884
inclusive). (Outline chart based on Bayfield survey, 1851.)

the east end of the lake. Both of these buildings, like the Main Station, were about three hundred to four hundred yards inland from the ocean beach and about the same distance from the margin of the lake.

Superintendent Hodgson's lifesaving crew comprised himself and four or five men. What distinguished his 1825 crew from Morris's was that three of the "men" were his sons: William, James, and George. William was an experienced Sable hand thirty years of age. The other two were hardly more than boys, James being a young teenager and George perhaps still a pre-teen. The only other member of the crew on record was a man named Michael Sheehan, age unknown. Also living at Hodgson's were his wife of thirty-two years and two unmarried daughters, one a minor. The three youngest children had been born on Sable Island. Five other Hodgson children, two of whom had been members of the lifesaving service, had left Sable to find work and found families on the mainland.

Clearly Sable Island castaways at this time were basically guests of the Hodgson family. They would swell the household by whatever their numbers might be. It is equally clear that much of the care of the unfortunate would become the province of the female Hodgsons, who were all rated as dependents. The Sable Island Commissioners maintained the myth that all females were non-working members of Establishment families, even though the demands made on them increased in direct proportion to the number of people saved from shipwrecks. Those demands would rise to new heights with a series of wrecks that began in the fall of 1825.

On the night of 10 September the English brig *Adelphi*, homeward bound from Saint John, New Brunswick, to Liverpool with a cargo of timber, ran aground. The brig, as Superintendent Hodgson informed the Commissioners,

> was Cast away on this Island, on the South side, by heavy weather, the Crew were saved with great difficulty, we got them on shore by ropes, the sea at the time running tremendous high.

The site of the wreck was about a mile east of Hodgson's Main Station across the lake. This stroke of good fortune led to quick discovery and the rescue of all on board: fourteen persons including the captain's wife and child. The vessel was a total loss, but the timber cargo gave promise of future salvaging.

A week after the *Adelphi* survivors landed on the island, they witnessed another wreck. At four P.M. on Sunday 18 September the schooner *Union* of Plymouth, Massachusetts, returning from a fishing voyage in the Gulf of St. Lawrence, "ran ashore on the North West Bar." The whole cargo of 650 quintals (about 65,000 pounds) of green fish was lost, while the Establishment crew—no doubt with the help of *Adelphi* seamen—managed to salvage some of the schooner's materials. Most important, all eight members of the *Union*'s crew were saved. The Hodgsons now had twenty-two strangers living with them.

Fortunately for all concerned, though unknown at Sable Island, help was on the way. Only hours before the *Union* struck Sable, the government armed brig *Chebucto*, commanded by Edward Potter, had sailed from Halifax for the island. Captain Potter's main purpose was to deliver provisions and other supplies plus two carpenters, a load of lumber, and other materials for building a new house on Sable Island. The weather played him false. He ran into a series of gales and took six days to reach his destination. At Sable he approached the north side under the lee of the land, but a fresh gale sprang up with heavy rain, forcing him to drop his best bower anchor half a mile from the usual landing place. When Potter saw that a fast-pulling boat could reach the shore only with great difficulty, he realized that he would not be able to land any of his cargo. Nor could he afford to remain at anchor. If the wind from the south should veer to the northwest, he might be driven onto a lee shore.

At this juncture, Superintendent Hodgson came aboard the *Chebucto* and reported the wrecks and the number of people marooned at his station. He told Potter "they would become a great burthen by remaining any longer on the Island." Hodgson's information persuaded Captain Potter to make a unilateral decision and alter his mission:

> I instantly determined on taking the whole of those unfortunate persons to Halifax direct, in three hours we had them all on board when I weighed Anchor and stood to sea.

The *Chebucto* arrived in Halifax four days later on 28 September after another tempestuous voyage. Captain Potter immediately sent a report of his voyage to Government House "for the information of His Excellency Lieu^r General Sir James Kempt." He knew that Lieutenant Governor Kempt would be keenly interested in news of shipwrecks at Sable Island.

∞∽

Sir James Kempt had returned to Nova Scotia in August 1825 after more than a year away on a visit to England. While Nova Scotia had been out of sight, for Kempt it was not out of mind. At the seat of empire, he had performed a signal service for the province, one that would have wide-ranging effects. Its benefits would be felt far beyond the limits of his colony.

Lieutenant Governor Kempt had made a sales pitch to Whitehall on behalf of the Sable Island Establishment. He may have been encouraged to take this step by the founding in 1824 of the Royal National Institution for the Preservation of Life from Shipwreck, which would become the Royal National Lifeboat Institution. It seemed possible that London might now be more receptive to the concept of the Sable Island Establishment.

Kempt presented an information package to Earl Bathurst, Secretary of State for War and the Colonies. The package included a written report about Sable Island and an annotated chart that graphically illustrated its dangers. The chart had been published in Halifax in 1824 by Capt. Joseph Darby, who was owner and master of a vessel that made frequent voyages to Sable Island for the Commissioners. Darby's chart presented a list of Sable shipwrecks since the founding of the Establishment, with locations for most of them. Kempt's report also stressed the number of ships lost at the island during the past quarter century. Kempt added that Sable was thought to have destroyed many more vessels than those documented, based on evidence frequently washed up on its shores: "dead bodies, pieces of wreck, and articles of merchandize." At the same time, he stressed the "extensive utility" of the Sable Establishment: the hundreds of lives that had already been saved and the potentiality for the future.

On the other hand—and here Kempt came to the point of his submission—although the Establishment had done a lot of good work and proved its worth, it needed to be better. Sir James mentioned some glaring deficiencies of the present Sable Establishment:

1. The houses, built twenty years ago, were in a state of decay. They needed to be replaced.
2. The government staff at Sable Island was too small. The coast guard required more men.
3. Communications with the mainland needed to be more frequent; failing that, the store of provisions on the island must be greatly increased.

In relation to the last point, Kempt used an argument that, while extreme, was to some degree prophetic. He said that with the increase of shipping, wrecks would probably become more frequent,

and it might so happen, that four or five hundred persons might be thrown on the Island about the same time, and obliged to remain there four or five months.

Since few of the vessels lost at Sable Island belonged to Nova Scotia ports, Kempt pointed out, the province's own people received little benefit from the Establishment. The provincial government could therefore not be expected to provide everything that was needed at it.

Having done so much in the cause of humanity, the Province thinks that it ought now to be relieved from a part at least of the charge of supporting it.

Kempt led logically to a practical conclusion in the form of a hopeful suggestion for Lord Bathurst, that

this interesting and humane establishment, which, if properly kept up, must assuredly be the means of saving thousands of lives, will be considered as a fit object for the protection of His Majesty's Government.

Without waiting around for a response to his presentation, which was dated 25 June 1825, Lieutenant Governor Kempt boarded a ship and sailed to Nova Scotia. He knew better than to expect Whitehall to act quickly.

Four months after his return to Halifax, having still heard nothing, he decided that he had waited long enough, that a gentle reminder was in order. He sent Bathurst a duplicate of his previous letter, memo, and plan of Sable Island. He also informed Bathurst of the loss of two more vessels, the *Adelphi* and *Union*, "the crews of which must have perished but for the Establishment in question, thus affording an additional proof of its Value and importance." This dispatch began the long journey to England just before Christmas.

∞

After the departure of the *Adelphi* and *Union* castaways, Superintendent Hodgson began preparing the Sable Establishment for the long winter season. Before the first cold spell struck, the island crew had harvested all the gardens and fields. The vegetables were stored in the root cellar, and hay for the livestock was stuffed into the loft in the barn or built into enormous haystacks. The large woodpile beside the house insured a basic supply of firewood; it would be replenished during the winter as demand required and the weather allowed. In October provisions delivered by another vessel from Halifax were safely lodged in the storehouse. Whether these preparations were enough to meet all Sable needs until the arrival of a relief schooner in spring, only time would tell.

This season's unscheduled demands on Establishment resources began in January 1826. The schooner *Brothers*, Captain McHarron, delivered the first customers, so to speak. Bound to Halifax from Newfoundland with a cargo of fish, the *Brothers* ran into a gale ten days out as it was passing to the north of Sable Island. Captain McHarron tried to keep the wind on the bow in order to prevent the heavy seas from breaking aboard. He left only enough sails set to make some headway as the schooner was falling away from the wind. But he was unable to make the vessel lie to. During the night of 23 January the gale drove it onto a lee shore: the north side of Sable Island. In the morning Captain McHarron and six of his crew managed to get ashore, bringing with them a 12-month old child. Two other hands and a female passenger were less fortunate—as they attempted to escape from the wreck the sea took them. The drowned passenger was presumably the baby's mother.

When the men from the Establishment discovered that the *Brothers* was stranded offshore, they repaired to the scene and helped salvage a large part of the rigging and sails. Afterward Captain McHarron and his seven fellow survivors moved in with the Hodgsons, where the care of the infant obviously became women's work.

The *Brothers* refugees had been on Sable Island about a month when the next wreck occurred, depositing more victims on the beach. The new arrivals belonged to the ship *Elizabeth*, Captain Liddell, of London. This ship was homeward bound with a cargo of timber, four days out of Saint John, New Brunswick, when it ran aground on the south side at the east end. Like the *Brothers*, it struck at night, on 27 February, but the crew hesitated to leave the ship even after the arrival of daylight. The reason for their hesitation, according to the account published later in a Halifax news-paper, was that they did not know whether the island was inhabited. But that was not the whole story.

The crew of the stranded vessel did try to abandon ship early on, but nothing went right. One of the ship's boats was dashed to pieces, and when they tried to lower another, it upset and they lost it. They feared to risk their last, the ship's longboat, until the weather should improve. Through the whole day and a second night they waited, huddled on the wreck. On the second day, Wednesday 1 March, the whole crew of eight-een reached shore safely, with belated assistance from Superintendent Hodgson and his party. Hodgson then took them to the warmth and com-forts of his house about seventeen miles away.

The Superintendent's remembrance of this wreck painted a somewhat different picture. Nearly five years later, in a retrospective account of his career, Hodgson recalled it. Although his memory lacked precision—he said the wreck was in January "about the year 1825"—his personalized description of the incident has the ring of truth.

Hodgson remembered how at news of the shipwreck he led his crew down-island to the site, "where I was exposed the whole of a long Winters Night & Day on the Beach, in a Dreadful Snow Storm." The night and day referred to would be Tuesday and Wednesday. Having reached the east end, the lifesavers completely lacked shelter; the nearest building was about nine miles away. The exposure took its toll.

I Succeeded in Saving the whole of the Crew, and the Materials of the Ship, but with the loss of my own Health, and the breaking up of my Constitution, for from the excess of fatigue, Cold & Suffer-ing that I experienced that Night, I have never got the better of.

Hodgson's claim about the salvaging was not only true but also under-stated. He and his men saved provisions from the ship's stores, which made an important addition to the supplies available at the Establishment. Since Hodgson was not a man to overstate his own accomplishments, he must have had good reason to claim credit for the rescue of the *Elizabeth*'s crew. He did, and stated it with characteristic directness: "it is my opinion that without the great exertions used by myself and my people the whole of this Crew would have perished as they were all in a State of Intoxication."

Hodgson was less clear whether the drunkenness happened before or after the wreck. At any rate, the seamen were in no condition to save them-selves even if they could reach shore in the longboat. The snow storm that caused Hodgson so much suffering would almost certainly have prevented them from finding shelter before they died of hypothermia. Instead the drunken survivors found themselves transported to a warm house to sober up. Here they joined the other castaways, bringing the total number of inhabitants to about thirty-five persons.

Since no relief vessel was expected at Sable Island before May, captains McHarron and Liddell decided to sail to the mainland and report their own wrecks. Superintendent Hodgson no doubt encouraged them, for this kind of adventure had by then become a time-honoured Sable tradition. McHarron and Liddell, like Morris and Burrows before them, renovated a boat from a wreck for the sea passage. They took the frame of a small boat from the *Adelphi* and, using materials salvaged from their own vessels, repaired, decked, and rigged it. In about a month the new vessel was ready, a sea-going boat "of 16 feet keel."

Manned by eight men—the captain and three crew members from each wreck—the boat sailed from Sable Island on Wednesday 5 April. It reached one of the nearest mainland ports, Fisherman's Harbour, the following night, and from there made its way along the coast to Halifax by Monday.

In Halifax the captains reported that eighteen of their men still remained on the island. The report caused no alarm, for they also said the supplies of food and fuel at Sable were abundant. Within three days, however, the *Chebucto* departed for Sable Island, and it was back by Sunday with all the rest of the castaways. The rescued people expressed gratitude for the role the Establishment had played in their survival at Sable Island. They referred in particular to Superintendent Hodgson's kindness. He treated them, said one, "as if he had been a father to them."

Such praise was all very well, but a general view was developing that something more than the stroking of local pride was needed. An editorial comment in the report of the wrecks *Brothers* and *Elizabeth* at Sable Island stated the case:

> These two accidents tend to show both the humanity and necessity
> of our establishment upon this dangerous spot, and at the same
> time…that the burden should no longer be supported singly from
> the revenue of this Province.

This message had of course already been delivered to London by Lieutenant Governor Kempt. And unbeknownst to anybody in Nova Scotia, it had taken effect.

Kempt's December letter with enclosures reached Lord Bathurst just before the *Elizabeth* struck Sable. The colonial secretary soon came to a momentous decision: he would commit the British government to support the Sable Island rescue service. After Bathurst set the wheels of the bureaucracy in motion, it took about three months to settle the matter. Bathurst's memo in favour of a grant for the Sable Establishment passed to his under-secretary, who wrote to the Treasury. The Treasury took its own good time to authorize the actual funding for the grant and then inform Bathurst's under-secretary, who told Bathurst, who then wrote to Kempt. The letter to Kempt took nearly another month to cross the Atlantic. By the time it reached Halifax, the list of Sable Island wrecks had drastically increased.

Superintendent Hodgson's family barely had time to put their house in order following the departure of the survivors from the *Brothers* and *Elizabeth* before they received more compulsory houseguests. On 27 April the brig *Traveller*, Captain Penrice, bound from Liverpool to Halifax with a cargo of salt, grounded on the outer end of the northeast bar. The vessel held together, and two days after it struck the bar, all fourteen of the crew landed safely on Sable Island. The captain wasted no time before preparing to make the trip to the mainland. He fitted out one of his boats and with six or seven of his crew put to sea about 15 May. Three days after they set out, they fell in with an American schooner, which took them all on board and, about two weeks after they had left the island, landed them at Eastern Passage in Halifax Harbour.

Captain Penrice brought plenty of news for the Sable Island Commissioners. He reported not only his own wreck but also another that had happened just before he departed from Sable Island. He in fact delivered a letter about the second wreck from Superintendent Hodgson's son. This son would be William, the eldest, who was probably filling in for his father because of the Superintendent's ill health resulting from his work at the *Elizabeth*.

William Hodgson informed the Commissioners that on Saturday 13 May the Establishment crew sighted the ship *Nassau* far out on the northwest bar. The ship was bound from Ireland for Quebec with a load of emigrants who, he said, totalled one hundred and forty.

The island crew and some of the *Traveller* survivors made all speed to the western tip of the island. Squinting seaward into the wind, from the dry sandbar they saw two boats some miles away heading for Sable Island from the wreck. As the boats drew nearer, the watchers on shore could see that they were filled with castaways. One boat pulled safely through the waves and right up on the beach. The other, the ship's longboat, also gained the island, but before the people on shore could reach it to help the passengers to disembark, it was "stove on the beach." The surf engulfed the smashed boat and its occupants. Five men and two women perished.

A total of thirty-seven castaways landed safely. They told the people on the beach that "upwards of 80" others, including the captain, remained on board the wreck. For recent arrivals and island residents alike, "it was indeed most dreadful, to see men, women and children, to whom we then could give no assistance."

Not until Monday was Hodgson able to send off two boats in hopes of saving the people still stranded on the northwest bar. The wreck lay "a considerable distance from the land—as far as the little island." This "island" was an exposed part of the bar about eight miles out to sea from the grass-covered hills at Sable's west end. The boats had not returned from their mission when Captain Penrice left the island with William Hodgson's letter. On his arrival in Halifax, Penrice expressed optimism about the rescue of the castaways because the weather had been calm for the first three or four days that he was at sea. Hodgson the younger was apparently not so hopeful. His letter as published in the newspaper on 1 June concluded with an obvious plea, "We shall look anxiously for relief."

The Sable Commissioners and others in Halifax realized that the survival of the eighty or so people still on the wreck would only add to the difficulties on Sable Island. The Establishment was not equipped to accommodate some one hundred and thirty people. So Lieutenant Governor Kempt immediately dispatched a schooner to bring off the castaways. If the cost of this voyage had to be paid by the people of Nova Scotia, who would object after reading of the *Nassau* tragedy?

By this time the situation at Sable was worse than anybody on the mainland realized. Another ship had gone down: the 519-ton *Agamemnon*, bound from New Brunswick to Glasgow with a cargo of timber. This ship had struck on 2 June and dumped another eighteen refugees on Sable Island.

Sir James Kempt's relief schooner was obliged to make two trips to remove all the stranded people, but they all reached Halifax without undue delay. Worst off were the hundred or so passengers from Ireland, as Kempt later informed Bathurst: "The Emigrants, in particular on their arrival here were in a most destitute state having lost all their Clothing and effects." He went on to say that he had advanced £100 from the provincial funds for their relief and that except for a few who had gone on to the United States the immigrants had obtained work and intended to stay in Nova Scotia.

The lieutenant governor no doubt took pleasure in reporting his recent efforts on behalf of victims of shipwreck at Sable Island, for he had received Bathurst's good-news letter on 4 June. Because of that letter, he also had no fear of complaints from the Assembly about the costs involved. Instead, Kempt enjoyed a moment of triumph with his announcement to the Assembly that his mission on behalf of the Sable Island Establishment had been a complete success.

Great Britain would henceforth provide an annual grant of £400 as long as Nova Scotia granted a similar amount. (The British grant actually amounted to about five hundred pounds because it was in sterling, then worth about 25 per cent more than Nova Scotia currency.) At one fell swoop, the funds for the rescue service at Sable Island had more than doubled, and the increase was virtually guaranteed in perpetuity.

Lieutenant Governor Kempt might justly take pride in the part he played on behalf of, in his words, "that most excellent, but expensive Establishment." He tried to ensure that Lord Bathurst and his colleagues in government would also feel satisfaction. In his letter of thanks to Bathurst for his "ready attention" to Kempt's proposal of a year earlier, Kempt enclosed a list of Sable wrecks since 1 September 1825. The list, drawn up by Michael

Wallace, Commissioner for Sable Island, contained some inaccuracies through error or design, such as deletion of the wreck of the American schooner *Union*. But it made some powerful points.

Wallace's list showed that five of six vessels had been lost on the run between ports in Great Britain and its colonies. From these wrecks, Wallace declared, 193 people had been saved. And 177 of them survived wrecks between January and June of 1826. During that period, the Sable lifesaving service was partly under the auspices of the British government, for the grant to the Sable Establishment authorized by Bathurst was retroactive to 1 January 1826. For Bathurst's benefit, Kempt underlined England's share in the recent humane work and pointed out the moral, as it were, of the story.

> The utility of the Establishment, and the necessity of placing it on
> a more efficient footing were never more obvious than at the
> present time,–nor could this liberality on the part of his Majestys
> Government have been evinced more opportunely.

The Lieutenant Governor of Nova Scotia was right to appreciate Britain's contribution to the lifesaving service, a contribution that has seldom if ever received proper recognition. Kempt also paid tribute to the people on Sable Island. Referring to the many ships lost in recent months, he added, "I am glad to say, with the loss of very few lives owing to the exertions of the persons belonging to the Establishment." Chief among those persons was the Superintendent, Edward Hodgson, who was then over sixty years of age. For him the year that promised to rejuvenate the Sable Island Establishment signalled the beginning of the end.

The unprecedented number of wrecks had brought trials and tribulations for the Superintendent of Sable Island. He had witnessed the sufferings of many men, women, and children, and the deaths of some. He had himself endured much hard labour and emotional strain, and had been ravaged by the elements. The British injection of funds would help provide new buildings and more hired hands for the Sable Establishment, but it could not restore Edward Hodgson's youth or health. The strong constitution that had served him so well over the years now began to break down. He became susceptible to injury, more inclined to a bout of illness after strenuous effort.

Despite the increased funds available, the Sable service during the last years of Hodgson's superintendency showed decline rather than renaissance. After the banner season of 1825–26, his greatest success lay behind him. Superintendent Hodgson embodied the human cost of that success, and, in a way, the largely anonymous victims of shipwreck at Sable Island.

Chapter Seven

The Triumphs of Joseph Darby

Joseph Darby was one of the most controversial characters in the entire Sable Island story, let alone in the history of the lifesaving Establishment. His career ended in disgrace when the reform government spearheaded by Joseph Howe dismissed him from the position of Sable Superintendent in 1848. Subsequent accounts of the Darby era have focused on his negative image, one of the latest referring to him as "The Rogue" and "a paranoiac who had dreams of absolute control of Sable." Darby has never received proper recognition in his native province for his contribution to the Sable lifesaving service. The greatest tribute paid him during his lifetime—or any time since—was by the government of France. The French Ministry of Marine singled him out for praise on two separate occasions. Each case involved a shipwreck. The two vessels, which ran afoul of Sable Island seventeen years apart, were the *Africaine* and the *Maria*.

Joseph Darby began his Sable Island career as a young man, before he reached twenty-one years of age. He served in the lifesaving crew under both of the first Superintendents, and Hodgson in particular spoke highly of his value on the island.

Hodgson was a man in his prime when he succeeded Morris, and he was likely to remain in charge of the island for many years. Every other member of the Establishment held an inherently dead-end job. Sable Island offered no opportunities for an ambitious man—like young Joseph Darby.

Darby had grown up in a small outport on the Nova Scotia coast, and he had some experience of sailing ships before he came to Sable Island. But when he left Sable, he had no intention of settling down in his native village. He sought out the capital of the province, the centre of government and business.

The young man spent some time working in the Halifax dockyard before taking up a full-time career as a self-styled "Mariner." Like his father before him, he became master of his own vessel. He married and began a family, and bought property in Halifax. Using local connections, mainly with Michael Wallace the Sable Island Commissioner, Darby operated a charter business. One of his regular charters was carrying goods and people to and from Sable Island.

In May 1822 Captain Darby sailed out of Halifax Harbour in his schooner *Two Brothers*, which was probably named for himself and his brother James, who also spent some time at Sable Island. The schooner was loaded with the spring supplies for the Sable Establishment. Included in the cargo were some loads of firewood and lumber for construction and repairs on the island.

When the island came in sight, Captain Darby made his approach from the northwest, heading for the Main Station near mid-island. All at once something caught his eye and drove away all thoughts of landing his cargo—a vessel aground off the south side.

The wreck was about three quarters of a mile offshore and four miles east of the northwest bar. With his intimate knowledge of the waters around Sable, Darby knew that he could sail around the west end of the island to go to the aid of the stranded vessel. Although the dangers of the northwest bar extended more than ten miles from the end of the island, just beyond the point of the visible dry bar a channel cut through it. Darby was sure that, so long as he kept to the deep part of that channel, the shallow-draught *Two Brothers* could sail safely through. Captain Darby changed course for the wreck.

The stranded ship was the French frigate *Africaine*, Captain Epron. It was on a passage from Martinique to Brest via St. George's Bay, Newfoundland, when it went aground. The ship's company comprised thirteen officers and more than two hundred and thirty-five enlisted men. Of this total, the frigate's boats could hold only about a third.

When the *Africaine* struck, some of the men piled into the available boats and headed for shore. They presumably intended to send the boats back for their shipmates. What happened next is an all too familiar Sable story. Some of the boats upset in the heavy surf, and a number of the men drowned. Others survived the dunking, thanks to Superintendent Hodgson and his crew, who waded into the breakers to drag them out of the sea. A total of about seventy landed safely. More than twice that number were still aboard the wreck, which the waves were pounding to death. As the castaways on the beach received attention from the islanders, their shipmates at sea looked to the *Two Brothers* for rescue.

When the schooner reached the wreck, Captain Darby saw at a glance that his loaded vessel could not accommodate the crowd on board. He made an instant decision. He ordered his crew to seize the firewood and lumber piled on deck and heave it overboard. Then he manoeuvred alongside the frigate.

The *Two Brothers* bounced on the waves by the stuck *Africaine*, trying to avoid smashing into its side. The trick was to lie close enough to allow the men to come off without actually bumping the frigate hard enough to damage the schooner. And there was no time to waste. The job required luck as well as skill, and on this occasion Captain Darby was blessed with both.

He removed the French sailors from the wreck, without any casualties, virtually as it was breaking up. Within an hour of grounding, the *Africaine* was in pieces. Darby retraced his course across the bar and sailed eastward to the landing place on the north side, where he put ashore the rescued men and delivered the remaining supplies for the Sable Establishment.

The Establishment lacked the facilities to look after such a large body of men, as Lieutenant Governor Kempt was to point out a few years later. Most of the *Africaine* refugees would be obliged to camp out while awaiting removal to the mainland. All except the officers would live and cook in little hollows and sheltered spots about the island, for want of proper buildings to house them. In the absence of indoor plumbing, these conditions were not the most sanitary. Weather also posed a threat. The usual Sable weather in May was likely to bring fog, cold, and storms, with heavy rain a virtual certainty and snow a possibility. For the benefit of all concerned, the top priority was to take the castaways off the island as soon as possible.

Immediately after the supplies were landed, Captain Darby took about half of the *Africaine*'s company—7 officers and 130 seamen— on board the *Two Brothers* and departed for Halifax. Captain Epron chose to stay with the men on Sable Island. The crowded schooner made a slow passage, and when it arrived in port on 26 May, the wreck survivors it discharged were "in a very wretched state." Darby delivered a dispatch from Captain Epron to Lieutenant Governor Kempt, who ordered the *Two Brothers* to return at once to Sable Island with another vessel and a supply of provisions and bring off the remainder of the castaways.

While Kempt awaited the arrival of the rest of the *Africaine*'s men, he arranged the best accommodation he could for those already delivered to Halifax. Most were put in barracks, but the sick were assigned a ward in the general hospital, where they might be under the care of their own surgeon. The lieutenant governor also ordered the commissariat to supply the shipwreck victims with provisions and any other necessaries they required. In response to Captain Epron's written request, he arranged for the hiring of a vessel as soon as possible to transport all the French sailors to Brest.

Kempt was well aware that these arrangements came more properly within the purview of the Naval Department, as he admitted in a dispatch to Lord Bathurst notifying him of events. But as he also explained, the admiral commanding on the Halifax station had gone to the West Indies, leaving not a single vessel of the squadron in Halifax Harbour. Exercising the usual bureaucratic caution, Kempt assured Bathurst that he would observe the strictest economy and incur only unavoidable expenses. Since Captain Epron was still at Sable Island and therefore unable to make an official report of the wreck to the Ministry of Marine, Kempt suggested that Bathurst might inform the French government of the disaster. Finally, with his dispatch Sir James sent a small parcel of letters from the officers and crew of the *Africaine,* and he told Bathurst that the men were anxious to have their letters forwarded to France at the first opportunity.

On 18 June Lieutenant Governor Kempt sent Lord Bathurst another dispatch, which detailed the outcome of this affair. He was happy to announce that all of the men rescued from the *Africaine,* 13 officers and 235 seamen, had sailed for France two days before. They departed in the *Victory,* a merchant ship of about three hundred tons burden, hired and fitted up as a transport for this service. Kempt assured the colonial secretary that, although the *Victory* was the only vessel in harbour capable of conveying so many persons, yet the freight charge of £800 was considered very moderate. He enclosed a general statement of all expenses, amounting to more than £2,000. These expenses related only to the provisions and other articles supplied in Halifax, plus money advanced Captain Epron. They included no charges for services at Sable Island. All the relevant receipts and vouchers would be forwarded later to His Majesty's Treasury to support a request to the French government for repayment.

When the British ambassador in Paris handed over copies of Kempt's letters and the accounts to the French government, they accepted the total with one minor change. By an agreement made prior to the *Victory*'s voyage, the value of the unused portion of the provisions supplied by Kempt that remained on board was deducted from the total expenses. The French Ministry of Marine issued an order for payment of the reduced sum. Nonetheless the ministry seems to have paid too much. It settled the account in francs at the exchange rate for the pound sterling. But Kempt's sums were presumably in Nova Scotia currency, which was worth less than sterling. At any rate, this payment ended France's obligation for the rescue and care of naval personnel from the wreck of the frigate *Africaine.*

∞∞

Fortunately for Joseph Darby, Captain Epron felt indebted for the rescue of himself and the majority of his men from the stranded *Africaine* at Sable Island. The debt was not the kind that was cleared by international banking. As an experienced sea captain, Epron appreciated the achievement of a fellow master, and he possessed the generosity of spirit to give credit to another in the face of his own misfortune.

In his report to the Minister of Marine about the loss of his frigate, Captain Epron highlighted the role played by Captain Darby. Epron made it clear that Darby had risked both his vessel and the lives of himself and crew to save the lives of the French sailors. He told the minister that Darby did not hesitate to enter the most dangerous passes with the schooner *Two*

Brothers, of which he was captain and owner, in order to come to the aid of the stranded vessel by the quickest route. In taking this route, Darby narrowly missed losing his schooner—it touched bottom twice—before he succeeded in picking up the shipwrecked mariners. Afterward, on the passage from Sable Island to Halifax, said Epron, Captain Darby lavished on the rescued men all the care that was in his power.

The Minister of Marine was so impressed by this testimonial that, as he informed Joseph Darby in a letter of 13 August, he brought Darby's "generous conduct" to the attention of the king. His majesty was "deeply touched" and ordered that "the memory of the honourable devotion" that Darby had shown toward Frenchmen be "consecrated by a gold medal." The king also directed, independent of the medal as testimony of his satisfaction, that a sum of 2,400 francs (about £94 sterling) be paid Captain Darby. The medal and money would be delivered in Halifax by Commander Béhie in the corvette *Egérie*.

The corvette arrived on 18 October. On the 22nd, in a ceremony in the Council Chamber, Captain Béhie presented the gold medal to Joseph Darby. Michael Wallace attended in his capacity of Commissioner for Sable Island and accepted "a similar medal and sum" for Superintendent Edward Hodgson, plus a gratuity to two of the Sable Island hands. Captain Béhie also delivered a dispatch from the French Minister of Marine to Lieutenant Governor Kempt. The minister told Kempt that the kind treatment of the shipwrecked men from the *Africaine* in Halifax had made a deep impression in France. So much so, that Sir James had been awarded the Legion of Honour. Kempt's interest in and support for the Sable Island Establishment may well have dated from this time, and he must have been aware that his glory arose in no small part from the actions of Joseph Darby.

The local prominence that Darby gained from this episode led to future accomplishments. A major of the Royal Artillery in the local garrison befriended him. Darby was impressed by the attention paid him by this officer and gentleman. The friendship that developed was, by Darby's own admission, the inspiration for his published chart of Sable Island. Encouraged by the officer to increase his knowledge of the island, Darby took soundings and plotted the Sable sandbars and currents in 1823. He then drew up the chart and published it in 1824 at his own expense. It cost him more than half the sum he had received from the King of France. His officer friend used his influence to advertise the chart in Halifax society. Even with this help, though, the chart was hardly a bestseller: Darby distributed no more than 200 copies.

In truth, the chief value of Darby's plan of Sable Island was not as a navigational chart. The useful information on it was less important for mariners trying to avoid Sable Island than for those who had already run afoul of it. Like its author, the chart was idiosyncratic. It presented Sable Island as a killer of ships and the home of the Sable Island Humane Establishment. In stressing the number of ships lost and lives saved, it was like a poster designed to publicize the worth of the government lifesaving station. Which is exactly how Sir James Kempt used it in his appeal to Whitehall for funding of the Establishment. The success of that appeal, then, may in large part be traced back to the wreck of the *Africaine* and its aftermath.

The *Africaine* incident also helped to determine Joseph Darby's future career. What that career might be, the focus of Darby's ambitions, is surely more than hinted at in the dedication on his chart.

To His Excellency Lt General Sir James Kempt G.C.B. Lt. Governor Of Nova Scotia the Honble The Members of His Majesty's council and the Gentlemen of the House of Assembly of this Province By whose Bounty and Benevolence This Most Excellent Establishment is supported and preserved This Chart And Description of Sable Island Is Dedicated with Great Respect by Their Most Obedient and very Humble Servant Joseph Darby.

When Edward Hodgson retired from the Sable coastguard service in 1830, his son William, who was still a member of the lifesaving crew, hoped to succeed him. But Commissioner Michael Wallace chose a Halifax resident as the new Superintendent of Sable Island: Joseph Darby.

∽∾∽

By 1839 Joseph Darby had more than eight years of experience as Sable Superintendent under his belt. He also had the benefit of an experienced crew of seven men. The Sable hands included one of his own sons and one of Edward Hodgson's. Some of the other men were related to the Hodgsons, the Darbys, or one another through the intermarriage that became a feature among the personnel of the Sable Island Establishment. One man who was not related to anybody else there was Martin Clye (or Cly). He was the only black man on the island, probably only the second in the Sable service—and the first known to have joined it of his own free will. Superintendent Darby had recruited him. Before Martin quit the service for good, another Clye would be working with him under Darby's command: James, who was probably his brother.

Superintendent Darby at the end of his career would call this 1839 group "the most efficient crew of men that was ever on the Island." They were each paid fifty shillings (two pounds ten shillings, or less than twelve dollars) a month. These wages were little enough for the work they were about to be called on to do when they rose from their bunks on the morning of Friday the 13th in September 1839.

Approaching Sable Island that morning was a ship about to reach the climax of a run of bad luck. Almost from the time the *Maria* of Havre, France, sailed out of its home port bound for New York, the fates seemed to be against it. Adverse weather capped by a hurricane battered the *Maria* all the way across the Atlantic until Sable Island delivered the *coup de grâce*.

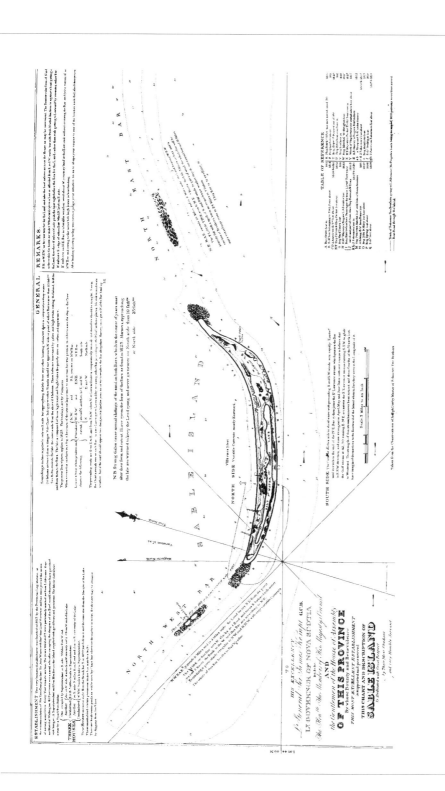

Chart of Sable Island by Joseph Darby, showing the track followed by the Two Brothers around the west end and going to the aid of the Africaine. (The information about other wrecks is not entirely reliable.)

The journey had consumed more than six weeks when the *Maria* ran aground off the south side of the island. For the ten-man crew and seventy passengers the stranding was the final calamity of a terrible ocean crossing. Many on board must have feared that it was their last misfortune, period. The raging seas denied any prospect of reaching shore alive.

Although the castaways were in no position to realize it, in two respects luck was with them. The *Maria* struck bottom less than three miles to the westward of the Main Station of the lifesaving service, and the ship held together long enough to allow the Sable crew to spot the wreck and transport men and equipment to a place opposite it on the beach.

The island lifesavers launched a boat and rowed through the surf to the side of the trapped ship. When the boat was loaded with castaways, the coxswain directed it back to shore. More trips followed. Back and forth, hour after hour, the boat crew rowed for their lives, and the lives they intended to save. Heavy seas tossed and pounded boat and wreck, threatening to throw the one end over end or to smash the other to pieces. And yet, by nightfall the whole ship's company was safe on Sable Island.

The Humane Establishment had grown under Superintendent Darby's command. There were now enough buildings for the eighty new arrivals to have a roof over their heads, if only that of a barn or outbuilding. In fact, the chief concern of the rescued people was the clothing and other personal baggage still aboard the wreck. So in the days following their rescue effort, though the sea remained high on the south side, the Sable boatmen time and again fought their way to the wreck to salvage these goods.

The salvagers were tempting fate. With each successive trip, the odds increased that something would go wrong. Finally it did. The sea flung the island boat awry, and in the blink of an eye Martin Clye had a broken leg. The surgeon who treated the injury described it as "a fracture of the leg & partial dislocation of Ankle joint." This doctor, who had the promising name of Fixotz, apparently arrived at Sable Island via the shipwreck. His technique for repairing the painful damage included "Bleeding." Martin Clye was the only casualty recorded in the loss of the *Maria*.

Captain Born of the *Maria*, like Captain Epron before him, provided a testimonial to the heroism of Joseph Darby. He included all the Sable lifeboatmen in his praise, granting Martin Clye special mention. Born's testimonial took the form of a certificate stating that he had received "every assistance possible" from Superintendent Darby and describing the work of the coastguard crew. Born told how the Sable boatmen had disembarked the castaways "through a frightening sea" and how the people's baggage was saved only by "the fearlessness and devotion to duty of Capt. Darby and his crew." He declared that the motivation for his testimonial was justice and gratitude, and a desire "that these brave mariners who in order to save us have so many times imperilled their lives" should receive "some reward or encouragement," which in his opinion they richly deserved. In conclusion, Born referred to Clye, albeit anonymously: "I particularly recommend the sailor who had the misfortune to have his leg broken in seeking to save our goods."

This glowing tribute might be thought suspect since Captain Born gave his certificate to Superintendent Darby before leaving Sable Island, though it is doubtful that Darby could translate the French. But when Born later made his official report of the loss of the *Maria* and the twenty-day sojourn of the castaways on Sable Island, he showed no change of heart. Witness the Minister of Marine's report to the king based on Born's information. The minister stated that Superintendent Darby and his crew had come to the wreck "to snatch from the jaws of death the unfortunate castaways" and that afterward they "did not cease from lavishing on them the most touching cares." He advised the king, on 11 May 1840, that "until now the recognition of these eminent deeds" had been the only reward for "this devotion to duty and this munificence." The minister therefore asked King Louis Philippe to authorize him to award a gold medal in the king's name to the foreign officer whose "noble and remarkable conduct" he had just pointed out.

The king consented to the award, as Ambassador Guizot informed Foreign Secretary Palmerston in London on 13 June 1840. Guizot enclosed a copy of the Minister of Marine's report to inform Palmerston of "the generous conduct of Captain Darby," with an addendum:

I must add that this officer having been strongly supported in his laudable enterprise by an English seaman (whose name is not indicated) who was injured at the time of the wreck of the *Maria* near Sable Island, the Minister of Marine has granted to this mariner a bounty of 300 francs, which he proposes to forward to him through the good offices of the French consul in Boston.

The consul informed Superintendent Darby of his award as well, but the actual medal did not reach Palmerston until December. He passed it on to Lord John Russell, the colonial secretary, who forwarded it to the Lieutenant Governor of Nova Scotia. In the meantime, the Sable Island Establishment had undergone a sea change.

∽

Shortly after the wreck of the *Maria*, Superintendent Darby sent an extract of Captain Born's certificate to the Sable Island Commissioners. They ignored it. They had little sympathy with Born's suggestion—and Darby's belief—that the crew of the Sable Island Establishment deserved some special reward or encouragement. In the Commissioners' view, the men who risked their lives to save life and property at Sable Island were simply doing their job. As government servants they were fulfilling the purpose for which the island settlement existed. Majority opinion in Nova Scotia might well have supported their position, if it had been known.

Back of Darby medal with testimonial about his aid to shipwrecked sailors. The inscription is somewhat misleading, since the vast majority of people rescued from the unnamed ship (Maria) were passengers, and the wreck occurred in 1839.

Front of medal struck for Joseph Darby showing profile of the King of France who awarded it.

Doing your duty for its own sake was a well-established Bluenose tradition. In this case, the Sable Commissioners occupied the moral high ground.

On the other hand, an experienced sea captain had viewed the actions of the Sable hands as beyond the call of duty. Should the men be expected as a matter of course and for low wages to risk their lives, or even serious injury, to save other people's property? What would happen to a man like Martin Clye if he were maimed for life? A working seaman like Born could appreciate the validity of questions like these. He knew the real danger faced by the coastguard crew. Men like the Commissioners, whose lives and welfare would never be subjected to such threats, probably could not. They could afford to view any special recognition offered men in the Sable Island service as the thin edge of the wedge of corruption. Their attitude would be more acceptable if the Halifax society in which they were so well placed had not offered numerous examples of the abusive combination of privilege and power that, as Joseph Howe pointed out, threatened to corrupt the whole province. There were clearly worse ways of seducing capable and ambitious men than by rewarding them for outstanding achievement in a good cause.

Superintendent Darby saw the Commissioners' lack of response to Captain Born's testimonial as directed against himself because he had come into conflict with them about other matters. Whether Darby was right or not, it is doubtful that he was the only one who took the Commissioners' lack of response personally. At the end of the winter season, in the spring of 1840, the crew of the Sable Island Establishment departed *en masse*. Only two continued in the lifesaving service. One was the least experienced hand, the other Darby's son. Martin Clye's resignation may have resulted from the injury to his leg, but the other departures bespeak disenchantment with the Sable Island service. The loss of experienced men of demonstrated ability and commitment must have been a blow to the Humane Establishment. All but one of the men hired as replacements were new to Sable Island and completely inexperienced. The exception, John Stevens, was another Darby relative, his wife's brother. The new Sable hands were each paid sixty shillings a month, ten shillings more than the former crew. These wages became the new standard for the Establishment.

The ease with which the Sable Island Commissioners signed on a new crew might be seen as a vindication of their attitude. No matter how many men resigned from Sable Island, there were plenty of others ready and willing to take their place if the money was right. The farming and fishing communities of Nova Scotia produced plenty of young men who, with a little experience at the island, might prove as worthy as the men they replaced. That the Superintendent of Sable Island was the one saddled with the job of moulding them into an efficient crew was not the

Commissioners' concern. Training new men was, after all, one of the duties of his position.

Superintendent Darby might console himself for the loss of the best crew he had known by looking at his dazzling gold medal—when it finally arrived in 1841. (The long delay no doubt explains why it was stamped with the wrong date for the wreck.) On the front was a stylized profile of King Louis Philippe, but for Darby, the main attraction would be the reverse side with its inscription:

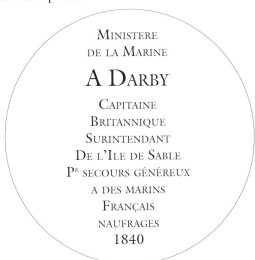

MINISTERE
DE LA MARINE

A DARBY

CAPITAINE
BRITANNIQUE
SURINTENDANT
DE L'ILE DE SABLE
Pr SECOURS GÉNÉREUX
A DES MARINS
FRANÇAIS
NAUFRAGES
1840

Superintendent Darby might also reflect on the irony of being a prophet in his own country. Like an Olympic champion he possessed gold medals representative of international recognition that nobody had the right to take away. And yet, it seemed that only a foreign power would pay tribute to his good work at Sable Island. The contrast with his native province—not to mention the Home government—was inescapable, and not a little galling for a loyal British subject.

In view of the bad press accorded Joseph Darby over the years, his exploits in connection with the losses of the *Africaine* and *Maria* deserve to be known. Of special note is the effect of his success on others. This reputed monomaniac was instrumental in securing a high honour for his lieutenant governor, and rewards of honour and money for fellow employees of the Sable Island Establishment. As Sable Superintendent, Darby took pride in the 300-franc award to Martin Clye—he resented only the lack of recognition for the rest of his faithful crew. It may be a coincidence that all the special awards to members of the Sable Island Humane Establishment up to Darby's time came from France. But was it mere coincidence that these awards were all linked to activities of "The Rogue" Joseph Darby?

Chapter Eight

A Season of Growlers
at Sable Island

For the outside observer of events at Sable Island, shipwrecks seem to be the most dramatic. For the people in the wreck, a better operative word would all too often be "traumatic"—unless it was "fatal." But for the people living on the island, in particular the Superintendent of the Humane Establishment, the wreck itself was sometimes less distressing than the aftermath. A case in point is the aptly named *Growler*.

The *Growler* stranded in close on the south side of Sable Island at 4:00 A.M. on 17 December 1849 during a strong gale from the south with heavy rain. When the wind moderated, since the beach was near, the whole crew were able to land safely and even salvage their kits. Meanwhile the people of the Establishment were unaware of the plight of these castaways.

The storm blew over about noon, but thick fog still blanketed the island. The Sable Superintendent, following what was now Establishment routine, sent out patrols to search for signs of wrecks along the shores. Also routinely since Darby's superintendency, these patrols travelled on horseback, using Sable Island animals that had been broken and trained as saddle horses. The Establishment facilities had changed in other respects as well, chiefly by simple expansion. Increases in personnel now allowed two inhabited outposts besides the Main Station. Both outposts were in the eastern part of the island, one at the foot of the lake, the other four miles away and within three miles of the east end.

In general, the Main Station patrols covered the western half of the island, both north and south coasts and the northwest bar. Under optimum conditions, the riders from headquarters were able to ford the lake at the shallowest part to the south beach. But that December day drift ice in the lake, and perhaps unusually high water, made the passage too difficult for the horses.

While one patrol headed eastward on the north side of the lake, the Superintendent himself scouted the west end. About three hours after the riders set out, one of them came galloping back from down-island to report the wreck on the south side, within five hundred yards of an unoccupied house of refuge. The Superintendent quickly took charge of the situation. He sent word of the wreck to the other stations, ordering the keepers to report for work at the stranded ship. He himself took six men in a boat, and they fought their way across the lake to the site of the wreck.

The Sable Superintendent at this time was Matthew D. McKenna. He was a no-nonsense Bluenose with definite standards and the determination to impose those standards on Sable Island. McKenna, in contrast to Superintendent Darby, has been the darling of most historians and others who have written about Sable Island. The author of the basic history of Sable Island, George Patterson, called him "simply the man for the place." One reason for McKenna's reputation is that his successful career is thoroughly documented. Included in the documents is the story of the *Growler*, remarkable in itself but a lowlight rather than a highlight of that career.

On arrival at the beach, Superintendent McKenna and his crew confronted a startling sight. Peering through the fog, they discerned a large white Newfoundland dog on top of the sea. It was the brigantine's figurehead, heavy with symbolism. The *Growler* was a sometime sealing vessel from St. John's, Newfoundland, and among the sealers the ship's name referred to more than an ill-tempered canine. A growler was also a mass of ice some twenty feet high detached from an iceberg, which also might be viewed as a watchdog for the parent berg. Local patriotism aside, the choice of a Newfoundland dog for a ship's figurehead was apt, for the breed is noted for its swimming powers. Since the Newfoundland dog is usually black, the white paint made the association with icebergs.

Soon after sighting the wreck, Superintendent McKenna met its master, Captain Robertson, and his crew on shore. Captain Robertson explained briefly how the calamity had happened. The *Growler* had sailed from Baltimore nine days previously on the homeward leg of its voyage, with a cargo classified as provisions, which included flour, corn, pork, and tobacco. While Robertson had known that he was in the general area of Sable Island, he did not know exactly where he had taken the ground. In fact, he had sailed nearly onto the beach, which at least enabled all on board to reach land unaided. The refugees from the wreck had then made their way to the house of refuge.

McKenna saw that the brigantine was well and truly grounded. Nothing could be done to get it off. On the other hand, the salvagers should be able to save pretty well all the cargo and ship's materials. The sea had now driven the wreck so far up the beach that the men could board it without using their boat. With darkness coming on, and the wreck not likely to suffer any great injury overnight, McKenna put off the salvaging. He deemed it best to take the shipwrecked seamen away from what he called "the wretched hovel" nearby to comfortable quarters at the Main Station. The salvage operation would begin on the morrow.

The 18th dawned very cold with snow squalls, giving a foretaste of what the salvagers would have to endure. On arriving at the wreck, they discovered that it now had about five feet of water in it at high tide. They set to work and by the end of the first day's labour had landed a hundred barrels of flour. Each barrel weighed about three hundred pounds. The weight and awkwardness of these and other casks added an element of danger to their labour. Sure enough, the next day one of the Sable crew, John Clyburn (or Clyburne), injured himself lifting one of them and was forced to return home. On reaching the Main Station, he discovered that the government schooner *Daring* had arrived. It was anchored in its usual location, but the sea was too high to allow anybody to board it.

On Thursday 20 December the *Daring* was able to take off the mate and six seamen from the *Growler* for the return trip to Halifax. Captain Robertson chose to remain on the island.

With the *Daring* looked after, most of the island crew went back to their salvaging. Two men were absent: Clyburn and one Henry Yorke (or York) who had been hurt in a fall from a horse before the wreck. The salvagers landed one hundred and thirty more barrels of flour. The working conditions were deteriorating. The cold had intensified to the point where the lake was completely frozen over. The ice was thick enough to prevent use of the boat but not solid enough to guarantee the men a safe walk across the lake. Then a change of weather typical of Sable Island brought a sudden thaw.

On Friday strong winds struck from the southward, with heavy rain. The men occupied themselves with various routine tasks close to home. Saturday saw another man on the limp, reducing the salvage party to six: Superintendent McKenna, Captain Robertson, and four others. This crew transported a quantity of the salvaged goods to the south side house and stored them inside. They also piled casks of flour close by the lakeshore and brought fifty-three boxes of candles, two boxes of tobacco, and a dozen brooms up from the beach. Sunday was a day of rest.

On Monday it was raining and heavy seas pounded the shores all around the island. Everybody except the two injured men went to the wreck, taking a boat and three teams. The hulk now had a large quantity of water in it, and a number of the remaining barrels were stove. The salvagers brought ashore about one hundred and forty barrels before the steadily rising sea became too high. Shifting their efforts inland, they carried another fifteen boxes of tobacco up from the beach.

That evening, Christmas Eve, Superintendent McKenna moved his family into a house that had been repaired recently for their use. (The McKennas had been living in an apartment at one end of the men's house). On

Contemporary artist's impression of the work of Sable Island salvagers at a vessel stranded like the Growler.

Christmas Day none of the men did any work—which was just as well, since all were sick with colds. But on Boxing Day it was business as usual.

The sea was still so heavy that the salvagers could work only at low water. They nevertheless landed another hundred and forty barrels of flour, much damaged, plus nineteen barrels of pork. At this point, a spell of miserable weather set in, with both snow and rain. The violent surf finally capsized what remained of the brigantine, which lay on its starboard side, the head offshore. The sea became so turbulent that boarding the downed hulk was impossible. The time had come to call a halt to this salvage effort.

In the privacy of his new quarters, Superintendent McKenna began the year 1850 by catching up on his administrative duties. His chief concern, partly because of the recent arrival of the castaways, was the rate at which the Establishment provisions were being consumed. He was not happy with the way things were going: "of late have found the consumption of small stores to be extravagant." So on 2 January, a Wednesday, he began a new system of rationing. He weighed out four pounds of tea, four pounds of chocolate, thirty-two pounds of sugar, and three gallons of molasses as a four-week supply for eight men.

The following Monday evening, a commotion arose in the men's house. The foreman of the headquarters crew, Gasper Graham, complained afterward that John Clyburn had taken hold of him, shaken him, and threatened further violence. After hearing Graham's report, Superintendent McKenna "investigated the matter" on Tuesday, presumably by interrogating eyewitnesses. He concluded that Clyburn "had committed the assault without justification."

On further inquiry, the Superintendent uncovered a more serious issue. Clyburn and three other men "had been finding a deal of fault with the provisions. They "had used abusive language," and three of them, without ever saying a word to McKenna himself, "had premeditated making a Complaint to the Commissioners with a view of effecting my removal." McKenna checked out their complaints and found not the slightest justification for them. He did discover, however, what he was convinced was the real cause of their discontent.

The great offence that McKenna had committed against the three intending petitioners, he declared, was "by not allowing them rum while the others were working at the Growler and getting what I thought proper to give them." Two of the complainers, Clyburn and Yorke, had been confined to the house with injuries, and the third, James Clye, whose job it was to take care of the livestock, did not work at wrecks. McKenna had therefore decided that they had no need for an issue of rum, which during the Age of Sail was considered the proper fuel for seamen and others engaged in strenuous maritime labour.

In his righteous anger, McKenna was determined to send the three men off the island, and he actually gave notice to Clyburn and Yorke. By thus confronting the men he saw as ringleaders of the discontent, the Superintendent thought that he had put an end to personnel conflicts on Sable Island. He would soon realize that he had made more than one erroneous assumption.

The next trouble came from a totally unexpected source and seemed to have nothing to do with any conflict between Superintendent McKenna and his men. In January, deep winter set in, with snow remaining on the ground, a sight not all that common at windswept Sable Island. On 25 January Captain Robertson set off eastward with a gun, apparently to do a little duck hunting. When he had not returned by midnight, McKenna became concerned. He and foremen Graham set off on horseback in search of the wanderer. They stopped off at the east end of the lake and had a chat with the outpost keeper. He told them that he or one of the others in his house had seen Captain Robertson rounding the foot of the lake the day before, heading toward the wreck of the *Growler*. Robertson was wearing neither coat nor "Jackcoat"—a seaman's thick, close-fitting serge jacket—but he still had the gun.

Since the snow on top of ice made night travel dangerous, McKenna and Graham waited until dawn to resume their journey. On reaching the south side house, they found Captain Robertson. The captain was missing his coats, "having left them on the road," but he had lit a fire in the cabin for warmth. McKenna chatted with Robertson for a while and came to a conclusion: "although evidently disturbed in his mind he seemed quite harmless." After "partaking of some refreshment"—perhaps a euphemism for a draught of rum, for medicinal purposes—which the two men had brought him, Robertson promised he would follow them home. When he reached the Main Station at 3:00 P.M, Robertson was injured, "having hurt his shoulder severely by firing his gun overcharged." Two days later the captain was still lame in the shoulder, and McKenna thought that his collarbone was broken. Otherwise, there seemed to be no repercussions from this bizarre incident.

Two weeks later, McKenna had a run-in with another of his crewmen. The men were sawing wood, but, in McKenna's opinion, not fast enough. When the Superintendent voiced this opinion, one of the men replied in highly insulting and abusive language. McKenna seems to have been as much puzzled as incensed by this latest insubordination. He had never before, not since he became Sable Superintendent in 1848, had any problem with his men.

Otherwise life on the island was tranquil enough, given the winter weather. The severest cold spell yet froze the lake solid, allowing men and horses to cross on the ice. Then a storm drove the sea through breaches on the south side, and a rise in temperature brought heavy rain followed by thick snow. The ice in the lake broke up and fog shrouded the island. During this period of time, the Sable crew attempted no projects beyond routine winter duties. Captain Robertson apparently spent much of his idle time sucking on his pipe, for Superintendent McKenna was obliged to weigh out twenty pounds of tobacco for him from one of the boxes salvaged from the wreck. Suddenly, with as little warning as a change in Sable weather, a storm struck indoors.

The incident began for Superintendent McKenna when Captain Robertson one day failed to appear for dinner or tea at his house according to the usual custom. When McKenna went to him and asked why he had not come, Robertson replied that he had been insulted by Sarah Ann Powell, one of two servant women at McKenna's. For a man like the Superintendent, that accusation struck too close to home, at his deepest loyalties. He checked into the matter on the woman's behalf and satisfied himself that "the insult given by her was in no degree equal to the insults he had given to her." By picking on one of the Sable Island women, Captain Robertson had gone too far.

Superintendent McKenna, now boiling with moral indignation, confronted Robertson and told him that he must conform to the rules of Sable

Island. According to McKenna, Robertson replied that "he would see me d——d first." Robertson's attitude convinced McKenna that "the mans mind was much disturbed."

Since Robertson refused absolutely to go again to McKenna's house, the Superintendent assigned some of the Sable hands to coax him to be their guest. Robertson went with them to their house but said he would not stay. The only housing for him on Sable Island, he said, would be in one of the outbuildings. These buildings, being unheated, were hardly suitable for living quarters in the dead of winter. McKenna tried talking to Robertson again but failed to achieve any better meeting of minds, so he gave it up as a bad job. He set men to watch over the sea captain, instructing them not to allow him to leave the house for the night.

At this point, his dander still up, Superintendent McKenna took pen in hand and recorded his problems with the captain of the *Growler*. In this retrospective account, hindsight may have played as important a part as the actual events. "The Conduct of Capt Robertson which has been of the baset Kind ever since he came here has this day become outrageous." (The misspelling and other errors in this journal entry—as well as the strong language—are unusual, and perhaps signs of McKenna's emotion.) McKenna related how Captain Robertson had come to live with him and his family after the *Growler* crew left Sable Island on 20 December. Robertson slept and ate there and also enjoyed the privilege of having his clothes washed for him. When not eating or sleeping, however, the captain spent nearly all his time with the island hands, "and as I had no trouble with my men before he came I attribute the difficulties I have since had to his example & precepts." Members of the island crew who had not been troublesome and who did not approve of Robertson's conduct told McKenna that they never knew a man who used such abominable language or boasted of such villainous acts. One phenomenon that exemplified Robertson's erratic behaviour was his mysterious disappearances. He often went missing in the early evening for no known reason. Only the evening before, Robertson had left McKenna's house about six o'clock and had not shown up at the nearby men's house until about nine-thirty. When he arrived, he was in a sweat and appeared to be much agitated. Having moved out of McKenna's house, Captain Robertson refused to have his belongings sent to him. He gave the impression that anything remotely connected with the Superintendent was abhorrent to him.

∽

When Captain Robertson took up residence in the men's house, Superintendent McKenna told Gasper Graham to put all guns and ammunition away upstairs, including a gun saved from the *Growler*. The foreman followed these orders. At the same time, he played the role of good cop toward Robertson in contrast to McKenna's bad cop. While Graham was chatting up the captain in the evening, he learned something that helped explain the man's insecurity. Robertson told him that he had "a quantity of hard money," the proceeds of the *Growler*'s cargo on the outward passage to Demerara. Robertson said that he did not wish anybody else on the island to know of it, but Graham naturally reported the information to Superintendent McKenna. The Superintendent concluded that "if true" this fact would explain Robertson's absences at night, "as no doubt if he has money he has it buried out in the Island."

The next day, Sunday, Captain Robertson was "a little less violent" though still "very uneasy." He vowed that "he would starve before he would eat any more of the Island provisions," so McKenna told the foreman to give him ham from the *Growler*'s cargo. Graham served the ham along with "bread tea &c" from the men's table, "and he ate hearty of them."

On Monday Superintendent McKenna took four men to the east end on a seal hunt. Before leaving, he instructed Graham to take advantage of their absence and cultivate Captain Robertson in an effort to find out how much money he had and where it was hidden. The Superintendent also told Graham not to allow Robertson to enter the house with McKenna's wife, daughters, and female servants.

When McKenna returned, Graham reported that Captain Robertson had demanded the clothes he had left at McKenna's and threatened to go in and take them. He "was advised by the foreman not to do so." Graham also said that when he asked about Robertson's money, the captain said he had a part of the proceeds of the outward cargo with him in gold, but he refused to divulge its value. He shrewdly quoted the saying that "a still tongue showed a wise head" and immediately dropped the subject. Clearly, although the captain may have lost his emotional bearings because of the loss of his ship— which by the rules of the game was his fault—he was no fool. Superintendent McKenna sent Robertson the clothes he had left on the bed he used in McKenna's house, plus a mattress for his chosen quarters among the Sable hands. Robertson continued to eat with the men but at a separate table, and he fed mainly on the ham salvaged from his own vessel.

Wednesday began with fog and rain and ended with snow squalls, but the lake was at last free of ice. For the first time since just after Christmas a boat was able to travel down to the wreck of the *Growler*. It brought back twelve sails, eleven dozen brooms, and some running rigging. On Thursday McKenna sent four men to the west end to collect wood for making shingles, always needed to replace those blown off the buildings by the winter winds. While the rest of his crew worked around the station, sawing wood and repairing a cart, McKenna spent some time "going through" the men's house. Here he made a disturbing discovery. At the head of what was now Captain Robertson's bed, McKenna found a gun.

It was the weapon from the *Growler* that had been put away.

When the four men returned from the west end, McKenna called his whole crew together and asked who had given the gun to Captain

Robertson. All denied having done so. McKenna reached the obvious conclusion: Captain Robertson "must have stolen up stairs unobserved" and retrieved it.

McKenna's shocking discovery had not really been by chance. Robertson had ignored his own good advice and talked too freely to the friendly island foreman. On Wednesday night Robertson had mentioned the gun to Graham, according to McKenna saying "that he would have her and that if I went to take her from him and she was loaded he would put the charge through me." Faced with such a threat, McKenna took all the guns in the men's house and locked them safely away in his own.

The climax of the drama with Captain Robertson had been reached, though McKenna may not have realized it at the time. Three days later the government schooner *Daring* arrived at Sable Island. As Captain Robertson was preparing to depart, he collected a chest that he had left in McKenna's house. He now said that this chest contained his money. The *Daring* sailed on 25 February, taking the captain of the *Growler* off the island and ending one of the more bizarre episodes in the history of the Sable Island Establishment.

Also departing on the *Daring* were two members of the Sable crew who had caused Superintendent McKenna trouble, but the terms of their leaving imply that he had had a change of heart. John Clyburn requested leave to go off on account of illness, and McKenna granted his wish. McKenna also allowed James Clye to leave, on the grounds that Clye had given the standard three months notice. Since three months back from 25 February would be prior to the wreck of the *Growler*, it seems likely that McKenna was here using a polite fiction to cover a parting by mutual consent without laying blame. The Superintendent had stated in January that he intended to get rid of Clyburn and Clye as soon as possible. At that time he had included a third man, Henry Yorke, among his candidates for firing, but he now allowed him to stay on the island. McKenna seems to have adjusted his thinking in the light of what he learned about Captain Robertson's bad influence. His lenient attitude toward these men, once his anger had cooled, does him credit.

Both Clye and Clyburn had been at Sable Island when McKenna came, and for more than a year he had found them satisfactory workers. Clyburn had served as McKenna's foreman before moving his wife to the east end to operate that station. When Clyburn's wife later left the island, he was obliged to return to the Main Station as an ordinary hand. Gasper Graham had replaced him as foreman. Then Clyburn injured his back in salvaging the *Growler*'s cargo. Superintendent McKenna no doubt took all these factors into consideration, as well as Clyburn's many years of Sable service. Instead of making a big issue of the recent unpleasantness, Superintendent McKenna simply let the matter drop.

In spite of the brief outbreak of discontent—which he had weathered with a minimum of difficulty—Superintendent McKenna had good reason to be pleased with his crew. They had performed yeoman service at the wreck of the *Growler*. The hundreds of barrels of flour and other goods landed from the wreck and transported to a safe place for storage speak for themselves. We may imagine the strain of heaving these awkward, heavy casks around while standing in a tossing boat or half-submerged in icy seawater. Even ashore the cutting wind and freezing temperatures would threaten the salvagers with hypothermia.

Superintendent McKenna himself admitted the extent of the labourers' ordeal when he was lobbying the Commissioners a year later for new buildings on the south part of the island. He said that in winter a wreck near either house on the south side or the Foot of the Lake Station would cause "a deal of suffering" for the island people. In bolstering his argument, he added:

> we can never again go through such fatigue and hardship as we
> endured last winter at saving the *Growler*'s Cargo, and she lay
> within 500 yards of the wretched hovel on the South Side.

In this same letter McKenna brought up another subject that has a direct bearing on the problems with his men. He complained that the winter supplies for the Establishment were being sent too late in the season. As an example, he said that the supplies for the winter of 1849–50 had been landed between 27 and 29 October and that a great part of them was lost in landing when the packages were broken and the articles soaked. In other words, McKenna's rationing of the small stores, which had aroused discontent in January 1850, was not a sign of stinginess. It resulted from a shortage of supplies caused by the losses of the previous October.

For the Sable hands, a reduction in their allowance of sweets like sugar and molasses just after they had been forced to burn up reserves of energy at the *Growler* was like adding insult to injury. McKenna's explanation that the real issue was rum is probably a partial truth. It is quite likely that the rum he dispensed at the wreck stimulated extraordinary efforts by his crew. A man need not be addicted to alcohol to place a high value on the issue of rum under those conditions. At the same time, by denying rum to the non-salvagers, McKenna was using liquor as an incentive to work. As a former seaman, he was following the tried and true mariner's tradition. His reasoning was understandable, but the denial of a tot of rum to men unable to work because of injury would only make them feel all the more left out and hard-done-by. During their season of discontent, the disturbed and disturbing Captain Robertson was there to play the role of agitator.

Indirectly, then, the wreck of the *Growler* contributed to the lowering of morale on Sable Island. As an instigator of complaints, it created a number of namesakes, not excluding the Superintendent of the Sable Lifesaving Establishment.

Chapter Nine

A Pair of Villains, An Angel, and the East End Station

Against the blinding snow of a northerly gale on 16 December 1852, a man was fighting his way from the East End Station at Sable Island to the lookout. Arrived, he peered seaward until the snow thinned for a moment and he glimpsed something—about half a mile to the west, close in to the north beach, a small schooner in the breakers! The man quickly scrambled down to the beach and set off toward the shipwreck. After only a few dozen plodding steps through snow and sand, he came upon two seamen from the stranded vessel. Both were wet and cold, and one man's feet were so badly frozen that he couldn't stand. Neither man could speak English, but their needs were clear: they must get to a warm place with hot food or drink as soon as possible. The Sable lifesaver took hold of the lame man and with the help of his ambulatory shipmate supported him up the hill to the station.

The outpost man, whose name was James Farquhar, sent off one of his children on horseback to report the wreck to Superintendent McKenna. The messenger had to ride twelve miles through drifting snow and sand to the Main Station. Meanwhile Farquhar mounted his own horse, Old Sam, and headed back to the beach. The two seamen had conveyed by sign language that some of their shipmates needed help at the wreck site. Farquhar aimed to bring back any other survivors.

He found the schooner driven up on the beach, though not free of the surging sea. He also found four more men on shore. From their actions and from the agonized screams he could hear above the wind, he learned that a fifth man was trapped aboard the wreck. This man could do little to help himself, for his leg was broken. All efforts by his mates to save him had failed. They had tied a rope around him and tried to drag him ashore but could not budge him. Now, with the temperature below zero Fahrenheit, the spray bursting over the stranded vessel was fast coating it with ice.

99

Farquhar realized that the only way to save the injured man was to go get him. Grabbing hold of the rope attached to the seaman, he pulled himself through the glacial surf to the wreck. On board he discovered that a bight had caught under a belaying pin and that the rope was frozen to the schooner's rail. He went to the crippled man, lowered him over the stern, and dragged him through the groundswell. As Farquhar staggered out of the surf with his burden, the seamen grabbed both men before the under-tow could drag them back.

With the help of one of the sailors, James Farquhar carried the suffering man to Old Sam and put him on the horse. He took the invalid as fast as he could over the treacherous terrain to the East End Station, where Farquhar's family helped minister to the injured and nearly frozen seaman. His right leg was broken below the knee. To counter the cold and pain, Farquhar plied him with the standard home remedy: brandy. Some time afterward, Superintendent McKenna arrived and Farquhar helped him to set the broken bone. Despite the brandy, this amateur operation was, as one eyewitness recalled, "a terrible ordeal for the victim."

After treating the wounded man, Superintendent McKenna turned his attention to the lost vessel. On arriving at the wreck scene, he found the schooner lying against the beach, with both masts down. The foremast was broken off near the top, while its lower part had come out of the step and was hanging across a sail. The mainmast was cut off at the deck. The deck was torn up, the vessel full of water. The only things that McKenna and his crew could salvage were some of the men's clothes and a few of the schooner's materials. Within twenty-four hours, the wreck was "beaten into staves."

One man failed to survive this wreck. Like his shipmates, he had lowered himself into the water from the stern, but unlike them, he had been caught in the backwash and carried seaward. He was never seen again, alive or dead.

Some of the survivors were able to communicate the story of their disaster. Superintendent McKenna recorded their account in his daily journal and in an official report to his mainland superiors. The lost schooner was the *Marie Anne* of St. Andre, Quebec. The ship's company totalled eight: Capt. Theophile Desjardins and his four-man crew plus three others who were working their passage to Nova Scotia. The schooner had sailed for Halifax from Placentia Bay, Newfoundland, on 9 December with a cargo of 1,200 quintals (120,000 pounds) of codfish. Approaching the coast of Nova Scotia, it ran into rough weather, with strong north winds that drove the vessel seaward. Captain Desjardins tried to lie to, had in fact done so for nearly two days. He and his crew were unaware that they were drifting inexorably toward Sable Island. When a northnorthwest gale struck on the 16th, they were so close to the island that the *Marie Anne*'s doom was sealed. Suddenly the eight men found themselves aground on the north shore of the island with the seas pouring over them. This assault by the

waves knocked down one of the regular hands before he could get free of
the wreck and threw him violently about the deck. He was lucky to survive
with only a broken leg. The man who escaped from the wreck but disappeared in the sea was one of the three working their passage. He was a
resident of Bay Verte known to the schooner crew only as Tom.

Superintendent McKenna believed that, all things considered, the *Marie
Anne* survivors had been exceptionally fortunate. If the schooner had struck
Sable Island further away from the eastern station, said McKenna, or if
Farquhar had not kept such a sharp lookout, spotted the schooner so soon
after it struck, and acted so fast, "I have no doubt but all on board would
have perished."

∽

James Farquhar was in many ways typical of the outpost men of the Sable
Island Establishment. They lived with their families separate from the Superintendent and his crew at the Main Station and kept no records of their
own activities. Seldom was their work mentioned in the Superintendent's
records.

But James Farquhar was also an exception. One of his sons, his name-
sake who grew up on Sable Island, in his old age wrote an autobiography.
Son James devoted considerable space to his family's Sable Island years.
These reminiscences offer a rare glimpse of the reality of the world of outpost keepers on Sable Island. The available official records show that in
general the younger Farquhar's account of such episodes as the wreck of
the *Marie Anne* is surprisingly accurate. The lack of pretension in the writing, the absence of grandiose claims of macho heroism on the part of his
father or himself, reflect the attitudes of this Sable family. The inevitable
errors of detail are more likely to be misremembered traditions than self-
serving distortions.

James Farquhar the outpost keeper was, according to his son, a Scots-
man of fair education, by trade a millwright. He immigrated to Nova Scotia,
where he married a local woman, Catherine Bayers. The couple settled on
a small farm on the Musquodoboit River twenty-eight miles from Halifax,
where Farquhar also owned and operated a small sawmill and grist mill.
Here they began raising their family, which eventually included seven children. And here James Augustus, who would be called Jim, was born on 12
October 1842.

When Jim was five years old, his father entered into a risky business
deal. Within a year he was bankrupt, losing his mills and farm. "Casting
about for a means of livelihood," Farquhar signed up for the Sable Island
Establishment. He went to the island alone, serving at first as a member of
the lifeboat crew at the Main Station.

In July 1849 Catherine Farquhar received a letter from her husband
telling her to catch the next boat for Sable Island. She and the children
were to join him at his new post in charge of the East End Station. She

immediately began making arrangements to move her family from the mainland. In a matter of weeks six-year-old Jim, his two brothers, and four sisters found themselves on the journey to Sable Island. The eldest child, Jim's sister Isabel, was then only sixteen. The first stage of the journey took them by land to Halifax in a hay wagon loaded with the family's few belongings.

After five days in what to the children was the big city, they departed in the schooner *Prince of Wales*, Captain Eisan, which was chartered to Sable Island for a load of wild horses. Three days later, on 31 August, they reached Sable Island. Only much later did Jim Farquhar appreciate the sadness of that journey for his mother, as she faced the prospect of living on this desolate island cut off from all her mainland friends. What he remembered was the excitement of landing at Sable. As the surfboat pulled ashore, hundreds of seals sported in the surrounding waters, filling Jim and the other children with delight.

At the Main Station Superintendent McKenna and his family welcomed the new arrivals and gave them a good meal to fortify them for the trip down-island. Then everybody was packed into another wagon to finish their journey the way they had started. Three Sable horses hauled the wagon over a road that was little more than a wheel track winding among the sandhills to the East End Station twelve miles away. By evening the whole Farquhar family was once again united. Early the next morning Jim's mother, with help from some of the children, began cleaning the house and trying to put it in order. Farquhar's station had served for some months as bachelor quarters.

The East End Station consisted of a group of wooden buildings nestled behind Sable's north ridge. The keeper and his family lived in a frame house covered with shingles from the ground to the peak of the low roof. A solid warehouse stored provisions and salvage; a combination barn and stable housed hay and livestock; and a shed served as a workshop. A small outhouse signalled the lack of indoor plumbing. At the flagstaff on a height a short distance north of the living quarters stood the lookout.

The East End Station was in truth somewhat misnamed. It was not at the east end proper. It was actually located about two and a half miles west of the eastern point of Sable Island. And this point, the end of the grass-covered land, marked the beginning of another three miles or so of dry northeast sandbar. To the westward of Farquhar's station dwelt the family's nearest neighbours, Mr. and Mrs. Stevens and their two daughters, about four miles away at the Foot of the Lake Station.

The setting of the Farquhars' new home resembled their farm on the mainland, if you ignored the lack of trees and the unceasing boom of the sea crashing on shore. These waves all too frequently shook the foundations of Sable like an earthquake. They were a constant reminder that James Farquhar's government job was, as his son said, "no sinecure."

Farquhar's wages of twelve dollars a month were little enough for a man who still had debts on the mainland. From this sum he had to buy bedding and clothing for his family, including his own workclothes, which wore out quickly under Sable conditions. The great benefit was security for his wife and children, the guarantee of a roof over their heads and free food—so long as the father remained healthy enough to perform his duty. For a man in Farquhar's circumstances, it was the best deal he could make. The duties of an Establishment outpost keeper also suited a man of his character and experience. He was able to empathize with victims of misfortune and sincerely wished to ease their suffering.

∞∞

Three of the survivors of the wreck *Marie Anne* were in such bad shape that they could not be transferred to the Main Station. The man with the broken leg was the worst case, but the one whose feet were frozen was a close second. The third, who had been found unconscious at the wreck, was simply worn out from shock and exposure. None was fit to endure a twelve-mile journey in an open cart under winter conditions. All needed a period of convalescence, which meant that the Farquhars would have to look after them.

At this time one of the older Farquhar daughters was living at the Main Station, helping out a married woman who may have been ill or pregnant. The addition of the three seamen therefore brought the total in Farquhar's house to eleven. Aside from the crowded conditions, the Farquhars faced the awkwardness of communicating with guests who spoke little or no English. For six weeks the family nursed the injured and frost-bitten men back to health, caring for all their needs. Catherine Farquhar and her young daughters did all their cooking and washing.

In fact, for a short while following the wreck, the Farquhars attended to all seven castaways, and the family's charity at this time cost them more than they could afford. The Sable Island Establishment of this era did not stock a supply of clothing for castaways. The outpost man and his family therefore provided the refugees with "dry wearing apparel and bedding and every other comfort within their reach." When the first group of survivors moved to the Main Station, and later when the other three followed along, they kept wearing most of the clothing Farquhar had lent them. Although part of the seamen's clothing was rescued from the *Marie Anne*, some of Farquhar's would never be returned.

Superintendent McKenna realized the situation and recognized its unfairness. He knew that the destruction of the *Marie Anne* was so complete that the Sable Establishment would realize next to nothing from the salvage. Nonetheless, in his report to the Chairman of the Board of Works—which had replaced the Sable Island Commissioners—he suggested that the Board should allow a small sum to compensate Farquhar for his loss. McKenna later suggested that four pounds would be appropriate (more

A Sable scene by Dr. J.B. Gilpin, who visited the East End Station when James Farquhar was in charge and his son Jim was still a boy.

than six weeks' wages). McKenna's intercession on behalf of Farquhar says something about both men. It points up the exceptional generosity of Farquhar and his wife and family. And it shows how Superintendent McKenna valued good works beyond mere duty.

In McKenna's case, the other side of the coin was that he had a low threshold of tolerance for behaviour that was by his standards improper. When the actions of the *Marie Anne* survivors offended those standards, the result was predictable: conflict. The preliminaries that led up to this conflict are, however, less than crystal clear. It apparently began with the man lost in the wreck. This death was the first in a shipwreck during McKenna's superintendency. (It would turn out to be the only one.) McKenna almost seems to have taken it personally, to have sought some cause of death beyond Sable Island. He developed certain suspicions about the tragedy.

The Superintendent's distrust arose from the little information he could glean from the survivors. One of the three men from Newfoundland who were working their passage, a man named Pierce, was supposed to have been the comrade of the lost man. Yet he insisted that he knew him only as Tom, with no last name. McKenna told the Chairman of the Board of Works bluntly, "I do not believe him." While salvaging the men's kits from the wreck, McKenna had inquired after Tom's belongings. The castaways at the Main Station told him that the only things of value that the man possessed were on his person when he went overboard. But much later, after Superintendent McKenna and Captain Desjardins had time to become better acquainted, the captain complained that some of the crew had taken Tom's clothes, which were "of some value." McKenna demanded the clothes of the men. When they denied having them, he left that issue to be dealt with in Halifax. Somebody else told McKenna that the drowned man had Mexican dollars worth about seven pounds and some papers of value, but nothing of the kind turned up at Sable Island.

Superintendent McKenna also reported that Captain Desjardins claimed to have 114 Mexican dollars, freight money he had received in Newfoundland. This money was in his trunk, which had been saved by the Sable crew and the *Marie Anne* crew working together. McKenna mentioned it to the Board so that they could inquire about it if they so chose. Desjardins "did not appear disposed to hand it over" to the Superintendent of Sable Island. McKenna sounded offended that the feelings of suspicion might have been mutual.

When the government schooner *Daring* arrived to take off the *Marie Anne* survivors on 29 March 1853, McKenna was glad to see the back of them. The letter he sent to the Board of Works in the *Daring* hinted at darker deeds than the ones he related in it. Reporting on the events of the past winter, he said vaguely, "I have had a great deal of very unpleasant duty to perform."

A follow-up letter offered an explanation of this portentous comment and also revealed McKenna's reason for going into detail about the matter. He thought that a complaint might have been made against him when the castaways reached Halifax. McKenna therefore took care to record his side of the issue and state his position in no uncertain terms. His conflict, he said, was not with any of the crew of the *Marie Anne* but with "the two fellows who were working their passage on board," that is to say, with Pierce and the third man whom McKenna never named:

> they are a pair of Villans and I believe would have given me some
> trouble while here if they could have raised a party sufficiently
> strong for their purpose and merely because I ordered all the
> Cards on the Island to be burned when I was informed by my
> foreman that those villans were playing them on Sundays – after
> which they grumbled about their provissions and many other

things…. I am willing to allow amusements in moderation at proper times but I will not allow Cards to be played on the Sabbath day nor will I allow any other games on that day where I am in authority let the consequence be what it may.

Today this passage might be read as the ravings of a religious fanatic, a man whose judgment was seriously unbalanced, even one who had completely lost contact with reality. Such a diagnosis would not only do McKenna an injustice; it would be seriously wide of the mark.

The issue was not as narrowly religious as might at first appear. Many Nova Scotians then and much later would have agreed with McKenna's attitude, a good percentage of them adults who seldom if ever saw the inside of a church. The explanation for the nickname Bluenose that it derived from the puritanical ways of the province's inhabitants is probably apocryphal, but its truth lies in the development of the myth, the creation of an explanation to fit the apparent reality. A strong Bluenose tradition held that the proper way to spend Sunday was not in fun and games, especially not games of cards. Extremists viewed cards, often associated with gambling, as the "Devil's Prayer Book." But even card lovers who liked nothing better than to while away the leisure hours with the province's favourite game of Auction 45s might refuse to play on Sunday. In short, McKenna's stance was as much cultural as strictly religious—akin to, say, today's political correctness. It bespoke a moralism greatly valued in his native province. He could be quite confident that the Halifax authorities would not condemn his attitude, whether they agreed with it or not.

Seamen in general, on the other hand, would find it hard to take. As men of the world, which most seamen were, no matter what their origins, they would find McKenna's reaction extreme. Even the villains of McKenna's story deserve sympathy. Marooned and often cooped up by weather and winter darkness for more than three months on Sable Island, they needed all the distraction they could get from their recent ordeal and present situation. By destroying all the cards, McKenna deprived them of what was doubtless a daily pastime. Whatever the reason for his action, the punishment was unfair. It hurt the innocent as much as the guilty. No wonder McKenna was subsequently forced to deal with a series of complaints. For the castaways, Sable Island was becoming less and less a place of refuge, more and more a prison.

James Farquhar and his family at the far end of the island played no part in the conflicts at the Main Station. For them the lasting memory of the loss of the *Marie Anne* was their care of the convalescents at their house. In future they could recall with pleasure the hearty thanks of the man Farquhar had saved from the wreck, whose broken leg was thoroughly healed by the time he left the island.

∾∾

A few months after the *Marie Anne* survivors departed from Sable Island, a rare visitor arrived. Any visit from the outside world caused excitement at Sable Island, especially for children like ten-year-old Jim Farquhar. In this case the event itself was gilded in memory by the fantastic aftermath. Jim never forgot the effect on Sable Island of this visitor, whom he would idealize in his memoirs. Her name was Dorothea Lynde Dix.

This woman would be linked to two Sable shipwrecks, one of them among the most famous in the annals of the island. It was also the most dramatic calamity to occur near James Farquhar's East End Station. The story of how Dorothea Dix was involved with these wrecks, and the work of the Sable Island Establishment, is complex, and so filled with coincidence as to rival the least credible Hollywood productions.

Dorothea Lynde Dix was a remarkable woman. She had spent a lonely and unhappy childhood under frontier conditions in Maine, from which she ran away at the age of twelve. Independent by nature, she became dependent upon wealthy relatives who took her in. She received an education and opened a school in Boston, intending to dedicate her life to teaching. After some years in this role, she suffered a long period of incapacitating illness, which today might be called burnout. About this time, her grandmother died and left her an inheritance that made her financially independent.

When Dorothea recovered her health, she volunteered to teach a class at the local jail. Here she saw mentally ill people locked away in a separate room under appalling conditions. Determined to change those conditions, she found that the only way to secure improvement was to take the jailer to court. At nearly forty years of age, Dorothea Dix had found her cause. By the time she came to Sable Island, she was well known as a reformer and philanthropist who had pressured state legislatures into passing laws on behalf of better treatment of "the insane."

In 1853 Dorothea Dix extended her mission beyond her native USA to Newfoundland and Nova Scotia. In Halifax the chief supporter of her efforts to found an asylum for the mentally ill was Hugh Bell. As Chairman of the Board of Works, Bell was also in charge of the Sable Island Establishment. Within a week of her arrival in Nova Scotia, Dorothea Dix was on her way to Sable Island. She landed from the government schooner *Daring* at noon on Tuesday 26 July. At 7:00 A.M. on Thursday a wreck occurred.

The schooner *Guide*, of London, Millichamp master, running in thick fog with a strong breeze from the southwest, hit a sandbar on the south side. The *Guide* was on a passage from New York to Labrador with a cargo of provisions. The location of the wreck was almost opposite the Main Station, from which it was discovered about nine o'clock. Superintendent McKenna and his crew rushed to the south side to rescue the people on the stranded vessel. Dorothea Dix followed on horseback and witnessed the

Dorothea Lynde Dix, the American philanthropist whose efforts provided a gift of lifesaving equipment from several U.S. cities that included the first rocket and breeches buoy apparatus at Sable Island and the lifeboats Reliance *and* Grace Darling.

work of the lifesavers. She watched from the beach as the Sable men manoeuvred their surfboat alongside the wreck and took off Captain Millichamp and his seven-man crew, then brought them safely ashore. By early evening everybody was back at headquarters, where the *Daring* still lay offshore. The castaways remained on the island to help salvage the vessel and cargo, but the *Daring* departed at 9:00 P.M. to report the wreck and take Dorothea Dix back to Halifax.

Through her conversations with Hugh Bell and Superintendent McKenna, plus what she had seen with her own eyes, Dorothea Dix realized that the lifesaving apparatus at the Sable Island Establishment was far from state-of-the-art. At the same time, she was impressed with the purpose of the Establishment and the work of the people in the Sable service. She decided to take a hand in furthering this good work.

Three weeks after her visit to Sable Island, having returned to Boston, Dorothea Dix consulted Robert B. Forbes, the chairman of the humane society, which was concerned with saving lives at sea. She presented her idea to him and gained his support. Leaving the technical details to Forbes, she went about her regular business while overseeing the project via correspondence. Before the end of 1853, she had raised enough money through subscriptions from "mercantile friends in the cities of Boston, New York, and Philadelphia" to provide four first-class lifeboats and other equipment. The other equipment included a mortar-and-life-car apparatus for firing a lifeline to a stranded vessel and hauling people ashore. The boats were all metallic, for lightness as well as strength, with special covered sections to increase buoyancy. She herself named them: the *Victoria* of Boston, the *Grace Darling* of Philadelphia, and the *Reliance* and *Samaritan* of New York. She called the life car *Rescue*.

Graphic illustration of the mortar firing the line to a wreck.

An ironic touch was added to the story when the ship carrying most of the equipment for relieving shipwrecks was wrecked on the coast of Nova Scotia. When the damaged boats were retrieved from the wreck, Dorothea Dix ordered them sent back to New York for thorough repair. Later problems with shipping arrangements caused further delay. So the first boats and other equipment did not reach Sable Island until a year after they were first shipped. One of the boats was the large lifeboat *Reliance*, which arrived on 11 November 1854.

∽∘∽

Early in the morning of 27 November 1854 James Farquhar and Old Sam were making their customary rounds of the east end of Sable Island. The thick overnight fog was beginning to dissipate. Sighting "fresh flotsam" in the surf, Farquhar rode on toward the northeast bar, his suspicion aroused. Through the lightening air he glimpsed the outlines of a vessel. As he rode nearer, his straining eyes discerned a three-masted tall ship looming out of the fog. It was the largest vessel Farquhar had seen at Sable Island—and it was stranded. Lying two hundred yards or more from the beach on the south side of the bar, listing seaward, it was caught by the stern, over which the waves were crashing. Farquhar could see dark masses in the forward rigging. He stared hard. The wreck was crowded with people!

James Farquhar turned Old Sam around and urged him home on the double. From his station he dispatched a messenger to Main with news of the wreck. The rider galloped the twelve miles at breakneck speed for such hazardous ground. By 9:00 A.M. the courier was making his report to Superintendent McKenna.

The stranded ship was the 715-ton *Arcadia*, a fine coppered vessel only five years old. It had been built and was still owned in Maine, Dorothea Dix's native state. Commanded by William Jordan, the *Arcadia* had sailed from Antwerp for New York on 29 October with 1,000 tons of cargo that included iron, lead, glassware, and measurement goods. The ship also carried 147 German passengers and a crew of 21 men. It had struck Sable's northeast bar at 6:00 P.M. the day before, while sailing into a strong southsouthwest wind in dense fog.

Superintendent McKenna lacked most of this information when he and his crew set out for the wreck with the Establishment's largest lifeboat, the recently arrived *Reliance*. On reaching the wreck site, McKenna saw a square-rigged ship,

lying about 200 yards from the beach, head to the Southward, settled deep in the sand and listed seaward, with her lee side under water, Main and Mizzen Masts gone by the deck, and a tremendous sea running and sweeping over her bows.

On the bar, he discovered the *Arcadia*'s mate and four seamen. They had landed in the ship's boat, then were unable to get off the bar to make the return trip.

The Sable crew immediately launched the *Reliance* and started for the wreck. The ship's mate, Dexter Collamore, went with them. The high winds and tide caused tremendous seas and a strong current that tossed the lifeboat around and carried it past its destination. Coping with these difficulties wasted precious time. The boat finally made its first contact with the wreck about three o'clock, when no more than two hours of daylight remained. With help from the *Arcadia*'s crew, the coxswain of the lifeboat took on a load of passengers and headed for shore.

When the *Reliance* neared the beach, James Farquhar and others waded into the icy water to haul it to safety before it could capsize or be dragged back off the bar. As soon as the drenched, shivering passengers were landed, the lifeboat again headed through the surf to the wreck. The lifeboat crew made six trips in all, bringing off "about 80 persons large and small." In two other attempts, "the oars and tholepins were broken by the violence of the sea," and the men finally had to draw up the boat. An attempt to run a warp from ship to shore failed because of the speed at which the current ran parallel to the bar. As night fell the seas rose.

The people on shore could hear, amid the thud and plash of wave on bar, the cries of castaways yet on the wreck, borne on the dark and piercing wind. To Superintendent McKenna these cries were "truly heart rending," as they were to the wreck victims already saved. And when they saw the boat pulled up for the night, a scene ensued, said McKenna, "that may be imagined but cannot be described." Families had been separated in the rush and confusion, with some members now ashore and some at sea. For the moment, nothing could be done to reunite them.

Superintendent McKenna concentrated on what could be done. He helped get all the new arrivals to shelter at the nearest station, Farquhar's, where they were served with refreshments. The house was too small to hold most of the castaways, and Farquhar's son later recalled, "we had to stow them in the barn among the hay for the night." McKenna also left the lifeboat crew there "to refresh themselves for the next day's work." The Superintendent mounted his horse and with his teamsters spent most of the night travelling to headquarters and back to bring metal tholepins for the lifeboat, plus the life-car-and-mortar apparatus. When McKenna arrived back before dawn, he found that the sea had gone down so much that there was no need for the life car. As soon as the men could see to work, the lifeboat crew again launched the *Reliance*. Before noon they made ten more trips to the wreck. They not only rescued all remaining passengers and crew but also salvaged all readily available clothing. When the sea be-

J. B. Gilpin watercolour showing the team hitched up and ready to haul the Sable surfboat during McKenna's superintendency.

gan rising again, the lifeboat crew drew up the boat and helped look after the most recent arrivals on shore.

With this second influx to Farquhar's station, most of yesterday's group were moved on to the Foot of the Lake Station for the night. By 2:00 P.M. every one of the castaways "was where they got a good fire to warm themselves by and plenty of Bread and water and some warm things to eat and to drink." The next morning some of the Establishment men began moving the refugees onward from station to station until they reached Main.

The weather had become mild, with a fairly smooth sea. So the Sable boat crew and the crew of the *Arcadia* boarded the wreck and saved barrels of bread and flour, plus more passengers' clothes.

In the midst of all this activity, the *Daring* made a providential appearance. With the assistance of the *Daring* crew, some of the Sable hands embarked eighty-seven of the castaways, and the schooner sailed for Halifax at 7:00 P.M. The rest of the passengers and the ship's crew remained at the Main Station to await the *Daring*'s return. About ten days later, the government schooner came back to free them from their accidental captivity.

By all accounts, in the disastrous circumstances of the *Arcadia* shipwreck, the people—ship's crew, passengers, and lifesavers—without exception did the best they could. Captain Jordan was knocked down by a wave, severely cut and bruised, and largely incapacitated early in the rescue effort. Mate Collamore took over the captain's responsibility and, Superintendent McKenna declared, "acted nobly throughout the whole business." The *Arcadia* sailors played their part well. The Sable hands "exerted themselves to the utmost"; the lifeboat crew "nobly stuck to their boat," refusing the mate's offer to spell them off with some of the ship's crew. Superintendent McKenna was particularly gratified that "the people of the Island both old and young, male and female, have shown a disposition to relieve suffering and to make the unfortunate as comfortable as circumstances will allow."

And yet, for McKenna the true hero of the occasion was the *Reliance*. The Francis Metallic Life Boat "Reliance" has done what no other boat could do that I have ever seen. It was a fearful time, yet the boats crew each took their stations readily and soon showed that they felt the "Reliance" to be worthy of her name.

By extension, McKenna's protagonist became the person who had sent the *Reliance* to Sable Island: Dorothea Dix. He was pleased to think that when she heard what the boat had done, she would feel more than compensated for "her great exertions on behalf of Sable Island Establishment." He was certain that many people had reason "to thank God that her good works have been felt on Sable Island." But his most heartfelt tribute to Dorothea Dix was expressed by his personal sentiments: "I shall think of her with feelings of gratitude while memory lasts."

Artist's sketch of the surfboat arriving at a wreck.

If Superintendent McKenna held such a high opinion of Dorothea Dix shortly after the loss of the *Arcadia*, he would later have cause to revise it upward. When Dorothea Dix heard the story of the *Arcadia*, she exerted herself even further on behalf of the Sable lifesavers. Through her offices, the Shipwrecked Fishermen and Mariners Royal Benevolent Society in London granted medals to Superintendent McKenna and the lifeboat crew: gold for him and silver for each boatman. In her letter informing McKenna of the awards, she told him she realized that no rewards or wages were equal to the services that he and his people performed. She nevertheless thought that they would value the medals highly as "evidence that your services in a lonely and desolate island are honorably estimated, and gratefully recorded."

Small wonder that the ten-year-old Jim Farquhar who had gazed upon the great lady remembered her fondly long after he himself became the

James Farquhar of his family. He recalled how she "quite captivated" the Sable residents and how the whole island later "rang with her praises." In the sentimental glow of reminiscence about his childhood days at Sable Island's East End Station, she became "Our Angel."

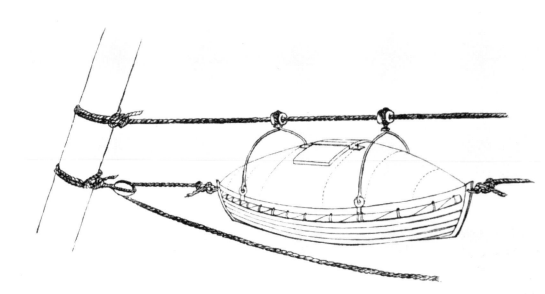

A life car like the one included in Dorothea Dix's gift to the Sable Island Establishment.

Chapter Ten

Women and Children First —Unfortunately

One of the great developments of the 19th century was the ocean-going steamship. With the increase in transatlantic travel, this development reached its zenith in the luxury passenger liner. Some people believed that in these marvellous vessels the ship had evolved to the stage where the ordinary dangers of the sea posed little threat. Free of the caprices of the wind that often forced sailing ships on unwanted courses, engine-powered steamships could, they reasoned, avoid known ocean hazards. One such hazard, known all too well, was Sable Island. Pessimists—or people who knew Sable better—thought that the fatal crescent of sand, which they expected to keep on wrecking windjammers, would also take its toll of steamers. And they feared that, given the number of people on board the new passenger ships, the human cost of shipwrecks at Sable Island might now be higher.

Such fears were of no concern to the people on board the passenger liner *State of Virginia* when it sailed from New York for Glasgow at ten o'clock in the morning on 10 July 1879. The *Virginia* was a fine iron steamship, 2,473 gross tons, rated A1 at Lloyd's. It was an impressive 331 feet long, 36 feet wide, and three decks high, designed to accommodate nearly 500 passengers: 62 first class, 32 second class, and 400 steerage. The hull was divided into six watertight compartments. As a precaution against fire, the ship carried fire engines operated by steam and an ample supply of hose, buckets, and other firefighting equipment. The second vessel put into operation by the State Line of Glasgow, the *Virginia* was only six years old.

This State Line ship was built not only for strength, speed, and security but also—to benefit the minority of passengers—for luxury. The main saloon was amidships, extending from side to side of the widest part of the vessel. It was elegantly fitted up and sported a piano and library plus seats for seventy-five persons. A "ladies' boudoir" adjoined the saloon at the front on the starboard side. Behind the saloon were the captain's cabin and the first class staterooms; in front of it, the second class staterooms on the starboard side and the dining saloon on the port. All the saloons and staterooms were decorated with English oak, maple, and rosewood. All the rooms were heated by steam and furnished with electric bells. On the top deck was "a nicely fitted up smoking-room for the use of the cabin passengers." From this description we may take the point that none of the luxury was intended for the steerage passengers. The best that could be said for their accommodation, it seems, was that separate apartments were provided for the married and single—with no indication of how many people were assigned to each "apartment."

One of the passengers in second cabin on the *Virginia* was a teacher from Niagara, Ontario, named Janet Carnochan. For years her great ambition had been to take a European voyage, and now in her late thirties she was realizing her dream. She was enjoying her first sight of the open sea and the experience of life in an ocean steamship.

On Thursday Janet spent her first night at sea stargazing. With the aid of the North Star, she established the points of the compass. She watched Venus sink slowly into the sea as Jupiter rose. She identified Cassiopeia and other constellations. In daylight on Friday she enjoyed many new and captivating sights: the antics of a shoal of porpoises, the spouting of a whale some distance off, and near the ship the fins of sharks cutting through the surface of the water.

The *Virginia* was making good time, almost maintaining its service speed of twelve knots. Then the fog set in. All Friday night and Saturday the fog whistle sounded to prevent collision with another vessel, the only danger feared on board the steamer. Since the fog prevented any observation Saturday at noon, the ship's officers were aware that their recorded latitude and longitude were unreliable. But Captain Moodie, who had commanded the *Virginia* for all the Atlantic crossings of its six-year operation, did not think that the ship's uncertain position was cause for worry. The passengers knew of no reason to be concerned.

On Saturday evening, to escape the chilling damp and gloom of the fog on deck, Janet Carnochan joined the other cabin passengers in the saloon. Here everything was bright and cheerful. In anticipation of Sunday service, the group sang hymns such as "Rock of Ages" and "Nearer, My God to Thee." About 7:50 P.M. the secure comfort of the singers was disturbed by a sudden jolt, then another. Alarmed, everybody rushed on deck.

One woman panicked, her face distorted in terror. She grabbed Janet's arm and asked her if the ship was sinking. Janet asked the man beside her, who replied that they had run aground, God only knew where. Janet herself, seeing the crew running about with ropes and chains, thought the *Virginia* had run down a smaller vessel and that these efforts were designed to save its crew. She did not yet know what Captain Moodie had already concluded: the ship had struck bottom at Sable Island. Janet's ignorance was, if not bliss, a comfort. As she watched the sailors dashing up and down the deck, she felt little fear.

The sailors strove to carry out the captain's order to try to work the vessel off the sandbar. The engine room crew stopped the engines, then reversed them at full speed. The seamen on deck dropped leads over the side to find the depth of water, lowered a boat, and sounded all around the ship. They ran a kedge anchor out astern to assist the engines. The ship refused to budge. Captain Moodie saw one remaining chance of saving his ship: it might float off when the tide reached its height at midnight. The crew prepared to help the forces of nature. They put out more boats, let cable over the side, and made ready to run out two more anchors.

Meanwhile, after the first shock, most of the passengers settled down. The danger seemed slight: the ship was apparently uninjured, and the night and sea were calm. Word went round that all they had to do was wait patiently for the tide to rise and lift them off in a few hours. Then came the second shock. It was more frightening than the first: the sound of grinding and crushing, as though the ship were being smashed on rocks. The rocks were imagined but the danger was real. The stern had swung around and struck the sandbar, breaking the rudder chain. As this news spread, Janet and her fellow passengers realized its import: "This was a new phase of our disaster; besides being imprisoned, we were now crippled." All efforts to free the *Virginia* were abandoned.

All night long the castaways waited, though they did not know what for. Some sat on deck, breathing the fog that dampened body and spirit. Some lay on lounges in the saloon. Some spent the time packing their valuables in anticipation of escape. Few took to their berths to sleep. Unable to see through the murky night, the wakeful castaways focused on what they could hear. Blind sounds aggravated frayed nerves: the hull grinding in the sand, which set the teeth on edge; the internal creaks and groans of the wounded ship; the waves lapping hungrily against its sides; the bullying boom of surf on an unseen shore.

Dawn of Sunday 13 July brought little relief until after breakfast, when the fog lifted for a spell. The people on deck sighted a lighthouse through the mist, and a low shore about half a mile away. The *Virginia* fired cannons to signal their distress. Then the fog closed in again. When next it began to lift, the straining eyes beheld a wonderful sight: men on shore with horses, a wagon, and boats. To Janet Carnochan the figures on the beach, distorted by receding fog and expanding hope, appeared colossal.

A surfboat soon came out from the Sable Island Establishment "with a message to land the passengers at once as the surf was constantly becoming worse." While the boat waited alongside, Captain Moodie renewed the attempt to free his ship.

The *Virginia* crew jettisoned part of the large general cargo, beginning with more than a hundred cattle penned on deck. The cattle swam around for hours trying to stay close to the ship, while casks, kegs, barrels, and cases of butter, fish oil, flour, and canned goods rained into the sea. Finally the terrified animals headed for shore, which sixty to seventy reached safely.

By this time some of the passengers were succumbing to nerves. Janet Carnochan saw one, "and not of the weaker sex," rushing from one officer or deckhand to another asking the same questions over and over. The disembarking of passengers began in the afternoon.

Janet was advised to go in the first boatload of women and children, plus the purser, doctor, and fourth officer. She decided to wait until the second boat. Upon further urging, she agreed to leave at once and descended the ship's ladder. Looking up, she saw the bulwark swinging in and out above her; looking down, she saw the lifeboat pitching and rolling on the waves below. Now committed to the venture, Janet let go. With a little luck and the help of the fourth officer, she landed in the boat. When nine more women and children were aboard, the boat headed for shore. The steersman said calmly, "I will do my best to take you all ashore, but it looks bad." For the first time, Janet realized that she might die.

Everybody in the boat was silent as the lifesavers rowed toward the breakers and the beach. When the coxswain gave the order to put on life preservers, Janet did not get one; the lifeboat carried only five, and none had been served out on the *Virginia*. As the men on shore signalled where to land, the boat twice started in, only to back off again. Line after line of breakers poured ashore while the passengers in the boat watched and waited. At last the lifesavers decided to make a try for the island. The rowers began to pull toward what Janet realized was "the one supreme moment of danger." As the boat sped toward the beach, one wave washed partly over it, but the next lifted it up and carried it right into the shallows. The men on the beach rushed into the water up to their waists to grab the boat. The lifesavers lifted out the *Virginia* people and carried them to dry land.

Exultant from adrenaline and relief, Janet was struck by a wry thought. She reflected that the poor fellow who carried her ashore must have been shocked by her weight, since she was wearing two dresses, an ulster, and a large shawl and was clutching a heavy valise.

Superintendent Duncan McDonald greeted the arriving castaways, then everybody turned their attention seaward to watch the rest of the passengers come off the wreck. After their own safe landing, Janet and her companions were unprepared for the horror that was to come.

The lifeboat returned to the *Virginia* and picked up another load, eighteen persons in all, including eleven women and five children. By the time the boat left the side of the ship, the surf on the beach had become worse. As the boat approached the point of no return, it hung back just outside the surfline, about one hundred and fifty feet from shore, waiting for the chance to make a run for the beach. Just as the lifeboat crew began to pull hard on the oars, a large roller caught the boat from behind. It flipped end over end, throwing everybody into the sea. Some people clung to the capsized boat, and when it righted itself in about four minutes, they climbed inside and helped others on board. The boat washed ashore, along with nine living *Virginia* castaways. Four of the women and all five children drowned.

Two of the ship's boats loaded with more passengers were following the Sable lifeboat toward shore. Seeing the accident, they turned back to the stranded ship. One of the male passengers, Thomas Peden, could only wonder in agony as to the fate of his wife and two children who were in the capsized lifeboat. He would discover soon enough that Mary, John, and Richard were all dead, leaving him "wifeless and childless." Three of the women who reached the island safely, two of them widows, each lost her only child. The three were Mrs. Widestrand of Chicago, and Mrs. Moutin and Mrs. Elizabeth Wilfson of New York. Mrs. Wilfson's husband had died in February, and she was taking her two-year-old daughter on a trip to Europe. The most touching story of all was that of Mrs. Moutin.

Mrs. Moutin was English, a native of Leeds who had married a Frenchman. Following the death of her husband, she had come to the United States with her small child some years ago. Since then she had lived in New York, where she maintained herself and her daughter, "upon whom she seems to have fairly doted," by doing needlework. In 1879 she answered an advertisement for a sewing woman by the wife of "a prominent officer of the State Line." Mrs. Moutin came to the woman's house for an interview and was hired. She did good work and was well-liked by her employer.

Upon discovering the husband's connection with a European steamship line, Mrs. Moutin told him how much she wished to visit Leeds and see her sister. She said that she could not afford the trip, even in steerage, without some discount in the ticket price. The man to whom she spoke, "seeing that she was a thoroughly respectable woman," arranged her passage with the company at a fare that she could afford, "and also placed her under the special charge of the purser, with orders to allow her all the privileges possible to a steerage passenger, and many which an ordinary steerage passenger could not afford." In fact, she was listed among the second-cabin passengers.

Mrs. Moutin thanked the man profusely, and just before embarking on her voyage, told his wife "that a special providence must have prompted her to answer the advertisement which had resulted in giving her and little Marie an opportunity to re-visit their native land."

When the news of the loss of the *State of Virginia* reached New York, the well-intentioned man's first thoughts, he told a reporter, were of little Marie and her mother. "It seemed to flash across me in an instant that mother or child, or both, were lost." A later report confirmed his fears. The *New York Times* reporter could not resist a sententious conclusion: "The special providence upon which Mrs. Moutin had relied with such touching faith had torn her child from her arms."

On Sable Island, right after the lifeboat disaster, Mrs. Moutin laid the blame elsewhere. Janet Carnochan described the scene as Mrs. Moutin and the other survivors struggled ashore. "The first words heard were from the mother of a beautiful golden-haired girl, gasping almost inarticulately, 'Oh, those cruel, cruel waves! My Marie is gone.' "

Superintendent McDonald and his crew, forced to abandon their efforts to rescue people from the wreck, turned all their attention to the castaways who had landed. All the surviving women and children except one were huddled on the beach. The exception was Kate Moodie, the captain's daughter, who remained on board the wreck with her father. The refugees on the island needed to be taken to lodgings as quickly as possible. Unfortunately the only available means of transportation to the Main Station about three miles away was an open wagon. This heavy, solidly built cart drawn by three Sable Island horses would have to make two trips to accommodate everybody.

In the first cartload went the seven women who had been thrown into the sea, some bleeding or otherwise injured. Janet Carnochan waited with the second group in the rain that had begun to fall. Some of the Establishment hands lit a fire to provide what comfort they might while waiting for the wagon to return. When Janet was finally on her way, she found that the ride only increased her discomfort. The extra-wide rims on the wheels, for travel through loose sand, gave the cart an unpleasant motion. For some of the women and children, the effect was all too familiar: it was like seasickness.

The horses walked right into the lake, taking a shortcut to the north side through its shallow west end. North of the lake they plodded eastward about three miles until, after climbing a small hill, they arrived within sight of headquarters. Janet and her companions saw a long, low wooden building that turned out to be the Superintendent's house. Several outbuildings of the same type huddled in the compound.

When the shipwreck survivors reached the house, Superintendent McDonald and his family welcomed them to their home. Janet and the other women soon settled in. Then they spent another anxious night, uncertain of the fate of friends and loved ones still on board the wreck.

Meanwhile on board the wreck, the men had tried to organize their escape. Further attempts to float the steamer had failed, so the ship's crew took to the boats. They stocked all eight boats with provisions and divided the male passengers among them. One boat remained alongside the *Virginia* to sound the steam whistle at intervals as a guide to the others.

The string of boats tried to row around the west end of Sable Island to the lee side, where they hoped to land safely. But when they reached the west point, they found the surf so heavy and the fog so dense that they could not round it. Guided by the sound of the fog whistle, they were obliged to return to the ship. There they spent the night.

Heavy fog closed in again, but the weather remained comparatively calm. The grounded *State of Virginia* seemed in no further danger at the moment. The pounding of the bottom on the sandbank had started some of the seams, and water invaded the hold. This leaking proved a blessing in disguise. The weight of the water inside kept the hull steady, and it did not bump as much as on the previous night.

On Monday morning the castaways at the wreck again headed for the west end and "after a hard pull" succeeded in rounding the point and crossing the northwest bar. They landed on the north side of the island but discovered that they were now further from the Main Station than at the wreck site. They put to sea again at once and rowed down the coast to the settlement. As boatload after boatload came safely ashore at McDonald's, Janet Carnochan and the other castaways from the house gathered to witness their arrival.

> They presented, to say the least, a novel spectacle: crew and passengers appeared almost to a man with boots off and legs bare to the knee, many of them wet to the waist. Added to this, some carried blankets, life preservers, and a heterogeneous collection of valuables.

What mattered most, of course, was that they were all alive.

Now that all the *Virginia* survivors were safely on the island, they began to consider their options. Since the government steamer was not due for at least two months, they faced the prospect of being marooned at Sable for the rest of the summer. The ship's officers took immediate steps to better the chances of early rescue. They spent the rest of Monday afternoon equipping one of the ship's boats for a passage to the mainland to report the loss of the *State of Virginia*. There was no lack of volunteers to man the boat. In the end the purser, John W. Robeson, and third officer John D. Jack took command of a picked crew and put to sea. They departed from Sable between eight and eight-thirty undeterred by either the approach of night or the thick fog.

The rest of the castaways resigned themselves to awaiting the outcome of this mission. They must call upon reserves of discipline and patience to endure yet another period of uncertainty. Along with the emotional strain, most of them would also have to accept a degree of physical discomfort.

∞

Facilities at the Sable Establishment had been somewhat improved since the Canadian government took over the lifesaving and coastguard service in 1867. The greatest, and most expensive, addition was two lighthouses, one at each end of the island. Both of these lights could be seen from a masthead eighteen miles to seaward in clear weather. In dense fog, as the recent disaster showed, the lights were all but invisible. (The *Virginia* had passed within one and a half miles of the west light.) The buildings at the Main Station were capable of accommodating a large number of castaways for a short-term stay, but the quality of the lodgings would not rate many stars in a tourist guidebook.

The women and children from the *Virginia*, about twenty in all, stayed at the Superintendent's house. Some of them had beds. The less fortunate ones, such as Janet Carnochan, slept on hay spread over the floor. The ship's crew lived in a house built for the purpose called the Sailors' Home. The male passengers slept in boathouse or barn on island hay, covered by blankets salvaged from the ship. For meals the shipwrecked crew did their own cooking; all the passengers ate with the McDonalds.

Janet Carnochan viewed these arrangements from a woman's perspective, but not only from the "poor castaway" point of view. She gives us a rare insight into a woman's lot at Sable Island, in particular that of the Superintendent's wife. If Janet and her companions felt the strain of not knowing how long they would be on the island, What, she asks, must be the worry induced in their hostess? Mrs. McDonald watched her house being taken over by strangers. For days, wet clothes hung drying everywhere in the kitchen, and in fine weather they filled the outside clotheslines as well. Since no dishes had been saved from the ship, all of Mrs. McDonald's were called into service—including her best china. During the first two days, the McDonald family fed all the passengers and officers, about a dozen at a time, so that each meal took two hours or more. Mrs. McDonald had never looked after so many people at once, "but all this she bore with the greatest good nature." After the first two days, the ship's cooks and stewards took over the preparation and serving of meals just as on board ship. They must, then, have taken over Mrs. McDonald's kitchen.

The people who ate at the Superintendent's table had a regular diet of bread, beef, potatoes, beef soup, tea, coffee, cheese, and sea biscuit or hardtack. A large part of these provisions came from the cargo thrown overboard from the wreck—including beef from the slaughter of cattle that had saved themselves from the sea.

Janet was moved to contrast the condition of the castaways with that of the steersman or coxswain of the lifeboat that had brought people off the wreck. She had seen him on the beach after the disastrous second trip, and he appeared devastated by the loss of life in the accident. Like the others in the boat, he had been thrown into the sea. Afterward he lay ill for days, "apparently suffering from diseased lungs." Janet could only pity the lot of the bunkhouse man. "As the unmarried men seemed to keep house for themselves, the utter discomfort to an invalid of this way of living may be imagined."

The Sable hands in general made a good impression on Janet Carnochan, who had plenty of opportunity to observe them up close as they went about their duties. She thought many of them "intelligent, as well as both physically and morally well-developed." She found it admirable that they would accept nothing in payment for services rendered. Janet herself saw one man quietly reject money offered by a "lady" for rescuing some of her belongings. Superintendent McDonald informed the woman, and Janet, that Establishment staff were not permitted to accept any such rewards.

The majority of Janet's fellows shared her appreciation of their treatment by the members of the Sable Island Establishment. On the Thursday following the wreck, they held a public meeting in the large boathouse and voted an address of thanks. The address stated that they were all the more pleased to express their appreciation to the Canadian government since only two of them were Canadians.

> To the Superintendent of the Island, Duncan MacDonald, his wife, and the faithful men who risked their lives to save some of ours, and who have done all that we could desire and more than we could expect for our comfort, we express the feelings that are in our hearts towards them of warmest gratitude and personal regard. We feel deeply the debt that we owe to them, a debt because of their sacrifice of ease and comfort in our behalf which we can never repay. We would commend the Government of Canada for its selection of a man to take charge of the affairs of this Island, where there is so much danger to those who follow the sea, so eminently fitted by his largeness of heart for the position that he occupies.

This address was not only a generous token of appreciation; it was also a sign that the *Virginia* castaways were maintaining good spirits in the absence of any news about their mission to the mainland.

The first night out on their mission to the mainland, the purser and his nine shipmates encountered a heavy sea. It slacked off Tuesday morning, and they aimed their open boat as best they could toward the nearest coastal point. Sighting a barkentine, they tried without success to attract its attention; it was too far off to notice their signals. Heavy fog set in again. For the rest of the day from about noon onward, they sailed blind. Wednesday morning was clear enough for them to make a landfall on the coast of Nova Scotia. They beached the boat and discovered that they were about twenty miles from Sherbrooke. Taking to the road, they walked for some miles before coming across a wagon, which they hired to deliver them to the nearest train station. The train landed them in Halifax on Thursday evening 17 July, the day their comrades delivered the address at Sable Island.

Purser Robeson immediately reported to the agent for the State Steamship Company. The agent hastened to make arrangements to bring the marooned people to Halifax. A newspaper story on Friday stated that the government steamer *Glendon* was expected to sail for Sable Island about noon. The paper speculated that, if all went well, the survivors would be in Halifax by Monday. The next day's paper updated the story, and the changes were not for the better.

The second report stated that the *Glendon* had indeed sailed Friday afternoon but to bring off only women, children, and the sick. Other passengers and crew would have to wait for the S.S. *Newfield*, another government steamer then on service in the Bay of Fundy. The majority of the castaways were now not expected to reach Halifax for a fortnight. The unexpected delay was given an ominous twist by another item of information. Either the purser or the company's agent had expressed concern that the people on Sable Island might be badly in need of water. A reporter put the question about the water situation to H.W. Johnston, the local agent of the federal Department of Marine and Fisheries, who was responsible for the Sable Island Establishment. Johnson said that he thought the island contained plenty of water, that there had never been any complaint of a scarcity, and that the many horses and other animals on Sable Island were proof of a plentiful supply. Agent Johnston's defensive reply was apparently good enough to scotch the alarmist rumour before it gained any force. That such an idea about Sable based on ignorant speculation should have any credence at all in Halifax is revealing; it argues that the island was still shrouded in an atmosphere of mystery and fear. A number of mainland observers expected every wreck of a passenger ship at Sable Island to lead to wholesale suffering and death.

A similar attitude underlay the editorializing in the newspaper story, but it did make a valid point. The writer stressed the providential aspect of the purser's open boat reaching the mainland. If disaster had overtaken the boat, the fate of the *Virginia* would have remained unknown for many weeks, until the next scheduled visit of the *Newfield* to Sable Island. And "during that terrible period," not only would the castaways suffer but their friends at home would also endure great anxiety when the ship was reported missing. The loss of the *State of Virginia* therefore strengthened an argument that had already been made by others: Sable Island should be connected to the mainland by telegraph.

If Haligonians waited in suspense for the return of the *Glendon*, their feelings hardly matched the restless impatience of the marooned people anticipating its arrival. When it was finally sighted off the island, the stranded passengers rushed to Flagstaff Hill to see if this unfamiliar ship would keep coming toward them. The *Glendon* anchored about a mile off the north side and sent a boat ashore. As the boat approached, some of the refugees with opera glasses recognized the face of Third Officer Jack from the *Virginia*. Only then did they feel sure of their deliverance.

For a number of the people about to be taken off, the idea of departure from Sable Island aroused mixed emotions. The only way to board the steamer was to go off by boat, and although weather conditions were good—for Sable—the surf was high. The baggage that some of the castaways carried into the surfboat included fear. An even heavier emotional burden was to be borne by the mothers of three lost children. They hated to leave without a final goodbye and the ritual comfort of a funeral followed by a proper burial, though they must have been told, as delicately as possible, that the bodies taken by the sea were gone forever.

The day remained clear and bright, and all the passengers plus the ship's firemen, seventy-nine in all, embarked safely in about five hours. Captain Moodie and his officers remained on Sable Island with some of the crew in hopes of salvaging more of the *Virginia*'s cargo. The *Glendon* sailed at 8:00 P.M. on Saturday 19 July—exactly a week from the time the *State of Virginia* had struck.

The *Glendon* made a fast trip to Halifax, but it tested the mettle of the castaways to the limit. The ship was overcrowded and in performance it compared badly with the luxurious *Virginia*. Even the uncomplaining Janet Carnochan, after being thrown about on the government steamer for twenty-four hours, declared that "though she proved a good Samaritan to us, yet did she pitch and toss and roll about in a most disagreeable fashion." Many of the passengers, though not Janet, were seasick. On Sunday night, all were glad to arrive in Halifax under cover of dark, "for we were truly a rather disreputable-looking collection of fagged out, dusty, in plain terms dirty individuals, with weary haggard faces." Many of the men had not shaved for a week, and to Janet they looked both wretched and hard. A week of Sable sun and fog had tanned some faces, reddened and blistered others; some people appeared to have erysipelas.

The captain and crew of the *Virginia* had praised the behaviour of the passengers throughout their ordeal, as did the officials on the *Glendon*. Now the survivors of the Sable catastrophe showed their true grit. Although nearly all of the baggage had been salvaged from the wreck, most of it was damaged. The passengers spent a few days in Halifax refreshing themselves and straightening out their possessions, replacing what they could of lost items. Then they boarded the steamer *Hibernian* and sailed once again for Europe. According to Janet Carnochan, only half a dozen or so abandoned their voyage.

Janet kept in contact with Sable through a correspondence with Mrs. McDonald. She knew that the bodies of two of the drowned women had washed ashore on the Monday following the wreck and that "they were buried quietly, no one being told." Janet herself seems to have been among the small group from the *Virginia* that conducted the burial service. The dead women were Miss Coleman, an elderly cabin passenger, and Mrs. Thomas Walker, a steerage passenger from Elmira, New York. Mrs. McDonald told Janet in one of her letters, "I have planted lilies on their graves which I keep in order, and often think of the sad fate of those beneath." In thus remembering the dead, the Superintendent's wife was maintaining a memorial of the *State of Virginia* disaster.

As an amateur historian, Janet Carnochan memorialized the calamitous shipwreck with her pen. After reflecting on her own experience and what she had learned from other sources, she pronounced her conclusion: "All honor then to our noble life-saving establishments, all honor to the men and women of Sable Island."

Chapter Eleven

Gross Inefficiency or Worse

Five years after the loss of the *State of Virginia*, another shipwreck at Sable Island demonstrated the exceptional demands on the lifesaving service in the era of luxury liners. The two catastrophes had much in common. Each of the wrecked vessels was a large steamship, one of the best of its kind, designed to carry hundreds of passengers. Each was commanded by an experienced captain familiar with the transatlantic run. Each ran aground at full speed, blinded by fog and oblivious of danger. More remarkable, however, were the differences between the two disasters. And in the loss of the second ship, those differences were what made news.

The S.S. *Amsterdam* was on the westward passage carrying more than two hundred passengers, most of them in steerage. In other words, the vast majority of the passengers were poor immigrants, at a far greater remove from the cabin passengers than a deck or two. The ship struck at the opposite end of Sable from the *Virginia* and not in line with the body of the island proper. It stranded well out on the northeast bar. The *Amsterdam*'s situation was more precarious, and it was much farther away—about thirteen miles—from the nearest likely spot for a safe landing. On board the ship, passengers of all classes reacted differently from those in the earlier wreck, as did some members of the crew. Unfortunately for the Sable Island Establishment, so did some of the men in its service.

Some cabin passengers testified later that the response of the Sable lifesavers gave cause for complaint. One passenger in particular voiced a litany of accusations to a reporter in Halifax. He gave the impression that he spoke for a group.

The first account of the wreck, in the *Morning Herald* of 7 August 1884, contained his remarks in a long section headed "The Story of a Passenger." This man was identified as Constantine Ludwig of New York, a freight agent who was the representative of Baasch and Rothenstein of

Berlin. The reporter presented the description of the wreck and subsequent events as one long quotation from Ludwig.

He said that the *Amsterdam* had experienced fog and rain during the entire passage from Europe up to the day before it struck Sable Island. On Tuesday 29 July the air cleared, and the captain took good observations at noon. The ship was then on "Newfoundland banks," meaning presumably the Grand Banks. On Wednesday night, in dense fog once again, it ran aground at full speed at 9:45 P.M. The ship struck three times but, because it was stuck in sand, the passengers did not realize what had happened for some minutes. "Then a panic ensued." Since the sea was comparatively smooth, Captain Lucas and his officers "succeeded in assuring the passengers."

Within ten minutes, all hands were busy throwing overboard a cargo of wire and 3,000 barrels of herring. This work continued until noon of the following day. Meanwhile, the ship's crew fired rockets to signal their distress and prepared the boats for launching. Captain Lucas realized that he was stranded far out on a Sable Island bar, where the surf was treacherous and any attempt at landing dangerous. He therefore kept all the passengers on board, "as the ship was not making water, and calm weather prevailed, although a heavy sea was beginning to run." But when the *Amsterdam* began to fill with water, Lucas decided to launch the boats. He had received no response to his distress signals, no sign of help on the way. By this time he could se the lighthouse in the distance. He hoped to land the passengers near it.

The first boatload included thirty-four cabin passengers plus women and children from steerage. Just as the loaded boat was ready to leave the ship,

a heavy wave dashed her up against a boat still swinging from the davits and smashed that boat to pieces, and caused the first boat to leak badly, but fortunately none of the passengers were injured.

The remaining five boats were then launched and boarded. Crowded with about two hundred castaways, the six boats battled the surf at night. The weather was now so clear that the people in the boats could see the lighthouse distinctly. The first boat succeeded in landing close to it about three o'clock in the morning. The last boat came ashore between five and six o'clock. One of the boats upset in landing, and two German passengers and a ship's fireman drowned.

The newspaper reporter here breaks into the story, with no indication by words, spacing, or punctuation that he is no longer quoting Ludwig. He says that the names of the cabin passengers were "Mr. and Mrs. Ludwig, three children and servant," Mr. and Mrs. Opfinger, the Rev. Mr. Carrmann, Mr. and Mrs. Fahrenwaldt, and Mr. Ulder. The impression given is that these twelve were the only cabin passengers on board. The reporter then returns to Ludwig's complaints.

"Mr. Ludwig referred to the want of facilities for saving life on the island." He said that the lighthouse keeper at the east end had seen the distress signals several hours after the *Amsterdam* struck but could not respond to them because he lacked the necessary rockets or other apparatus. When the keeper sent a messenger to report the wreck, the man took five hours to reach the Main Station. "There is no telephone or telegraph communication." Ludwig also made pronouncements about Sable Island. He said that the weather there was rarely fine as it was at this time. "Had the ordinary heavy surf prevailed, but few of the passengers could have been saved."

Some of Ludwig's comments were direct charges against groups of people. When the six boats left the *Amsterdam*, some passengers and crew remained on board the wreck, and they "broke into and rifled the ship." None of the baggage was saved. What provisions were salvaged and brought ashore "were taken possession of by the people of the island, many of whom became drunk and riotous from the liquor obtained from the ship."

Ludwig concluded with a few bouquets. He praised the extraordinary courage and coolness of Captain Lucas. He spoke highly of "the governor of the island, Garroway, and officials Desbrisay and Allan," as well as of Captain Guildford of the steamer *Newfield* and Mr. Hutchins, the lighthouse inspector who was on board the steamer that eventually came to the shipwrecked people's relief.

∽∽

The loquacious Mr. Ludwig was clearly a journalist's dream. The *Herald* hastened to interview him again and published his further comments with provocative headlines:

Sable Island's Life Service
Complaints of Gross Inefficiency
By a Wrecked Passenger

The journalist set the scene in a brief preamble:
> The stories told by passengers of the inefficiency of Sable Island officials and their treatment of the surviving passengers and crew have caused a sensation in this city, and lighthouse inspector Hutchins has gone down to investigate the reports. The whole story is brought out in an interview with Constantine Ludwig, the New York representative of several German houses, and who with his wife and children were cabin passengers.

The rest of the article consisted of a series of leading questions by the reporter and Ludwig's responses.

How do you account for the steamship Amsterdam being so far
out of her course, when she struck on Sable Island?

"By the extraordinary current." Ludwig said that Captain Guildford of the
Newfield, who had half a century of experience on this coast, told him that
the current at Sable this season was stronger than he had ever known it.
Captain Lucas of the *Amsterdam* was in his regular course. He had made
monthly trips across the Atlantic for four years but this time was greatly
deceived in his reckoning by the unprecedented current. At the moment
his ship struck, Captain Lucas thought (according to Ludwig) that he was
thirty-five miles south of the Sable lighthouse, on the basis of observations
he had taken the previous day.

What are the facts about the steerage passengers and crew left on
the ship Thursday night, breaking into the cabin and rifling the
baggage?

"Simply this: That when these people landed we found them possessed of
jewelry and clothing left in the trunks of the cabin passengers."

What did you do about it?

"Nothing. The steerage passengers and some of the crew acted very ugly.
We saw that to complain or demand our own would cause trouble and
probably precipitate a riot or mutiny, and so we gave everything up for
lost."

Was the captain powerless?

"No. The captain did his duty to the utmost. But he was only one man
against 250." After this contradictory answer, Ludwig went on to say that
an address agreed to by nearly all the passengers expressed unqualified confidence in Captain Lucas's courage and seamanship and absolved him of
any blame for the calamity.

Do you consider that the officials on the island made proper efforts
to rescue the passengers from the stranded ship?

"No." The ship struck at 10 P.M. Wednesday and, said Ludwig, the lighthouse people admitted that they saw the distress signals at noon on Thursday, when the castaways could in fact see the lighthouse with the naked
eye. "But it was 10 o'clock Friday morning before their boat came to the
rescue of the ship," thirty-six hours after the ship struck and sixteen hours
after the boats had left the wreck for shore. Nearly twenty-four hours passed
from the admitted sighting of the distress signals to the arrival of the island
boat. If the weather had been stormy instead of calm, Ludwig doubted
that a single person of the two hundred and sixty on board would have
survived. If the boatmen of the Sable Island Establishment took thirty-six
hours to reach a wrecked vessel in a dead calm, Ludwig questioned what
good they would be in a storm. "This matter requires thorough investigation in the interests of humanity."

What reason did they give for the delay?

According to Ludwig, they said it took five hours to spread the news from the lighthouse to the lifeboat stations and ten more hours to get the boats launched. "There are not enough men on the island in case of emergency." Because a certain number of men were absolutely necessary to handle the boat, when one or two of the men got sick, in Ludwig's opinion "the whole crew are demoralized."

How were you treated after you did land?

"The acting governor, assisted by two others, Desbrisay and Allan, did all he could for us." The castaways at the Main Station had plenty of food, "but the passengers billeted at the minor stations were in want." After the captain and the rest of the crew were brought ashore in the island lifeboat, this boat and one of the ship's boats returned to the wreck for provisions. "The crew of the life boat came back drunk," and they were still drunk when Ludwig came off the island in the *Newfield*. The ship's boat had not yet come back from the wreck.

Where not some of the passengers threatened by the officials of the island?

"Yes." While Captain Lucas was at the wreck trying to save some of the small luggage, "we prepared supper for him." A party of the island hands "came and stole the food—the whole of the food we had." The next day, a complaint was made to "the governor," and two days later two of the lifeboat crew came to Ludwig and asked him if he was the complainant. They "threatened that they would kill the man who had made the complaint. They swore that he would never leave the island alive."

Were they drunk?

"No, perfectly sober." Part of the *Amsterdam*'s crew as well had joined with the island hands in stealing the provisions and liquor landed from the wreck. In conclusion, Ludwig said that Captain Lucas and part of his crew were still on Sable Island, "but how they will fare among the liquor crazed islanders until the return of the Newfield God only knows."

∽

If Constantine Ludwig had been a woman, his more extreme claims might have been attributed to hysteria. (On hearing that only women and children had died in the wreck of the *State of Virginia*, the agent of the company in New York had said, "I can account for this only on the supposition that a panic must have ensued among the women, and that probably, after being placed in the boats, they capsized them, and were lost in that way.") But no such suspicion could apply to a solid citizen who was himself a member of the shipping fraternity.

Yet the report of C.A. Hutchins, the lighthouse inspector on board the *Newfield*, contrasted markedly with Ludwig's. The 7 August newspaper quoted his version. When on 5 August the *Newfield* anchored off the Main Station at Sable Island in the evening, said Hutchins, he discerned through the fog a crowd of people on the beach and the banks above. He went ashore in the ship's surfboat to find out what had happened. As he landed, he was greeted by cheers. (Ludwig's comment to the reporter: "you can imagine why we cheered the arrival of the Newfield."

Hutchins then learned of the wreck of the *Amsterdam*, which he said had sailed from Amsterdam on 19 July with 212 passengers and a crew of 48 "all told." The weather throughout the journey was variable. The day before the ship ran aground was fine and clear but shut down thick about eight o'clock in the evening. Because of the fog, the wreck was not seen from the island until 1:30 P.M. the following day. As soon as the wreck was sighted, a messenger started off for the Main Station. Before the island crew arrived at the east end, the captain on the wreck decided to send the passengers ashore in the ship's boats. Six boatloads left the ship at 6:00 P.M. and headed for the lighthouse. They remained afloat all night and landed about six o'clock the next morning. In landing, one boat capsized and three of the people in it were drowned. Meanwhile the Establishment life-boat had put off to the ship about 3:00 A.M. The captain and all others remaining on the wreck came off in this boat and one of the ship's boats, landing on the north side of the island.

When all the castaways were ashore, they were distributed among the different stations and made as comfortable as possible. "Amongst the passengers there are a goodly proportion of women, 27 children and 11 infants." Besides the deaths, "A few slight casualties occurred, one man loosing two of his fingers, and another breaking an arm." The steerage passengers were chiefly "German and Dutch immigrants and about 25 Polish Jews."

The crew of the *Newfield* hastened to take on board all the *Virginia* passengers and some of its crew. Hutchins and Captain Guildford prepared quarters below deck for the women and children that were as comfortable as possible. Despite thick fog, all were safely embarked by midnight. The government steamer then departed for Halifax. Captain Lucas remained at Sable Island "to look after the ship until further arrangements are made." Most of his officers, including the ship's doctor, and part of the crew stayed with him.

At Halifax, Hutchins took part in the further arrangements. He sailed again for Sable on 7 August. With him in the *Newfield* were the agent for the Netherlands-American line and one James Farquhar. Farquhar was the former Jim who had grown up at the East End Station. Now in his forties, he was an experienced sea captain and also a deep-sea diver. On this occasion he was returning to Sable Island on business: he was to supervise any diving necessary at the wreck of the *Amsterdam*. A number of diving schooners were fitting out for departure the following day. The Nova Scotia government also sent a crew of men to help salvage the ship's cargo. Everybody realized that time was of the essence. "The ship will be buried in the sand by the first storm, so that whatever is done must be done quickly."

On reaching Sable Island, the *Newfield* anchored about a quarter of a mile from the wreck, in five fathoms of water. To one observer on board, the *Amsterdam* looked "as if she were just ready for sea,"

> The smoke rolls out from her smoke stack, and with the exception
> of a slight lift of her stern showing a couple of feet of her red
> bottom aft, and a slight list to port, she is on an even keel.

The government steamer was well equipped for the salvage operation, better than any other available ship. It possessed cable-laying gear capable of exerting enough of a pull to start the wreck off the sandbar. It carried surfboats well-adapted to handling cargo safely and efficiently in rough waters.

Inspector of Lighthouses Hutchins took charge of the salvage operation. He directed the labourers who removed the cargo, and he managed the attempt to refloat the wreck. The labourers worked for twenty-four hours straight, with brief pauses for meals, "rowing and pulling and hauling until human endurance is at an end." They hoisted out one hundred and fifty tons of cargo, transferred it to the *Newfield*, and stowed it away. In order to remove the water from the hold of the wreck, they put on board a steam engine and two steam pumps.

The five-ton engine gave the most trouble. As the *Newfield* rolled from side to side and the boats rose and fell as much as five feet, a winch lifted the engine from the deck and lowered it over the side. To receive the awkward load, the labourers placed two boats side by side, joined them by lashing two spars across their ends, and fastened planks across the space. On this mobile platform they transported the engine to the wreck.

When the pumps began spilling water out of the hold on the evening of 14 August, everybody looked forward to the next high tide for a trial at getting the *Amsterdam* off. Then heavy fog set in and shut them down for two days. The removal of cargo and water had considerably lightened the ship. It pounded heavily on the hard bed of sand, but on the seventeenth it also moved twenty-five feet toward deep water. "Success seemed certain."

Although a heavy gale sprang up that night, the salvagers kept at work discharging cargo in anticipation of high tide. The *Newfield* had two hawsers fastened to the wreck ready to help pull it off when the tide came. Instead, the *Newfield* nearly joined the *Amsterdam*. The current became so strong that the government steamer dragged its anchors and was fast drifting onto the bar. To save their own ship, the salvagers cut the hawsers and abandoned the *Amsterdam*. All hands were called off the wreck, and the *Newfield* steamed to a safe anchorage.

In the light of day, as the steamer and four wrecking schooners tossed about in choppy seas, the salvagers assessed the situation. They had saved all the cargo except a load of iron and a few packages. During the night, the *Amserdam*'s bows had buried in the sand. The stern had raised four feet, but the hull clung to the bar amidships. The ship was sunk too deep in the bar ever to float again. And the wreck itself showed signs of a general collapse. So the salvagers pronounced the *Amsterdam* a hopeless case and sailed for home.

∞

While Captain Lucas and his crew were trying to help the salvagers recover his lost ship and its cargo, the *Amsterdam* passengers continued their journey. The steamship company gave them the options of travelling onward by another steamer or by rail. A party of cabin passengers who chose the train arrived on 10 August at Grand Central Station. The group, according to the *New York Times*, comprised Mr. and Mrs. Ludwig and their two children (not three, as reported in Halifax), Mr. and Mrs. Adolph Opfinger, Mr. and Mrs. H. Fahrenwaldt, Rev. Joseph Carrmann, and Christian Ulder. The Ludwigs were met by friends and taken to their home; Ulder quickly disappeared into the crowd. The others stayed overnight in a hotel. Carrmann was on his way home to Louisville, Kentucky; Opfinger was a life insurance agent who lived in Brooklyn; Fahrenwaldt, a civil engineer from Berlin, had come "to try his fortunes in this country." That evening, "the Rev. Father Carrmann," in the presence of the other two men, "related the melancholy story of their adventures" to a *Times* reporter.

This third version of the *Amsterdam* story supported and elaborated upon Ludwig's. None of the added details favoured the Sable Island Establishment. Father Carrmann's story—no doubt aided and abetted by the journalist—supplied plenty of drama for the New York audience.

Carrmann began like Ludwig with the passage from Europe. The first clear sky they saw was ten days out from Amsterdam on Tuesday 29 July. The officers took two observations, and the ship stopped for an hour and a half "to buy fish of a fishing smack." About 4:00 P.M. the steamer stopped for another hour when "something went wrong with the machinery" and repairs were made. Wednesday was rainy right up to nightfall, when fog set in again.

Father Carrmann said that he was seated at the supper table Wednesday night with two other cabin passengers when one of them asked if the ship had struck something. A pregnant pause ensued, "and then I distinctly felt the boat strike the rocks." At that moment the engines stopped. Everybody crowded on deck. When the fog lifted, they found that the ship was on a sandbar. The ship's crew quickly opened the hatches over the hold; cabin and steerage passengers "went vigorously to work, hoisting and throwing overboard the packages of iron wire which chiefly constituted the vessel's cargo." When a gleam of light flashed across the water, Captain Lucas told the passengers that they were aground at Sable Island.

As the fog settled in again, the men kept at their labour. They worked hard all night. "The women were crying in the cabin," and nobody went to bed. About 8:00 A.M. on Thursday the first officer and some seamen put an anchor in a boat and started for the island. They intended to secure the anchor on land, then use a windlass to haul the ship inshore. "The sea was running mountains high, however," so the sailors ditched the anchor and came back to the ship. At noon the weather cleared, and the castaways saw better where they were.

"The captain at first did not know what to do. We prevailed on him to lower the boats." The cabin passengers "and as many of the women and children as could crowd in" were lowered in the first boat at 6:00 P.M. "The waves caught our boat with a receding motion and raised us high above the vessel. We all cried out: 'We are lost!' " Just then, the crowded boat smashed against another being lowered and rebounded off it on the waves toward shore. "Had it not been for that collision, our boat must have been swamped, and many of us must have found a watery grave."

All of the boats were eventually launched, and Carrmann and his companions reached Sable Island "at 5 o'clock on the following afternoon." (This error for morning must be the reporter's.) As they climbed out of the boats, their feet sank into sand two feet deep. "We were now terrified at the idea that it might be quicksand."

One of the boats was swamped, and "a fireman and two young men, passengers" drowned. (The lost men were elsewhere listed as Hendrick or Heinrich Schellenberg, a twenty-five-year-old farmer on his way to Wisconsin to join relatives; Hans Dix or William Dicks, a butcher from Germany; and Franz Van Bomel, twenty-one, a coal trimmer on the steamer who was from Amsterdam.) Carrmann attributed their deaths to exhaustion. He was slightly acquainted with one of the victims, who was about twenty-two years old "and had worked bravely to help lighten the cargo." This young man "like others," had eaten nothing after the vessel grounded but had drunk "considerable wine, which naturally must have affected his head." Carrmann believed that all three of the lost men were the worse for wine; otherwise "their lives would have been spared, as all of the little children, and there were many, who were in the boat were successfully rescued."

The three deaths were, for Father Carrmann as for Constantine Ludwig, far from the climax of the *Amsterdam* disaster. "After we reached the island we were in danger of starvation." The 260 castaways, who found "only 18 persons residing on the island," had eaten nothing for three days and were obliged to wait another day before they received their first meal on Sable Island. (Carrmann's timing was off. Since he was at supper when the ship struck Wednesday evening, everybody had presumably eaten a noon meal, so when they landed on Sable early Friday, they had been without food not three days but less than two.) On Saturday the slaughter of two calves finally supplied them with meat. By then the sea was less threatening, so Carrmann and others returned to the wreck to try to save some of their possessions. On climbing aboard, they received a shock.

We found that our baggage had all been broken open, and all portable valuables had been stolen. There were a number of Russian Jews among the steerage passengers, and they had stolen everything they could secure.

Carrmann later added others to his list of villains. "The steamer's crew…helped themselves liberally to such articles of the passengers' baggage as they desired." He exempted only the ship's officers from this accusation. They had helped Captain Lucas, who did all he could, but "after that every one was looking for spoils."

Father Carrmann also had nothing good to say about the Sable Island Establishment. The "British Government" was, in his opinion, "lamentably delinquent" in providing neither telegraph nor telephone on Sable Island. It ought at least to furnish rockets to "the alleged Life-saving Service." The first boat from the lifesaving station had not left for the wreck until about the time that the ship's boats were landing on the beach. "To procure even that amount of assistance, an old and feeble man had been compelled to walk a long distance to the signal station."

Like Ludwig, Carrmann thought that Captain Lucas should not be judged too harshly for being so far off course. The captain of the *Newfield* had told Carrmann that "the vagaries of the Gulf Stream" this year had carried other vessels many miles from their intended route. One person seems to have stirred some Christian compassion in Father Carrmann: his fellow cabin passenger Mr. Ulder. Carrmann said that Ulder was a musician, an orchestra leader from Bolivia, who spoke only Spanish and Dutch. Both of Ulder's trunks, one containing several hundred dollars, "were despoiled by the thieves who plundered the wreck." Ulder also lost "a traveling bed" that cost $200 in Paris. All he had left was the few dollars in his purse.

The *Times* reporter secured a few quotes from Mr. Opfinger about his situation. The Opfingers had gone to Holland about two months previously because of the fatal illness of his father. After the funeral, they had gone on a buying spree, and their baggage on the *Amsterdam* consisted of eighteen trunks. "'Every portable article was stolen,' said Mr. Opfinger, 'and my wife saw a new Winter hat which cost her $40 on the head of the stewardess.'" One thing that Opfinger did not lose was his sense of humour. He told the reporter that the day before the wreck, in a conversation with the ship's doctor, he had said that he would like to see Sable Island. The doctor told him that the *Amsterdam* would not go anywhere near it. "'I had the melancholy satisfaction before leaving Halifax,' said Mr. Opfinger, 'of telling the doctor that he was mistaken.'"

～～

Any attempt to make sense of the criticism of the Sable Island Establishment by Ludwig and Carrmann must be based on what is known of the actual Sable setup. The total population of the island at the time of the *Amsterdam* wreck was recorded as forty-six souls. About seventeen of these, the paid members of the coastguard crew, were adult males. The others were women and children. The men and their families were spread about the island, at five separate stations, including the lighthouses at the two ends. At the east end were the light keeper and his assistant plus one or two other men. The Main Station was fifteen miles away, but between the East Light and it were two other stations. One was four miles from the light, the other six. At each of these intermediate stations were two men.

So much for the formal arrangements. Perhaps more important was the organization of the Establishment personnel. In the spring of that year, Duncan McDonald had retired from the position of Superintendent, which he had held for more than ten years. His replacement, J.H. Garroway, was a former member of the lifeboat crew who was now only an acting Super-intendent.

From the point of view of the Sable Establishment, the wreck of the *Amsterdam* presented one of the worst possible scenarios. The ship went aground in fog at the least accessible part of the island from the Main Station, which housed the chief resources of men and equipment for deal-ing with a wreck. In the aftermath of the stranding, hundreds of survivors landed all at once at the far end of the island. When the people came ashore, most of the headquarters crew were at sea in the lifeboat going to the wreck. The stage was set for confusion and discord. Not least among the problems was the attitude of many of the castaways.

The confused reports of Ludwig and Carrmann as presented by jour-nalists with their own axe to grind—sensationalism has always sold news-papers—are difficult to interpret. Some of the claims, however, are clearly ludicrous. Others are so biased as to destroy credibility. That Sable people needed to virtually take food out of the mouths of castaways makes no sense. Nor does the threat of starvation: nobody ever starved to death in three days. That the island lifeboat crew got drunk on board the wreck is possible, but that they all remained drunk until Ludwig left the island is unlikely. If they did, where did the two perfectly sober ones come from who threatened him? The notion that "liquor crazed islanders" were a threat to Captain Lucas, his officers, and a large part of his crew, who outnumbered them about three to one and who also had the support of Garroway and at least two of his men, is silly. If the threat existed, Ludwig should not have praised Inspector of Lights Hutchins, who sailed away without taking any steps to eliminate it. The implication that the only way to report the wreck to the Main Station was for an old man to walk to it from the lighthouse ignores two realities: the manned stations closer to the east end and the Sable Island "pony express."

The image of Sable Island in these newspaper stories was like a throw-back to the days before the founding of the Lifesaving Establishment. The island was pictured as a desolate place inhabited by a race of barbarians who, like the mythical wreckers of old, indulged inhuman appetites at the expense of the victims of disaster at sea.

And yet, even the Ludwig and Carrmann versions show that all the wrecking took place on board the stranded ship. Only a half dozen Sable hands went off to the wreck, and the only thing they were accused of stealing was liquor. No explanation was offered as to why Captain Lucas and his officers were unable to control the rest of the ship's crew or why the passengers could not be prevented from looting the baggage. It seems clear that the majority of the sailors, possibly even some officers, must have been either among the looters or indifferent to their duty. In other words, the discipline of the ship had broken down. All subsequent riotous behaviour was an outgrowth of this beginning. To blame the Sable Island Establishment for the worst features of the *Amsterdam* debacle makes about as much sense as the good Father Carrmann's singling out Russian Jews—who were twenty-five in all, many of them women and children—as the chief culprits.

∽∽

At the opposite extreme from Carrmann and Ludwig was the public defence of the Sable Establishment by an official of the Canadian government. William Smith, the Deputy Minister of Marine, made light of the whole *Amsterdam* episode in a speech to the British Association in Montreal in September, which he later published.

> With reference to exaggerated statements which appeared in some of the New York papers, to the effect that the natives of Sable Island had ill-used the passengers in the *Amsterdam*, and had got possession of liquor which was in the vessel, and otherwise behaved in a riotous manner, I may say that no credit should be given to such statements.

The lack of candour in this strong declaration appeared from the flippant explanation that followed it: "there are only a few natives on the island, and they are children under ten years of age."

More seriously, Smith offered a partial explanation of what happened. Two of the Establishment men had behaved "improperly"; as a result, they were suspended and removed to Halifax. Since no liquor was allowed on Sable Island, said Smith, few complaints had ever been brought against Sable hands. When, however, liquor reached the island from a wrecked vessel, "it was possible some misconduct might take place." Without saying so, Smith was admitting that the two men were drunk.

As for the complaints of some passengers and crew that the Establishment people took too long to provide them with food, Smith quite reasonably pointed out that the castaways landed fifteen miles away from the main stock of provisions on the island. And it was a long fifteen miles, "the road being over heavy, soft sand." Under the circumstances, it would take some time to prepare meals for over two hundred and fifty people and serve them. The deputy minister explained that the government kept plenty of provisions in store on Sable Island, besides forty or fifty head of cattle and two hundred or more wild horses. It was therefore unlikely that any large number of immigrants wrecked on Sable would suffer greatly for want of food. Specifically in the case of the *Amsterdam*, "their complaints had no substantial foundation."

Much later, almost as an afterthought, Smith mentioned two things needed to make the Sable lifesaving station more efficient: telephones from one end of the island to the other, and a telegraph cable to the mainland.

If the newspaper accounts of the disastrous loss of the *Amsterdam* are viewed as sensationalism, Deputy Minister Smith's effort must be seen as a whitewash. The truth lies somewhere between the two.

No likely explanation springs to mind for the long delay in reporting the wreck to the Main Station or in dispatching the lifeboat to its assistance. The charge of inefficiency seems valid. The Establishment crew also displayed a lack of discipline; some of them were guilty of wilful neglect of duty. A likely explanation for this state of affairs lies in the recent retirement of Superintendent McDonald.

Acting Superintendent Garroway had not had time to consolidate his authority before he faced a challenge that would have tested any Sable Superintendent. The loss of the *Amsterdam* turned out to be one of the most complex and controversial shipwrecks in the history of the Establishment. Garroway, as a man raised from the ranks on Sable Island, was called on to command men accustomed to think of themselves as his equal. Through no fault of his own, he might find that some of the Sable hands viewed his authority as merely temporary and took advantage of the situation. When Garroway said jump, they would be inclined to stroll. The men least committed to the Sable service would indulge their independence even further. The weakest, or least principled, would succumb to the temptation presented on board the stranded luxury liner in the form of freely available liquor.

Personnel problems, then, were one cause of the *Amsterdam* fiasco. Ludwig and Carrmann had pointed out, and Smith virtually admitted, another: the lack of fast and easy communication between stations and to the mainland. An underlying cause that related to both of these problems was not made public. It had to do with the organization of the Sable Island Establishment.

Because of the great expense of lighthouses, Smith and his colleagues had tended to look for means of cutting other costs or of actually making money for the government by exploiting Sable resources. One possibility was the expansion of island agriculture, including livestock raising. Duncan McDonald's original appointment was as an acting Superintendent "and farmer," and each of the outposts was staffed by a farmer with assistants.

In short, the Department of Marine shifted the focus from "lifesaving station" to "farming settlement with lifesaving equipment."

The rationale behind this new emphasis was that the lighthouses would prevent most shipwrecks. The loss of the *State of Virginia* could be viewed as a rare freak accident, but the *Amsterdam* wreck with all its bad publicity was not so easy to disregard. Hence Deputy Minister Smith's exercise in damage control.

A corollary of the domestic livestock program was the removal and sale of the Sable Island wild horses. Smith in effect announced a reversal of this policy. He gave a public assurance that the Sable horses "to the extent of 200 or 300" would remain on the island, because "in case of an emigrant ship being wrecked there, they might prove useful as food for the emigrants, if they should fall short of provisions." (We might wonder how a future Mr. Ludwig would react on being served a dinner of Sable horsemeat.) The loss of the *Amsterdam* thus played a key role in the survival of the race of Sable Island horses.

The connection of the *Amsterdam* with other developments at Sable Island is less explicit. Suffice to say that before the end of 1884 the Minister of Marine appointed a new Superintendent, and a whole new era in the history of the Sable Island Humane Establishment began.

Chapter Twelve

A Lone Survivor

Following the wreck of the *Amsterdam* and the dismal aftermath, life at Sable Island returned to its usual routine for about three months. The mainland authorities, however, were mindful of the need for a change. Their top priority was to find a new Superintendent for the Sable Humane Establishment. In November they found their man and appointed him to the post. His name was Robert J. Boutilier.

Nothing on paper showed Boutilier to be an exceptional catch, and the custom of the time made it likely that his appointment had a political dimension. Born at St. Margaret's Bay, Nova Scotia, he had experience with boats and fishing. By trade he was a carpenter and builder who also had a good knowledge of business. Physically he was impressive, broad shouldered and deep chested. Surprisingly he was young.

Boutilier was thirty years of age when he officially took control of Sable Island at 9:00 P.M. on 5 December 1884. He had arrived at 2:30 that afternoon on the S.S. *Lansdowne* . His wife and children were to follow some months later. Like the Farquhars thirty-five years earlier, the Boutilier family had found a new home where the father was beginning a new career. The roles of the two fathers were marked by one great difference: Boutilier was the Superintendent of Sable Island, theoretically master of all he surveyed. It remained to be seen whether he could make good on that authority.

One thing the Sable Superintendent could not control was the surrounding ocean, and recent events had amply demonstrated that the fortunes of the seas might have serious effects on the island. All that a Superintendent could do in advance of a shipwreck was try to be prepared for the event. With the example of the *Amsterdam* fresh in his mind Superintendent Boutilier knew that improvements in the Establishment were necessary. He tackled the job without delay. His first reports show a confidence and a decisiveness that had been missing at Sable Island. They evince intangible

C.G.S. Lansdowne, *built at Maccan, Nova Scotia, the steamer that brought Superintendent Boutilier to Sable Island and later took off the only survivor of the wreck* A.S.H.

traits that are difficult to prove objectively or validate with statistics—presence, charisma, leadership.

Superintendent Boutilier began his new career by assessing the Sable Establishment from the viewpoint of what was available to do the job. In the first week of his superintendency he visited all the outlying stations and the two lighthouses. He found everything in fairly good condition but not necessarily to his satisfaction; for example, the readiness of the lifeboats and their crews. Although there was a lifeboat at the east end of the island in good repair, it was not readily available. To put it in use required seven men: six to handle the boat and one to attend the horses used for its transport. Station #4 housed the boat and only two men. The rest of the crew that was needed to activate it must come from other locations. Four lifeboatmen lived to the westward at stations #3 and #2, and two to the eastward at the lighthouse. The farthest away was Station #2, seven miles distant. If a wreck occurred at the east end and one of the men from #4 rode all the way to #2 to report it, he would have travelled fourteen miles before he laid a hand on the boat. Not the best preparation for hard lifeboat service. So Boutilier suggested placing two more men at Station #4 and using the second man from the lighthouse as a messenger. This arrangement eliminated the need for boatmen from the station farthest away and would also allow the messenger to continue on to report the wreck to the Main Station.

Boutilier applied the same logic at headquarters. The lifeboat here was, in his opinion, "entirely too heavy." In rough weather, all of the island hands would be needed to launch it. In ordinary use, it required a crew of seven, two of whom lived at Station #2 seven miles away. Since he was stuck with the boat for the present, Boutilier decided that a full crew of seven able-bodied men, plus an extra man as cook, should be kept at the Main Station. This thinking led to an obvious conclusion: the Sable service needed an increase in personnel. In his first report to H.W. Johnston, Nova Scotia Agent for the Department of Marine, the new Superintendent therefore recommended that the crew at Sable headquarters be increased by two, "more especially as I am informed that in time past, the Staff at the Main Station consisted of nine men."

Two other items of equipment occupied Boutilier's attention. He examined the rocket apparatus (for shooting lines to vessels, not signal rockets) and thought it looked all right but characteristically reserved final judgment until he had an opportunity to test it. On finding that the carriage for transporting the apparatus to wreck sites had been broken up, he recommended that it be replaced.

One aspect of Sable Island itself was of particular interest to Boutilier: the wild horses. From the beginning, he showed signs of making them a special project. Estimates at the time of his coming to the island put the total number of wild horses at four hundred or more. Boutilier already had fixed ideas about them. He considered them inferior: "inbreeding has greatly deteriorated the Stock, and given us the present generation of smaller & weaker ponies." To remedy the situation, he recommended the introduction of some "entire horses"—uncastrated stallions—of some "superior breed." His stated goal was to increase the value of the whole stock by producing "a better breed of larger and stronger draft horses." In pursuit of this goal, he intended to remove all uncastrated wild stallions from Sable Island.

Boutilier had heard that "the Department" intended to connect the Sable stations by telephone, and he was all for the idea. A telephone network would abolish the need to send messengers to the other stations to report a wreck and would enable all the men on the island to know at once where they, and perhaps their lifeboat, were needed. Boutilier had already scouted out a good route for telephone lines from end to end of Sable Island.

Superintendent Boutilier's first report showed that his primary focus was undoubtedly the lifesaving service, not farming. In a second letter to Agent Johnston a few days later, Boutilier assured him that the Humane Establishment did not need any more provisions for castaways. With some eighty head of cattle on the island, he had no fear of running short of food. "In fact," he told Johnston with some exaggeration, "there are so many cattle at present that the men's time is almost entirely occupied in their care." The top priority, he stressed, was not provisions but personnel: "I greatly feel the need of more men for the boats." Meanwhile Boutilier made sure that he would get the best possible performance out of the men

Supt. R.J. Boutilier near mid-career with his second wife and the four children still living on Sable. Left to right: (back row) Dick, Bertha, Jim; (front row) Mrs. Margaret (Maggie) Boutilier, R.J., Beatrice (Trixie). Two older sons were then off the Island. Only Jim was born there. The children's mother died on Sable Island in 1894, as would their stepmother in 1906.

he had. On 17 December he began regular lifeboat drills with the Establishment boatmen.

It might be said that the new superintendency had an auspicious beginning. But the real test for the young Superintendent would be his first shipwreck. It was not long in coming. It happened two weeks after Boutilier came ashore at Sable, less than a week before Christmas. And even for Sable Island it was horrible.

∞

On Monday 15 December a French brigantine named only by initials, the *A.S.H.*, sailed from St. Pierre-Miquelon with a full cargo of 2,700 quintals (270,000 lbs.) of fish consigned to Delong and Seamen of Boston, Massachusetts. The commander of the brig, Captain Lemarchand, was a native of St. Malo, France, but the vessel belonged to Omeyers et Cie of St. Pierre. The first day out, the winds were moderate westerly and the weather fine. On Tuesday a strong breeze sprang up, increasing to a gale on Wednesday, with snow. The winds continued without letup, gaining force. By Friday they had reached hurricane force and were driving the battered brig, which was now well off course, toward Sable Island. At 4:00 P.M. that day, despite a snowstorm, the crew of the *A.S.H.* sighted the west Sable lighthouse to the southward. The seas were mountainous in the bitter cold. The cold had already taken a toll: the whole crew were suffering, one seaman's hands and feet were frozen.

Seeing that they were going to run aground, the desperate sailors tried to tack off, but a heavy squall threw the windjammer on its beam ends. Waves broke over the upset vessel and washed off four seamen, including the boy apprentice. The three who remained—captain, first mate, and a seaman—put off in a ship's boat. The boat at once capsized and dumped the mariners into the frigid water. The mate, a veteran of twenty years at sea, found himself cast up on the beach. He saw no sign of the others. What he did see was the West Light, a beacon whose source was about a mile away. Although more dead than alive, he set an agonized course for the lighthouse. The long last quarter mile he crawled on hands and knees. At 11:40 P.M. he reached the lighthouse door.

The people of the Sable Establishment, for obvious reasons, knew nothing of the *A.S.H.*'s plight. Superintendent Boutilier's journal entry for Friday 19 December says simply: "Wind N. Blowing Gale. Blinding snow storm. Cattle would not leave the Barn." Technically the day ended at midnight, but when Boutilier retired to bed, his day was far from over. At nearly 1:30 A.M. William Merson, Keeper of the West Light, arrived at the Main Station. He informed Superintendent Boutilier that he had opened his door about two hours earlier to find a shipwrecked sailor, "exhausted, one foot bare, nearly gone. A Frenchman, could only say 'Ship, seven.'" Merson had left the suffering castaway to the care of his wife and fought his way four miles through "a fearful night to venture out in" to report the wreck.

145

Sable wild horses rounded up in Number 2 Pound for culling. Superintendent Boutilier leans over the rail with Egan of that station to decide on the individual fates of the animals.

Boutilier at once aroused the Main Station crew. He told some of them to ready the rocket apparatus, then stand by, but it would soon become clear that the rocket was of no use that night. Taking two others with him, Boutilier headed for the lighthouse with Merson.

On the way, they sighted the wreck—what was left of it. The heavy seas had smashed the brigantine to pieces. The chief wreckage lay on the north shore near a spot called the Highlands, about three miles west of Main. Boutilier and his three companions searched the area as best they could. Shielding their faces against the wind-driven snow and sand, they patrolled along the beach and climbed up the banks. Scarcely able to see each other in the raging dark, they saw no sign of the lost seamen.

The Superintendent sent a message back to headquarters for his men "to scour the beach at daylight." He himself continued on with Merson and reached the lighthouse about 4:00 A.M. There he met the French sailor, "who in his suffering condition could merely make signs, and spoke no English."

Superintendent Boutilier's lifeboat crew at drill in the Grace Darling.

At daybreak Boutilier resumed the search for possible, though unlikely, survivors. He soon found two bodies, "apparently dead for some hours." One was on the cliff side, the other over on the lakeshore, both of them "barefooted and sparely clad." The mate's two companions had reached shore alive and, like him, tried to make their way inland. Unlike him, they died in the attempt. Boutilier made no further discoveries on his way home.

After a brief rest, the Superintendent took three men and a team to the wreck site in the early afternoon to pick up the bodies. "The storm was so severe that one of the bodies had to be chopped out of the ice into which it was firmly frozen."

Papers found in the clothing on one of the bodies revealed that the dead man was Captain Lemarchand. Also in the pockets were 400 francs in silver, gold, and paper, and a small amount in cents. Superintendent Boutilier sent the bodies back to the Main Station for burial while he continued to the West Light. For the second time that day he visited the man who, he was sure, was "the only survivor of that sad disaster"; then Boutilier returned home, where he could catch up on his rest.

On a bright, calm Sunday, the Main Station people buried the two bodies found near the wreck. The graves were close by the resting place of the two victims from the *State of Virginia*. The second body from the *A.S.H.* was identified as "Baptiste the steward & 2ᵈ mate." This identification may have been made by the mate, since Boutilier fetched him from Merson's on Sunday, perhaps with this need in mind.

The mate was certainly at Main in time to identify the next corpse, which arrived later in the day. One of the outpost men had reported a dead man found near "the Eliza Gulch," a landmark seven or eight miles east of the *A.S.H.* wreck site. Boutilier expressed no surprise at the location. The strong inshore current to the eastward on the north side of Sable Island often carried pieces of wreck and bodies far down-island. The Superintendent, with a team of draft animals and a few helpers, fetched the corpse up to Main in a cart. On Monday the islanders buried this third seaman "in the same corner of the little plot north of the Main Station." They placed his grave "at the foot of the other two, northward." This man was listed in Boutilier's records as "a sailor from Britanny in France" named Noblong or Noblanc.

The lone survivor from the wreck, who gave his name as Thomas Huet, apparently knew enough English to be able to give Boutilier some information about the recent disaster. (Boutilier, despite his Acadian name, was not a francophone, though he may have understood some French.) In response to questions, mate Huet supplied his name and rank and said that he came from a small place in France near St. Malo. He told Boutilier that the total complement on board the *A.S.H.* was seven, including Captain Lemarchand and the apprentice boy.

With the human beings from the *A.S.H.*, living and dead, looked after, Superintendent Boutilier turned his attention to salvaging. He and his men took a team to the wreck to save whatever they might. Given the type of vessel and its cargo, plus the extent of the destruction, the prospects were not good. And the weather was no help. Monday began mild and hazy, but by the time the salvaging was underway, it had deteriorated to rain with squalls. Tuesday brought high winds, and even though they blew from the south, the surf on the north shore was heavy. The salvage effort, in fact, was short-lived.

About three o'clock Tuesday afternoon, the Canadian government steamship *Lansdowne* hove into sight off the Main Station. Boutilier signalled in code from the flagstaff that the surf was too high to go aboard, so the steamer anchored for the night. On Wednesday the Main Station boat crew rowed Thomas Huet out to the *Lansdowne*, and he was soon on his way to the mainland. The only survivor from the shipwreck of the brigantine *A.S.H.* arrived in Halifax on Christmas Day after dark.

The *New York Times* of 26 December 1884 carried a report of the loss of the *A.S.H.* datelined Halifax. The story purported to be the tale of the wreck as told by the mate, whose name was given as Le Pierre. The *Times* account differed from Superintendent Boutilier's official report in several details. It said that the *A.S.H.*'s sails had been blown away, making it unmanageable; that it struck while the captain and crew were still on board and was dashed to pieces; that six men tried to reach the island on floating planks but only two succeeded; and that the captain reached shore alive but soon died of cold and fatigue. It also said that the whole crew except the captain belonged to St. Pierre. This story ignored the existence of the Sable Island Establishment, except for one oblique reference: "The mate managed to reach the lighthouse, where he was cared for."

Superintendent Boutilier viewed the matter differently. In his report to H.W. Johnston with all the seamen's personal effects and papers picked up on the island, he made a point of praising the conduct of his men. The Main Station crew had shown prompt attention to his orders and willing obedience. Boutilier rightly gave the most credit to William Merson.

> Much praise is due Wm. Merson, Keeper of the West End Light, for the prompt manner in which at the risk of his own life, he set out alone, and brought word to me as soon as possible, as I could not afterwards with my men, without the greatest difficulty and risk, find the wreck.

Merson's effort admittedly did not save any more lives—but it might have. If any of the other castaways had been able to survive on shore, Boutilier and his men might have found them. The fact remains that Merson had risked his life ploughing four miles on foot through a blizzard to deliver his report. His accomplishment contrasts starkly with the incompetent communication at the time of the *Amsterdam* catastrophe, which took place at the height of summer. Merson may well have had that example—and the resulting controversy—in mind as he trudged toward the Main Station.

Not to be overlooked, incidentally, is the role played by Mrs. Merson. With the departure of her husband for headquarters, she was left alone to try to restore life to the apparently dying seaman. Whatever ministrations and home remedies she applied, then and afterward, worked. They were also taken for granted, apparently deemed unworthy of official comment.

The good work of Keeper Merson and Superintendent Boutilier did not go unrecognized. In some official circles, the two men were actually given more than their due. A list of awards for gallant and humane services in saving lives from shipwrecked vessels published by the Department of Marine included their names. The problem was the citation. It stated that a gold medal awarded to Boutilier and a silver one to Merson were "for services in rescuing the crew of the French schooner A.S.H." of St. Malo. If only it were so.

The medals were real enough, awarded by the government of France. France thus continued a tradition of honouring the work of the Sable Island Establishment on behalf of its shipping and mariners. In this case, two points stand out: 1. The lost vessel was a humble merchant vessel with a small crew, operating out of St. Pierre/Miquelon. 2. Most of the men on board the lost brigantine (not schooner) died. The clear implication was that the honour of the work lay not in the social importance of the victims or in the degree of success of the lifesavers. What mattered was the risks undertaken and the good will demonstrated by the attempt. This attitude was realistic; it also aimed to encourage the work of the Sable Island Establishment.

Superintendent Boutilier showed the same approach toward the men under his command. His official report of the wreck praised the willing performance of duty by his entire crew and gave proper credit to William Merson. That the Sable hands received no award at all or that the Superintendent's medal was more prestigious than Merson's was not Boutilier's fault. It was simply the way of the world.

∽∽

On 25 March 1886 the *Newfield* arrived at Sable Island, and Superintendent Boutilier went aboard according to custom. This time, however, he met with a surprise. He discovered that, fifteen months after the loss of the *A.S.H.*, the medals had arrived. Captain Guildford was under instructions to make an official presentation on behalf of the Department of Marine. On hearing this news, Superintendent Boutilier immediately sent the boat ashore to bring off his staff to witness the ceremony and help celebrate the occasion. Captain Guildford did the honours with "a lengthy address" and a formal presentation to Boutilier and Merson in front of the small assemblage.

One incident marred the ceremonial atmosphere of the day and proved to be a forerunner of tragedy. A member of the Sable staff, William Guinan, got drunk. This minor incident reveals a major fact: even Superintendent Boutilier could not banish drunkenness from Sable Island. A week later the Superintendent reported Guinan sick from the effects of a cold caught while he was drunk on "Steamer Day."

Steamer Day was the customary source of liquor for men deprived of alcoholic drink on Sable Island. When the government steamship anchored off the Main Station, the boatmen would travel back and forth to it loading and unloading. It was no great trick to take advantage of this situation. The boat crew might sneak a drink or two on board the steamer, and with the connivance of members of the ship's crew, they could also smuggle the odd bottle ashore. Within limits this behaviour became hallowed by tradition, but in some cases it got out of hand. William Guinan was one of the unfortunate cases. Ordinarily Guinan caused no trouble. Between visits of the *Newfield*, he simply went about his business. Steamer Day, however, proved his nemesis.

On another Steamer Day that year, in September, Guinan disappeared. Superintendent Boutilier had sent him to the south side with a team of oxen to haul up a ship's boat. When he failed to return, Boutilier sent some of the other hands to look for him. From the signs that they discovered, Boutilier reconstructed events. Apparently Guinan had completed the job he was sent to do and then headed home. Boutilier concluded that the oxen must have taken him into the lake, where he drowned. The body was nowhere to be seen.

This explanation leaves a lot to be desired. To picture slow-moving oxen pulling a man, or a cart with a man in it, into deep water before he could let go of the reins or jump out is difficult, if not impossible. Boutilier's reticence is suspicious. The likely explanation would seem to be that Guinan lacked full physical control at the time of the accident. But if overindulgence in liquor was the cause of Guinan's tragedy, Superintendent Boutilier saw no point in revealing it in a public record.

About two weeks later, a teamster found Guinan's body washed up on the lakeshore and brought it to the Main Station. Superintendent Boutilier wrapped the corpse in canvas, put it in a wooden coffin, and buried it in the little graveyard.

The story of William Guinan's death at Sable Island may be just one more island mystery. On the other hand, the likely manner of that death lends a sad irony to the burial of one of the Sable lifesaving crew among the victims of the *A.S.H.* and other shipwrecks. It also shows that improvements in the Establishment such as more frequent visits by government steamers like the *Newfield* were not an unmixed blessing.

On the whole, however, Superintendent Boutilier benefited from the timing of his term of office. The Department of Marine and Fisheries was at this time more aware of the need to improve the lifesaving service at Sable than in most other eras. The mainland officials were therefore more likely to be open to suggestions from the man in charge on the island.

Boutilier was fortunate in other ways as well. His first wreck as Superintendent might have been viewed as an unmitigated disaster because of the loss of life. Instead it turned into something of a triumph. The generous action of the French government reflected well on Boutilier's superiors in Halifax and Ottawa. Because of this happy result, they were inclined to be well disposed toward the Establishment on Sable Island and especially toward its new Superintendent.

At the same time, knowledgeable men in the department could see that the *A.S.H.* only reinforced the lesson of the *Amsterdam*. Telephone communication between the various Sable Island stations was an idea whose time had come. Rather, it was overdue. The old system, which relied on one well organized crew at the Main Station and little more than lookouts

A team of Sable oxen like the one Guinan was driving at the time of his death.

at outposts around the island, was no longer good enough. In an emergency, the Superintendent needed to be able to marshal his forces from all over the island, acting on specific instructions. Or looking at the situation the other way round, he had to know as quickly as possible when, where, and what help was needed. The quickest possible way to communicate such orders and information was by telephone. The telephone would also increase the Superintendent's powers of supervision. With it, every outpost keeper could be held to a schedule for reporting observations from patrols in his specified area. And he would be continuously on call.

No single fact or event accounts for the coming of the telephone to Sable Island. But two events should not be overlooked. First, the arrival at the end of 1884 of a young, dynamic Superintendent. Second, the *A.S.H.* tragedy, which had the heavier impact. It gave rise to speculation: a telephone call from Merson might have summoned help in time to save two more lives. And it demonstrated a certainty: a telephone service would have lessened Merson's own peril.

The summer after the loss of the *A.S.H.*, a crew of telephone installers came to Sable. Superintendent Boutilier and his men helped them to put up posts and to string lines from one end of the island to the other. By September 1885 the telephone system of the Sable Lifesaving Service was in full operation.

Chapter Thirteen

Grace Darling, the Rocket Apparatus, and the Destruction of Sable Island

Shipwrecks at Sable Island in the last decade of the nineteenth century benefited by new technology such as the telephone, which enabled the Superintendent and lifeboat crew from the Main Station to reach the wreck faster. But once at the wreck, success depended on efficient use of more traditional equipment. And efficient use depended on the organization, training, and, most of all, calibre of the men. Two wrecks of this period illustrate the quality of service available at the lifesaving Establishment, as well as the international scope of Sable Island's deadly toll. One was the Norwegian bark *Gerda*, the other the Italian *Raffaele D.*

Dense fog pressed down on Sable Island all day Sunday 27 July 1890 despite strong southwest winds. The Main Station hands and the outpost keepers patrolled the shores. On returning to their stations, they would phone Main and report no unusual sightings. About two or three o'clock in the afternoon, John Donaldson, keeper of #3 Station, telephoned Superintendent Boutilier. Donaldson's outpost was located at the foot of the lake, and he was calling to report a horn heard on the south side of the island. About fifteen minutes later, after further checking, he phoned again. He had found a boat on the south beach with its stern out.

That news was enough to galvanize Superintendent Boutilier and his headquarters crew. They took the Francis metallic lifeboat out of the north side boathouse and launched it in the lake. The boat was named *Grace Darling*. The men loaded it with equipment and set sail eastward and across to the other side of the lake. The chief item of equipment was the rocket apparatus, a later version of the life car and mortar provided by Dorothea Dix. It included a propelling device or launcher, lines of different weight and strength, and a breeches buoy.

The lifesaving crew beached their boat in the lake near the scene of the wreck, about three quarters of a mile west of #3 Station. They hauled the

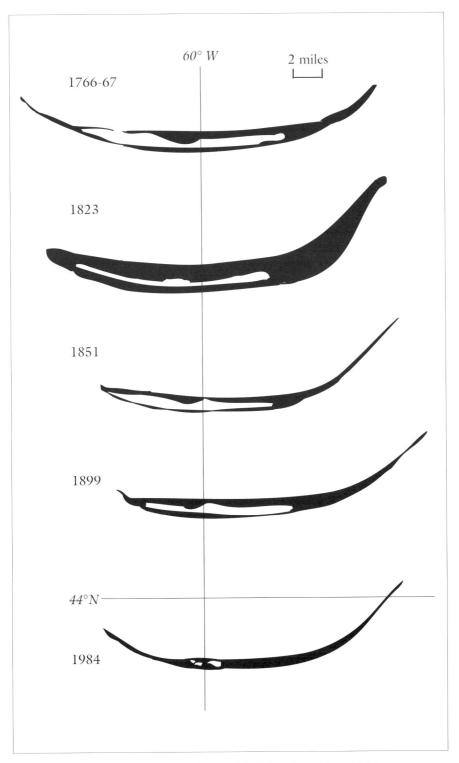

"Lateral movement" of Sable Island 1766 to 1984.

Number 3 Station in the late 1890s.

rocket apparatus from the lake beach to the seashore. The strong south wind was chasing such high seas ashore that the surf was too heavy for the Establishment men to launch the lifeboat. Since the rocket apparatus was their only hope, they quickly laid it out on the beach. It comprised the gun known as a costain gun; rocket projectiles; a light line rove through a single block, the whole called a whip; a heavy line or hawser at least five inches in diameter; a block known as a traveller; and the breeches buoy.

The first step in the use of this equipment was to fire a rocket to or over the target. Attached to the rocket was the whip. The people on the target—the stranded vessel—would grab hold of the whip and secure its block on the wreck. They would then use the endless line to haul out the rest of the necessaries. When the hawser arrived, they would attach their end of it to some solid part of the ship well above sea level to form a jackstay. The other end of the hawser or jackstay was firmly fixed on land. Along the jackstay rode the travelling block, pulled by the whip line now attached at one end to the landward side of this block and at the other to the seaward side. From the travelling block hung the breeches buoy, which is pretty well described by its name: a pair of breeches hanging down from a lifebuoy that forms the waistband. A person to be rescued would step into the breeches, and the lifesavers on shore would haul on the landward whip line, pulling block, breeches, and body ashore. Then a pull on the seaward whip line would haul the empty breeches buoy back to receive another passenger.

Under the right conditions, the rocket apparatus worked well, but conditions at Sable Island were seldom right. Boutilier and his men soon discovered that this wreck was not one of the lucky ones for use of the breeches buoy. The first rocket, fired about six o'clock, missed the target. The second put the whip line on board the wreck, and the castaway seamen made fast its tailblock. The next step was to use this line to haul out the hawser. All efforts to do so failed.

Boutilier and his men were hampered by a strong current running along the beach as well as by the fog that prevented those on shore from seeing what was happening on the wreck. Because the strain on the hawser was so great, Boutilier concluded that the castaways had hold of it "but that it was foul on the wreckage alongside." He feared that efforts to clear the hawser might break the whip line and lose the connection with the stranded ship. He was also leery about hauling men through the surf in the dark. Since the vessel showed no signs of breaking up, Superintendent Boutilier decided to cease operations until daylight.

While the Superintendent and crew from Main were working at the wreck site, two other Sable hands were doing their duty elsewhere. Donaldson from #3 Station was on patrol with E. Hansen, whose #2 Station had just been closed down for relocation. As they scoured the south beach, they sighted two men struggling in the surf. Hansen and Donaldson rushed into the water, fought their way through the waves, and dragged the floundering men ashore.

The two rescued men, it turned out, had been in a boat alongside the wreck when "the sea tore away the stern." Both seamen, surprisingly, could swim and each had a cork lifebuoy, so they struck out for shore. But the strength of the current alongshore and the power of the incoming waves were too much for them. Each man struggled as hard as he could to reach the safety of land. Neither succeeded. Both reached a state of exhaustion. They were so weak when Hansen and Donaldson got to them that, as Superintendent Boutilier stressed later, on their own they would probably not have made it to the beach alive.

At the wreck site, Boutilier and his men remained on the beach all night. By 3:00 A.M. the surf had "somewhat subsided," and on Monday morning

Dramatization of a breeches buoy apparatus in operation during the Age of Sail.

The Breeches Buoy

daylight "broke clear," so the Superintendent ordered the *Grace Darling* hauled over from the lake and launched. The lifeboat crew comprised Stephen Small-combe the coxswain, G. Bungay, William Horne, Maurice Noonan, John Cleary, Donaldson, and Hansen. (Standard procedure dictated that the Superintendent not leave the island on such occasions.) Approaching the wreck, the lifeboatmen saw at once that they would not be able to pull in close to the hull. The heavy surf was dangerous enough, threatening to smash the lifeboat against the side of the vessel. Worse

William Horne, another member of the lifeboat crew that aided Gerda *castaways.*

was the tangle of spars and rigging alongside the wreck, a trap to grip their boat while the sea mounted its attack. Having sized up the situation, Smallcombe and his crew saw what they must do. Since they could not go to the stranded seamen, they must bring the seamen to them. Success in their mission would require courage tempered by caution.

Keeping their boat a safe distance from the wreck, the Sable lifesavers threw a heaving line—a light line with a weighted bag attached—to the castaways. With this line they hauled each man through the sea and into the lifeboat. In less than two hours from the time the *Grace Darling* was launched, it rescued eight seamen and landed them "all well" on shore. Superintendent Boutilier took the new arrivals to Station #3, the nearest house capable of supplying their needs.

The lost vessel proved to be the bark *Gerda*, Captain Klaus F. Olsen, of Drammen, Norway, bound from Barbados to Quebec with a cargo of sugar and molasses. The cargo was obviously a total loss, but Boutilier returned to the wreck site and waited around for several hours in hopes of salvaging "the Cabin furniture." A rising sea dashed any hopes of boarding the wreck, so around noon Boutilier called it a day. He picked up the castaways at the foot of the lake and carried everybody up to Main in the island sloop. Captain Olsen moved into Superintendent Boutilier's house as his guest. The seamen took up quarters in the Sailors' Home.

On Wednesday the *Gerda*'s captain and crew went down to the wreck with Boutilier and four of his men. Using the *Grace Darling*, which had been left hauled up on the beach, they brought ashore some personal effects and some canned goods from ship's stores. Most of the crew's clothing had been lost in the boat that was smashed by the surf on Sunday. By the end of the week, the *Gerda* was breaking up. Strewn all over the beach to the east of the wreck were empty casks that had held the molasses cargo.

When a schooner captain came ashore for a Sunday visit on 3 August, Superintendent Boutilier gave him a telegram to be sent from Canso. The telegram notified Agent Johnston of the loss of the *Gerda* and told him how things stood at Sable Island. Boutilier made it clear that there was no state of emergency. Since the *Newfield* had visited the island less than three weeks earlier, he did not expect it to come right away to pick up the marooned seamen.

If Captain Olson was too impatient to wait around for the government steamer, Superintendent Boutilier had a suggestion. Under Boutilier the Sable Establishment maintained a boat called the *Despatch*, which was suitable for an ocean voyage. A shipwright had come in the *Newfield* on its recent trip to make repairs on this boat. He was now almost finished. When Boutilier advised the *Gerda*'s captain that the *Despatch* would soon be available, Olsen gladly took advantage of the offer. On 9 August, with the *Despatch* thoroughly shipshape, Captain Olsen and most of his crew departed for the mainland.

The departure of the *Despatch* also solved a problem for Superintendent Boutilier. One of the men in the Sable crew—not one of the lifeboatmen—had been causing trouble. The other hands had complained to Boutilier about his "disagreeableness." So the Superintendent made a deal with Captain Olsen and one of his seamen. Olsen took off the troublemaker and Boutilier hired Adolph Christiansen from the *Gerda* in his place. Christiansen thus became one of the few non-Canadians (including colonial Nova Scotia as Canadian) in the Sable service, and probably the only Scandinavian citizen to be a member of the Sable Island Humane Establishment.

Captain Olsen performed another service for Boutilier by delivering his report of the recent wreck to Agent Johnston in Halifax. This report, as we might expect, was positive, but it contained a few surprises. Superintendent Boutilier praised his lifeboat crew—and others.

I cannot close this Report without mentioning the excellent
behaviour of the men & the assistance of Mr. O'Connor & the
four carpenters During the time of the work at the wreck.

William O'Connor was, of all things, a schoolteacher. Boutilier had brought him to the island only twelve days before the loss of the *Gerda*. The carpenters had been there longer, repairing buildings and equipment. They built a new men's house at the Main Station that summer and a new east end house at #4 Station.

A Sable Island lifesaving crew in the 1890s. Two of the back three, George Bungay on the left and Maurice Noonan on the right, served in the lifeboat that rescued survivors from the wreck Gerda.

Superintendent Boutilier was following his usual practice of giving credit for good work, but his highest praise was for none of these men. It was for the lifeboat. "I cannot speak too highly of the way the Boat acted in spite of the fact that the steering iron broke in getting her off the beach." This lifeboat, the *Grace Darling*, named after one heroic woman by another (Grace Darling was the poetic yet real name of the daughter of an English lighthouse keeper who risked her life to save castaways in the Farne Islands), was one of the gifts from Dorothea Dix. Its service in saving the seamen from the *Gerda* was its last hurrah. At this time the gallant boat was thirty-six years old, a veteran of many years of rough usage. The breaking of the steering iron as it left the beach for the wreck was a symptom of its weakened condition; also, the forward air tank leaked. Although Boutilier subsequently kept this boat on the island, assigned to the station at the foot of the lake, it was no longer a first-class lifeboat.

Rather than think of the *Grace Darling* ending its Sable career on this note, we should perhaps recall its success. Superintendent Boutilier long considered it the best boat on the island for lifesaving duty; yet when he first saw it, the boat was already thirty years old. He preferred it to two self-righting, self-bailing lifeboats sent to Sable in his time. He never used these marvels of scientific boat-building, because they were too heavy to drag across the beach to launch. The *Grace Darling* was ideal for a case like the wreck *Gerda*, of which there were many at Sable Island. It sailed well enough to take the men down the lake to the wreck site in a hurry; it was light enough to haul quickly overland from the lake to the beach; and it was strong and buoyant enough to survive in a cruel sea.

Considering the fame that has been granted the sister boat *Reliance*, it seems only fair that the *Grace Darling* be remembered as well. The role the *Grace Darling* played in saving the *Gerda* seamen also makes another point. It is a happy reminder of how long the good works of Dorothea Dix lasted at Sable Island.

∽∾

Mrs. Egan, wife of the Keeper of Station No. 2, wondered why her dog was acting up. Looking through the window, all she could see was dense fog and rain. Although pregnant and nearing her term that July day in 1896, Mrs. Egan went outside to scout around. She thought she heard cries in the strong southwest wind, borne from the other side of the island. She went back inside and telephoned Station #3, nearly five miles to the eastward and past the foot of the lake.

At Number 3 a patrolman mounted his horse right away and headed westward along the south beach. After a time, he sighted several men in the distance and rode up to them. The men spoke little English, but they managed to tell him that they were from a vessel wrecked farther to the west, which was fast breaking up with the captain and four men still aboard. The Sable hand galloped back to his station.

At 5:15 P.M. the telephone in the Main Station rang. When Superintendent Boutilier answered it, he found himself talking to Station #3 and listening to the report of a wreck. Boutilier reacted to the news at once. He ordered a team hitched to the rocket wagon, then gave the alarm to the other outposts so that they could dispatch men to the wreck. In fifteen minutes the Main Station crew had caught the workhorses, hitched them up, loaded the lifesaving apparatus into the cart, and taken off at speed.

Although the wreck site was known to be west of Station #2 and only about four miles east of Main, the wagon had to travel about eleven miles to reach it. The cause of the detour was the lake. The team's route lay about seven miles down-island on the north side to a ford only about two miles from the foot of the lake, then through the shallow water to the south side, and finally back up the beach. The wagon reached the wreck in less than two hours.

The scene in front of them was recorded by an eyewitness:

The dim outline of the vessel's hull loomed through the fog, which was now lifting, showing the forms of five men clinging to the mizzen chain plates on the upturned side of the ship. The seas were bursting over her constantly, drenching in a smother of foam the unfortunate men in their perilous position.

(The chain plates were short lengths of chain, iron, or bronze on the outside of the hull, just below the level of the deck. Their lower end was attached to the side of the ship, the upper end to the standing rigging, in this case the rigging for the mizzen or rear mast.) All the spars had fallen, and the vessel listed seaward. It was rapidly breaking up.

With no time to lose, the Sable crew quickly set up the rocket apparatus with its lines laid out, aimed the gun, and fired. Only the day before, Superintendent Boutilier had put the men through a full-scale drill with this equipment. Now the practice paid off. The rocket shrieked through the air, trailing its light line, which was appropriately known as the lifeline. The men on the beach watched with bated breath to see if their aim held true. It did. The line fell among the stranded seamen, who seized it and anchored the block for hauling out the hawser. Meanwhile the lifesavers had connected the hawser and its block to the other end of the lifeline. The seamen on the wreck began to drag the heavy cable to them. Although the vessel was aground only two hundred yards from the beach, the line seemed to take forever to reach it.

Slowly the line crept out under the hard conditions of the hauling, the men having to hold on for their lives by one hand while they hauled with the other, while the seas made complete breach over them.

Finally the end of the heavy line reached the wreck, where the castaways made it fast to the chain plates. With the other end anchored firmly ashore, this line now formed a reliable jackstay. But before the stranded seamen could set up the breeches buoy, one of their own number threatened the whole rescue effort. Wearing a lifebuoy, he insisted on going ashore on the whip line. Luck was with him and the line held. His heedless rush to save himself, however, inspired no rejoicing. It caused a delay that might have proved fatal to his shipmates. When at last the breeches buoy began its work, darkness was closing in.

This was not a classic example of the use of the breeches buoy. With the masts gone out of the vessel, the chain plates were the highest point available for anchoring the jackstay, and their elevation left something to be desired. Each man rescued in the breeches buoy hung down so far that he was literally dragged ashore through the sea. The first man hauled ashore was the steward, "in an exhausted condition and almost naked." On the third trip came the captain. He had been injured on board when a spar and its rigging fell on him. Then he was somehow wrongly positioned in the breeches buoy, so that he overturned twice in the surf. When the lifesavers waded into the breakers and dragged him clear, as they did for all the rescued men, the captain was nearly unconscious.

As each survivor was guided to dry land, he was handed over to other Sable hands on the beach who "administered restoratives." Before the last man staggered ashore, night fell. Shortly afterward the wreck broke up.

Superintendent Boutilier sent the refugees, soaking wet and some nearly naked, to Stations #2 and #3 for the night. The next day he brought them all to his own station. Here another welcome change from the old days of the Sable Establishment became clear. Boutilier issued to the castaway seamen whatever clothing they needed: underclothing, jackets, pants, shirts, socks, boots, caps, and even vests.

The sailors also benefited from what might be called an accidental service at the Main Station. Staying with Superintendent Boutilier at that time was a visitor to Sable Island, Dr. S.D. Macdonald. He was the eyewitness referred to previously. Dr. Macdonald had landed from the *Newfield* on 3 July to remain until the steamer's next visit. He naturally treated the wounds of the shipwrecked captain and incidentally learned the story of the disaster. He wrote an account of the shipwreck that was published in a contemporary Halifax newspaper.

The lost vessel was the wooden bark *Raffaele D.* of Genoa, Italy, Captain G.B. Caprile. It was fifty-four days out from Genoa bound for Bathurst, New Brunswick, in ballast when it struck Sable Island. Captain Caprile said that for the previous six days he had had heavy southwest winds and dense fogs. He had not seen the sun for two days, and by dead reckoning he thought he was about fifty miles east of Sable. At the time of his unfortunate grounding, he had most of his sails set and was steering a course northeast by east. Like many another sea captain since the sixteenth century, Caprile sailed right at Sable from the southward. Being unsure of his position, he ordered the lead to be thrown—too late.

One of the seamen sighted broken water to windward (southwest), then Captain Caprile saw "shore breakers" dead ahead. Before Caprile could react to the danger, the bark's keel grated on bottom. Shortly afterward the bow struck the inner sandbar off Sable Island's south side. Held fast in front, the *Raffaele D.* swung broadside to the incoming waves. As the bark hung helpless, the seas poured over her fore and aft,

and she thumped heavily. This started the deck and all hands took
to the rigging. An unusual heavy sea threw her on her beam ends.
At the same time the main and mizzen masts went by the board
lifting her outward.

Trapped in the falling rigging, Captain Caprile was thrown into the lee scuppers, injuring his arm and face. One of the crew saw the captain lying against the bulwark and came to his aid. The seaman, according to Macdonald, used what seems like an unorthodox method of rescue: he put a rope around Captain Caprile's neck and hauled him to safety. (Remembering how Caprile was placed wrong way round in the breeches buoy, we might wonder about the relations between captain and crew.)

In the meantime seven of the crew threw the ship's small boat overboard. They jumped in and were towed astern for a few minutes until they cut the line to the vessel. The boat hurtled shoreward until the surf overturned it. As the boat rolled over and over and narrowly missed smashing the men in the water, the waves repeatedly threw the sailors ashore and dragged them back. At last a huge breaker tossed them beyond the reach of the sea, and they struggled up to the beach.

Their shipmates aboard the wreck hung on for dear life, even as the sea was pounding the bark to pieces. Masts, spars, and rigging tumbled about in the water near the stranded men, threatening to knock them off their perch. The sea tore planks out of the deck and sides. Seeing all this debris in the water between ship and shore, the sailors feared that their rescue by lifeline and breeches buoy was impossible. They nonetheless took off most of their clothing in preparation for a journey through the watery turmoil. Some of them remained virtually naked for three hours before they all reached shore safely.

Even if the *Raffaele D.*, which was nearly thirty years old, had been able to stand up to the all-night pounding of the seas, the five men on the wreck would have been dead before morning. So said Superintendent Boutilier:

It is a matter for congratulations that we were able to get the five
men off the wreck before night otherwise there is no doubt of
their being washed off during the darkness and lost.

If not for Mrs. Egan and her dog, help might have arrived too late.

On the second morning after the loss of the *Raffaele D.*, having attended to all the seamen, Superintendent Boutilier returned to the wreck scene. He took a team in case horsepower might be required for salvaging. He need not have bothered. The wreck had all but vanished from the surface of the sea. The broken pieces lay scattered along the beach for a mile or more. Only the bow failed to come ashore, being fastened to the sandy bottom of its ocean grave by an anchor and chain. The salvagers collected "nothing of any Value."

The steamer *Newfield* arrived on 22 July and took off Captain Caprile and his crew. It also took Mrs. Egan, who was going home to Ottawa until after the birth of her child, and Dr. Macdonald.

∽∾∾

Dr. S.D. Macdonald deserves special consideration quite apart from the medical services he performed on Sable Island. He was one of the pioneers of Sable research. Macdonald was fascinated by the island, in particular by the destruction associated with it. Two kinds of destruction captured his interest: the annihilation of ships (and people) by Sable Island and the wasting away of Sable itself by the forces of nature. By the time of his visit in 1896 Dr. Macdonald had devoted a good deal of time and effort to his chosen subject over many years. He had published some of the results of his research.

In 1882 Macdonald unveiled a wreck chart, an outline map of Sable Island that purported to show the locations of the known wrecks on Sable and its bars. The legend on the chart stated that it was "compiled from official reports," and Macdonald declared elsewhere that the chart had been "submitted to the three superintendents that have had charge of the Island." This declaration implied that the chart had been verified by men with firsthand knowledge of its contents. The claim was misleading. All the superintendents up to 1848 were long dead. The only Sable superintendents who might have viewed the 1882 chart were McDonald, Dodd, and McKenna. It is doubtful that any of these men kept an accurate record of the locations of wrecks during their time on the island, but if they did, it could only cover the years from 1848 to the date of publication. Yet Dr. Macdonald's list has been accepted as the official record of Sable wrecks, and every wreck chart published since—and there have been more than a few—has been based on it directly or indirectly, with or without acknowledgment. This list, with subsequent updates by Macdonald and others, has generally not been questioned as to authenticity.

Macdonald's other contribution to Sable lore related to the island itself. He published a series of articles documenting the shrinkage of Sable Island over time. From records of the Sable Establishment, he concluded that between 1801 and 1886 the area of the island had shrunk by half. This "discovery" encouraged him to project the reduction of the island back through its history. His Sable studies prevented him from taking too simplistic an approach: he did not just multiply average annual wastage by number of years. He had learned that the rate of wastage was not constant—during long periods of time, Sable appeared not to shrink at all. So in his projections Macdonald allowed for "periods of comparative repose it

*Team hitched to loaded rocket wagon in front
of horse barn at Main Station.*

may have enjoyed." (He nonetheless exaggerated Sable's size in previous
centuries.) His stated conclusion was, he said, his most conservative judgment on the matter. Macdonald believed that in the sixteenth century,
around the time of the wreck of the *Delight*, the dimensions of Sable Island
were

> at least equal to an area of 80 miles in length, 10 miles in breadth,
> and a height not less than 300 feet, with an extensive harbor,
> having a northern entrance and a safe approach.

He did not see how a smaller island could have survived for about three
hundred years.

Macdonald then looked in the other direction in time. He extended his
findings into the future and reached a doomsday conclusion: Sable Island,

> exposed to the full force of the unbroken waves of the Atlantic,
> before whose power its sand cliffs melt away in a manner that must
> be seen to be understood, must and will soon disappear beneath
> the waters.

The key phrase here perhaps is "must be seen to be understood." One of the reasons Macdonald went to Sable was to observe the destruction of the west end of the island. He was clearly impressed by what he saw. Without doubting his sincerity, we may also note that Macdonald was conscious of his privileged position as a writer—few others shared his experience of Sable Island. But that very experience misled him. S.D. Macdonald stood too much in awe of the Sable devastation he had observed at first hand.

For nearly a century Dr. Macdonald's alarmist opinion dominated the thinking about Sable Island, until more scientific studies demonstrated that its destruction was not imminent. His wreck chart and its offspring have also retained credibility, though it too in unreliable. The original chart and its updated copies contain many errors of omission and commission. As a list of known wrecks, it is far from complete, and as a map of wreck locations is it quite inaccurate.

Of course, nearly all wreck locations at Sable Island must be approximations, but the relative positions should wherever possible match the documentary evidence. The whole matter is greatly complicated by the "movement" of Sable Island. Changes in Sable itself have altered the locations of

The Main Station in the year before the Gerda *came ashore.*
Left to right: flagstaff and Men's Home, horse barn, smoke house,
cow barn, Boutilier's house and outbuildings.

wrecks vis-à-vis the ends of the island and their bars. A ship that struck opposite the island proper might be shown well out to sea on a modern chart. The *State of Virginia* is a case in point. The *Virginia* went aground well to the east of the west point of the island, but it should be shown well west of it on today's chart. In other words, the only way to give a proper understanding of where a vessel was lost is to plot it on both a chart reasonably contemporary with the wreck and the latest available chart of Sable Island. The Macdonald chart and its clones are inconsistent in this regard.

Just as Dr. S.D. Macdonald was appreciated on Sable Island for his medical care of inhabitants and castaways, we should remember his positive contributions to Sable Island studies. His concern for the fragility of the landscape was not misplaced. The new environmental awareness in recent decades has validated his fears, though for different reasons. The island's value as a base for humane service to victims of shipwreck is today less important than its value as a foundation of life, a unique homeland for numerous species of plants and animals. Sable is recognized as having worth in its own right. This recognition has the force of law: strict regulations limit access to Sable Island and prohibit activities that destroy its terrain.

Superintendent Boutilier's Main Station in the late 1890s.
On the left is the Sailors' Home for castaways with lake in background.

Macdonald's wreck chart possessed two signal qualities: uniqueness and visual appeal. As the only one of its kind—whatever its errors—it provided information made public nowhere else. And this chart was the most graphic statement of Sable's toll on shipping to that time. It has been revised and expanded since but never replaced. All successors are simply variations of Macdonald's original concept.

Dr. S.D. Macdonald deserves to be acknowledged today for his Sable Island work just as he was (though inaccurately), along with others, in 1896.

A week after the *Newfield* took Macdonald and his companions off Sable Island, a Halifax newspaper printed the following item:

The Thanks of a Shipwrecked Crew

To the Editor of the Herald:

Sir,—I beg leave, through the columns of the HALIFAX HERALD to acknowledge with heartfelt thanks the gallant services rendered myself and crew by the superintendent and officials at Sable Island on the occasion of the wreck of the Italian barque "Raffaele D." on the 8th inst. Had it not been for their prompt, skilful and effective assistance we would certainly have perished. I wish also on behalf of myself and crew to return thanks to the captain and officers of the steamer Newfield and to Dr. J.D. MacDonald, the former for their great kindness to us while under their care, the latter for his skilful attention to myself and others injured on the wreck.

G.B. Caprile
Captain of barque
Raffaela D.

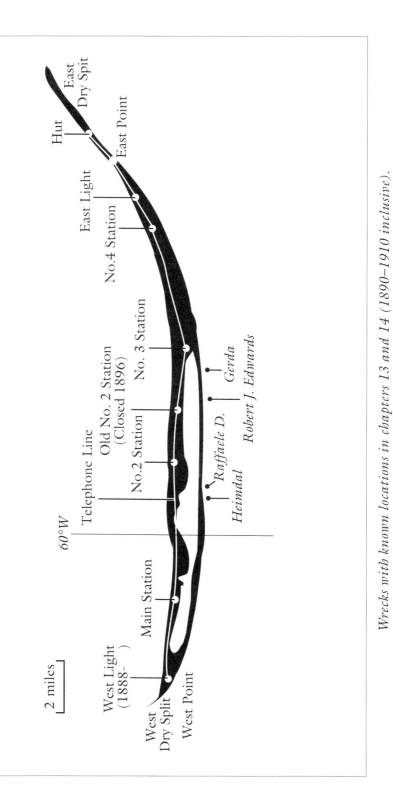

Wrecks with known locations in chapters 13 and 14 (1890–1910 inclusive).
(Outline chart based on Anderson survey, 1899.)

2 miles

West Light
(1888-)

Main Station

West
Dry Split

West Point

60°W

Telephone Line

Old No. 2 Station
(Closed 1896)

No.2 Station

No. 3 Station

Raffaele D.

Heimdal

Gerda

Robert J. Edwards

East Light

No.4 Station

Hut

East Point

East
Dry Spit

Chapter Fourteen

The End of an Era and the Beginning of a New Age

In the 1890s news of shipwrecks travelled fast on Sable Island, thanks to the telephone. But reports to the mainland lacked electronic assistance. A wreck in the last decade of the century might remain unknown almost as long as in the first.

The chief argument in favour of faster communication was that it could bring aid to stranded passengers and crew of lost vessels. Another argument applied to one class of vessels that was now more prone than most to meet disaster at Sable Island. Schooners from western Atlantic ports that were employed in the banks fishery or, during the off season, in the coastal trade often found themselves in Sable waters. Their work demanded that they be there, and sometimes the fortunes of the sea dictated that there they remain. If mariners had to die, it was best that their fate be known. The fast delivery of bad news was an act of kindness for family or friends at home awaiting the return of a loved one. It relieved unbearable suspense— the all-but-certain uncertainty about those who had gone missing.

From the beginning of Superintendent Boutilier's career, the Canadian government was aware of the need for a means of quick communication with Sable Island. The possibility of laying a cable between Sable and the mainland was mentioned, discussed—and ignored. The stumbling block was cost. Since the Ottawa mandarins found the cost of cable communication prohibitive, they were open to other, cheaper suggestions. In 1890 a new idea came to the fore, one that met their bottom-line standard: airmail by carrier pigeon. They decided to give it a try. The author of an official history of Canada's coastguard services refers to this episode as "an odd facet of the long struggle to save ships and men from the insatiable appetite of Sable Island." We may see it as a Sable tragi-comedy.

The idea originated with a military man whose government connections insured that it would receive a full test and more. The pigeon fancier was Maj.-Gen. Donald Roderick Cameron, Commandant of the Royal Military College at Kingston, Ontario. More important in the present context, he was the brother-in-law of Sir Charles Hibbert Tupper, who happened to be Minister of Marine and Fisheries.

Cameron himself did not apply his idea specifically to Sable Island in his original brief to the government titled "Messenger Pigeons: a National Question." He made claims and quoted examples to show the immense capabilities of messenger pigeons. For example, in North America pigeons had carried messages as far as four hundred miles; in Europe, flights of five hundred miles were common. Homing pigeons had enabled the Rothchilds of London to receive news of the Battle of Waterloo several days before the arrival of the government messengers and thereby make a killing in government bonds. Records showed that messenger pigeons were capable of speeds of sixty miles an hour over distances of nearly two hundred and fifty miles.

Agent Johnston of the Department of Marine in Halifax, perhaps with some prompting, took up Cameron's idea. He suggested to the Deputy Minister of Marine that pigeons be used for reporting wrecks at Sable Island. Ottawa not surprisingly approved the idea, and the department ordered a pigeon loft set up in Halifax. They hired "an experienced naturalist," Andrew Downs, to train the birds and supervise their breeding. On taking charge of "the carrier pigeon station," Downs declared his optimism to Agent Johnston:

> From my many years' experience with bird life, I have no reason to fear that the experiments proposed by the Dominion Government will be other than successful, and the result be the saving of valuable time in making communication between the mainland and the much-dreaded Sable Island

In the summer of 1891, the Department of Marine sent Major-General Cameron to Halifax to report on Down's progress. Cameron was reasonably satisfied with the loft and the care of the pigeons but not with their training or Downs's record-keeping. The loft had begun with seventeen birds from England and six of a different strain from New Brunswick. Some of the English birds had outstanding pedigrees, and the New Brunswick birds were "of the best Belgian breed." But Cameron found that the two groups and their offspring had been indiscriminately mixed, and most of the forty-one that he saw were not marked with legbands. In training, no bird had yet flown from seaward. Noting that "the results hoped for are yet far short of realization," Cameron laid down rules for future training.

Following Cameron's visit, the care and training of the pigeons became the responsibility of soldiers stationed in Halifax. The man in charge was Capt. L.J. Dopping-Hepenstal of the Royal Engineers, who was Superintendent of Signals. When troop transfers removed pigeon-training personnel from the Halifax station, other soldiers took their places. In October

1892 Sgt. Uriah Mulholland, R.E., the Director of Signals, took charge of the project. Mulholland's assistant was Private Weaver of the 1st Liverpool Regiment.

Sergeant Mulholland took nothing for granted. He started from scratch, treating all the birds—thirty-two when he took over—as completely untrained. He also relocated the pigeon loft, moving it from the Marine and Fisheries wharf to the signal station on Citadel Hill. On 11 February 1893 he began the actual training. It consisted mainly of taking (or sending, when ocean-going ships were used) pigeons farther and farther from home, releasing them, and recording the results. By the end of June the results were far from encouraging. The greatest distance from which any pigeon had been released was twenty-five miles to seaward, and only four of eleven had returned. Three of the returnees came back within five days; one took three weeks. Gradually, "with perseverance and patience," Mulholland and Weaver by the end of the summer produced some birds with better records. The next step was to subject them to the supreme test: the flight home from Sable Island.

In November 1893 Sergeant Mulholland boarded the steamer *Newfield* with seven pigeons. On the twenty-third he landed at Sable Island, where he turned the pigeons over to Superintendent Boutilier. Mulholland travelled down to #4 Station with Boutilier, which was about all the sightseeing he had time for, and explained what Boutilier needed to know about handling and releasing the pigeons. Then he boarded the steamer and sailed back to Halifax to await the arrival of his prize pupils.

Superintendent Boutilier released the seven pigeons on 28 November. Five of the birds were never seen again. Two completed the flight to Halifax, one arriving on the twenty-ninth, the other on the thirtieth. The distance covered was about 170 miles as the pigeon flies. These times represented speeds of about 7 and 3.5 miles an hour, not even close to Cameron's claims of 60 miles an hour over 250 miles.

Mulholland was nonetheless encouraged by the performance of the two successful pigeons. He sent them back to Sable Island. Known only as Number 113 and Number 119, they arrived at the beginning of January. This time the Sable Island messengers were reporting to Superintendent Boutilier for serious duty.

∽∾∾

Thursday 11 January 1894 was a rare day at Sable Island: it was nearly calm. In retrospect, Superintendent Boutilier could see that this was the proverbial calm before "the most violent and prolonged storm I have experienced." Coming from a man who had spent nearly a decade on Sable Island, these were not empty words.

On Friday morning snow began to fall and the wind to rise. At 7:00 A.M. the wind blew at forty-four miles an hour. At 2:00 P.M. the snow changed to heavy rain, with winds of seventy-three miles an hour. The barometer reached the lowest point in Boutilier's experience. The wind had hauled around from the east through south and southwest to west. The temperature dropped to the freezing level, the rain ceased, and at five o'clock the snow began again. At 7:00 P.M. the wind reached eighty miles an hour—full hurricane force. The snowfall became a blizzard, with winds from the northwest, which lasted for the next twenty-four hours.

Superintendent Boutilier added up the hourly wind readings from noon Friday until the wind "moderated" to gale force about noon Saturday. He made the total 1515 for that period, "400 miles more than ever before recorded here in 24 hours." His average hourly speed of sixty-three miles was sixteen miles an hour faster than the previous high for the same period of time. The barometer reading, which Boutilier gave as "27.870 corrected," was "nearly one inch lower than ever before." He thought that this low might be a record not only for Sable Island but also for the whole nearby coast.

Given these meteorological conditions, the only hope for shipping was that no vessel be in the Sable area. As Boutilier and his island companions would discover to their sorrow, such was not the case.

During the entire period of more than thirty-six hours, visibility for the island lookouts was nil. Driving rain or snow, flying sand, and ocean spray filled the air. The drifting sand and snow blocked off beach patrols. On Saturday, the first hint of disaster reached Superintendent Boutilier when the Keeper of Station #3 reported. He said that the storm had blown shingles off his barn and cut a gulch or channel through the south side into the lake near its east end. More ominously, he reported that deck plank from a vessel was coming ashore on the south beach. Soon other discoveries would confirm the worst.

On Sunday the northwest wind continued strong but the day dawned clear. The patrols from the various stations made their rounds. Throughout the day, the telephone at Main kept ringing and one after another the lookouts reported in. Station #4: saw bottom of schooner on south side keel up. Main Station patrol: found wreckage on south side. Number 5, the East End Light: saw wreckage on south side and discovered body of man on northeast bar. This news confirmed a disaster. Later a chest found on the south beach revealed the name of the lost vessel. The chest's contents showed that it belonged to Captain Edward Bibber of the schooner *Robert J. Edwards* of Gloucester, Massachusetts.

Another body came ashore Monday on the northeast bar. Both corpses were taken to Station No. 4, and Superintendent Boutilier drove down to bury them in its graveyard. In a letter to Agent Johnston, the Superintendent described the bodies for the purposes of identification:

No. 1. Medium size, light complexion, heavy moustache and hair turning grey, age about 50, tatooed on right arm, – AUGUSTA. T., on left arm, – LULU, dressed in ordinary fishermans clothes. Nothing found on person.

No. 2. Young man about 25 years old, brown hair, 5 feet, 10 inches high, dressed in ordinary fishermans clothes. Found on person a pocket book containing $5 in gold and papers that would show he was Malcom Mc Master, and probably a native of Cape Breton. A jack knife was also found on him with letters cut in the handle M.M.M.

That a Cape Bretoner such as Malcolm McMaster would be working on an American schooner was not at all unusual. Generations of Nova Scotians travelled to Boston to seek berths on its fishing schooners or those of famous outports like Gloucester. Many settled in the Boston area and founded American families. The Boston connection was so close for so long that Cape Bretoners and other Bluenoses often referred to the USA as "the Boston States."

On Tuesday Superintendent Boutilier and his men patrolled the whole island in search of more bodies. They found none, then or afterward. The only wreckage of any value picked up was a barrel of flour "and two tubs olemargarine." A few barrels of herring "seen in the wash" led Boutilier to conjecture that the *Robert J. Edwards* might have been loaded with frozen herring from Newfoundland. A corollary of this speculation is that the schooner sailed from home on a fishing voyage but caught little, and so decided to salvage something from the trip by calling at Newfoundland for a cargo of frozen fish. Since the schooner was never seen by anybody on Sable Island, Boutilier could also only guess at the specific time and place of the wreck.

I conclude she struck about 2 miles west of No. 3 station sometime before noon of the 12th and with the sea running there at the time it would be a matter of a very few minutes until she was broken up.

He pointed out that the south side bar and beaches were entirely submerged during the storm and that wreckage was washed into the lake and scattered the whole length of the south side.

Boutilier seems to have reasoned somewhat as follows: with such strong easterly winds at the time the schooner broke up, the wreckage would have been driven generally west and northwest; within four or five hours, however, the wind had virtually reversed direction, so that it plus the inshore current would drive wreckage back the other way. Boutilier located the point of stranding west of the foot of the lake, off the south beach. It was in fact near the midpoint of the island east to west. From this point, the current tended to run eastward, which would explain the arrival of the bodies at the northeast bar. If the schooner had struck more to the westward, the winds at the time would have driven most of the wreckage still farther west, and the subsequent winds would have deposited it at the west end or on the northwest bar.

The Superintendent wrote his detailed report of the loss of the *Robert J. Edwards* for the record. He knew that months might pass before he had a chance to send it to Agent Johnston. Yet he did have hope of dispatching news of the wreck to the mainland. It was a job for the newest members of the Sable Island Establishment: Messenger Pigeons 113 and 119.

∽

Superintendent Boutilier drafted a message in telegraphese on both sides of a small piece of paper. On the front:

Sable Island, 9:30 A.M., 21st, 1.94, E. 30 minutes, 113 and 119 together. American schooner Robert J. Edwards lost with all hands, south side, southwest hurricane. Jan. 12, R.J. Boutilier, to H.W. Johnstone, all well.

And on the back:

January 12th, bar 2 P.M., 27.39, wind S.E., 75 to 80 miles. No. 962,831 W., 75 to 80 car to sea eve.

This somewhat confused message was the version printed in the newspaper. Most of it can be deciphered by using the information in Boutilier's records, though they do not include the complete text of his message.

Superintendent Boutilier is advising Agent Johnston of the place, time, and date (21/1/94) of release of the two messenger pigeons. The next point refers to the wind at the time: from the east at thirty miles an hour. (He doubtless intended to write "W 30 mi E," and may have done so.) The second major point is the description of the wreck. The date at the end obviously belongs with it, not with Boutilier's sign-off. He had already dated his message the twenty-first. The details on the back seem to refer to the weather on Friday, when the schooner was lost. Boutilier's record shows the barometer at 27.89 at 2:00 P.M. The last sentence is garbled and strangely repetitious, but the intended meaning seems to be that the wind blew at seventy-five to eighty miles an hour until evening. If the large number is a code referring to the hurricane, the message may be that it was carried out to sea, away from the mainland, in the evening. But these minor points of detail hardly matter. The chief message was all too clear: a hurricane had sunk the *Robert J. Edwards*, and everybody on board was dead.

Pigeons 113 and 119 took off from Sable Island at ten o'clock on Sunday morning. Each carried a copy of this message written on linen paper. With a thirty-mile-an-hour tailwind, if all went well, they would both arrive in Halifax before evening. But all did not go well. Not for Superintendent Boutilier, not for mainland Marine officials—and not for the pigeons.

More than two hundred miles westsouthwest of Sable Island at the moment that the messengers took flight, the fishing schooner *Mabel B. Leighton* was going about its business. It was still in the area at four o'clock that afternoon, its position logged as "latitude 42 degrees 30 minutes, longitude 65 degrees 5 minutes." All at once something strange happened. With nothing but open water between them and the horizon on all sides, Captain Crittenden and his crew looked on in wonder as a pigeon landed on the *Leighton*'s deck. The fishermen noticed the flat ring on the bird's leg and realized that it was a messenger pigeon. They could also see that the winged courier "was greatly exhausted, as if it had come from a long distance." Crittenden removed the note attached to the pigeon and read it. He rightly concluded that two birds had been sent out at the same time from Sable Island with this dispatch to government officials in Halifax "who could readily decipher the code on the message." He and his shipmates understood enough of the message to know the worst, that luck had run out for some of their fellow fishermen. They also realized that the bird's mission was to deliver the sad news to the mainland.

The sympathetic fishermen kept the exhausted messenger on board for fifteen hours and did everything they could think of "to resuscitate it." Finally, Captain Crittenden concluded that the feathered mail-carrier was too far gone to complete its mission. He removed the pigeon's ring—which identified it as Number 119—and the note, then set it free. Number 119 tried gallantly to take off but soon fell into the sea. The schooner was plunging and rolling before a driving wind, and the fishermen could not rescue the fallen bird.

The *Mabel Leighton* remained at sea until 11 February, when it returned to Gloucester. Captain Crittenden reported the loss of the *Robert J. Edwards* and of Messenger Pigeon 119. He also revealed the contents of the message to the press. The newspaper report from Gloucester was picked up by the papers in New York and Halifax. It was also later printed in the annual report of the Department of Marine and Fisheries. So Number 119, despite the failure to complete the mission, achieved a brief fame. By stretching a point, we might even argue that the winged messenger died a hero's death.

Certainly the new Superintendent of Signals, Captain D. Mills, made a point of defending the honour of his charge. In his report to the department on the messenger pigeon service, he stressed several points: 1. The delay in reporting the wreck was not the pigeon's fault, since Captain Crittenden waited three weeks before sailing into port. 2. If the wind had been from the eastsoutheast instead of the east, both messenger pigeons would have made the trip to Halifax in good time. 3. If Number 119 had not flown on board the schooner, the wreck of the *Edwards* would not have been known until some months later.

While Mills was no doubt right to point out the extenuating circumstances on behalf of an obscure government servant—we do not even know whether Number 119 was male or female—he was too sanguine about the messenger pigeon service in general. The sad truth is that no other bird would come close to emulating Number 119's achievement. (Incidentally, according to the time and location reported by Crittenden, this messenger's flight was no mean feat: an average speed of about forty miles an hour for six hours.)

∞

In the summer of 1894, the messenger-pigeon trainers took thirty-three birds to Sable Island. When the pigeons were released, only seven completed the flight to Halifax; the other twenty-five were lost. Captain Mill's successor, Capt. H.V. Kent, blamed the failures on the prevalence of fog on the coast plus "the persecution of sea gulls." At Sable Island the gulls would circle around the released pigeons, confusing them and driving many back down to the ground. And yet, on one banner occasion in further trials five of six birds released under the best conditions at Sable reached Halifax. Kent therefore thought that though the service was unreliable attempts should be made to improve it, for "one successful message from Sable Island may mean the saving of many lives." He suggested that the pigeon loft be located closer to Sable Island, say at Canso. The new Nova Scotia Agent, Jonathan Parsons, seconded this idea, so the pigeons were bundled off to Hazel Hill near Canso. The pigeon loft at the Citadel was demolished on 22 December 1895.

At Hazel Hill, a Mr. S.S. Dickenson took over responsibility for the department's problem children, so to speak. The birds were housed comfortably, and they thrived. But their training did not go well. Dickenson blamed prevailing dense fogs and high winds, and even more "the large number of hawks and other wild birds" that "infested" the wilderness area. The outdoor feathered breeds intimidated the government house-dwellers. The coddled pigeons, when let out, became frightened and immediately sought cover. The bottom line was that in two years only two of Dickenson's trained birds had returned from as far away as five miles. The Department of Marine began to consider discontinuing the non-existent messenger pigeon service. It took them another two years to make the final decision. By then Dickenson's pigeons had become so timid that they refused to leave their roosts in the loft unless forced to do so, and when taken outside, ducked back in at the first opportunity.

Finally Dickenson decided that the department needed a nudge. Although some of his messenger pigeons had flown as far as thirty miles, he saw little promise in their efforts, since Sable Island was more than three times that distance away. Noting that Hazel Hill stood about one hundred and fifty feet above sea level with no intervening land between it and Sable, he added a suggestion to his report:

> you will perhaps pardon me for expressing the opinion, that I think
> your department might profitably direct its attention to wireless
> telegraphy as a means of establishing communication with Sable
> Island. Within the past few months, Signor Marconi has amply
> demonstrated, that his system of wireless telegraphy is both practi-

cable and reliable, as a means of obtaining communication between points separated by considerable stretches of water. Within a
distance of about eighty miles, it is no longer an experiment, and
Signor Marconi firmly believes that he can increase this distance.

In January 1900 Deputy Minister Gourdeau reported bluntly to the
Minister of Marine and Fisheries about the messenger pigeon service: "This
service will be discontinued." He did not mention any plan to install a
Marconi Wireless Telegraph station at Sable Island.

∽∾

The Marconi Company established the first radio communication in Canada
in 1901. Of more importance for the Sable Island Establishment in that
same year was Marconi's first transatlantic radio signal from Cornwall,
England, to Newfoundland. It was followed two years later by the first
transatlantic message, from Glace Bay to Cornwall, 15 December 1902.
The Canadian government had subsidized Marconi's work at Glace Bay,
and in 1904 the Department of Marine and Fisheries began building a
chain of Marconi stations or marine radio stations. One of them was on
Sable Island. The Sable station sent its first official wireless messages 27
June 1905. Coincidentally one of these first messages was to the inventor
of the telephone, Alexander Graham Bell. Bell had visited Sable some years
earlier and struck up a friendship with Superintendent Boutilier.

From the middle of 1905 onward, then, the Sable Island Establishment
enjoyed the fast communication with the mainland that was so important
should a wreck occur. No longer were large numbers of people likely to be
stranded on the island for weeks or months at a stretch. In some cases, help
might even be summoned soon enough to get the stranded vessel off. The
first use of the Sable radio to call for this kind of help occurred in 1910 in
connection with the stranding of the steamer *Heimdal*.

The *Heimdal* was in fact only the second vessel to go aground at Sable
Island since the Marconi radio station was set up. This 1,857-ton Norwegian steamship was bound from Santos, Brazil, to New Brunswick when it
struck the south side of Sable Island in a dense fog. Neither weather nor
sea threatened the wreck, so the captain, named Gabrulsen, came ashore
on 19 June to send a message to the owners. He then returned to his ship
until he should be compelled to abandon it. The wreck was located about
four miles to the eastward of the Main Station, offshore on the south side.

From the Sable Island wireless station, messages went to a station at
Camperdown Hill about ten miles from Halifax. This station was well within
the 300-mile range of the Sable equipment. From Camperdown the news
of the *Heimdal* was quickly transmitted to Halifax, where various wrecking
concerns were always on the alert for business. On this occasion, two com-
panies, Chas. Brister and Son, Ltd. and the Halifax Wrecking Co., reacted
first. Each sent out a tugboat full speed ahead for Sable Island. On 20 June
the two tugs anchored off the *Heimdal*.

Captain Gabrulsen was still reluctant to abandon his ship. He was waiting for instructions from his company. When no news came by 23 June, Gabrulsen asked Superintendent Boutilier and a Captain Ford from another ship to survey the wreck. They "held a survey and condemned her." Boutilier then notified the Department of Marine and Fisheries that he would begin the next day to salvage what he could from the wreck. The following morning, Boutilier ordered all hands to the wreck, where they landed "boats, oil, sails, and hawsers." That night, the Superintendent received a message from Agent C.H. Harvey to await further instructions. He would later learn that another company had closed a contract to salve the *Heimdal* under an arrangement of "no cure no pay." On the twenty-fifth Captain Gabrulsen received orders from his owner to remain by his ship.

These events make it clear that one result of improved communications between Sable Island and the mainland was that shipwrecks were becoming much more complicated affairs than in the past for the people on the spot at Sable. But quick reactions from the mainland were no guarantee of success. The *Heimdal* is a case in point. The outcome of its stranding was no different from that of most similar cases in the previous history of the Establishment. All efforts to refloat the steamship failed, and like so many vessels of the old days at Sable Island, the *Heimdal* became a total loss.

A point worth mentioning about the *Heimdal* is the lack of a radio on board, for the new invention was at least as valuable at sea as on land. It enabled a stranded ship to call for help at Sable Island when, like the *Heimdal*, it was invisible from shore. It might also prevent a wreck by warning of danger.

To prove a negative is difficult, and prevented wrecks fall into this category. The Sable Island records support few such claims. On the other hand, statistics do seem to indicate a new trend with the installation of a marine radio station at Sable Island. In the fifteen years following the first radio message from Sable Island, only half as many wrecks occurred as in the fifteen years that preceded it. The latter fifteen years saw far fewer wrecks than in any fifteen-year period in the previous history of the Sable Establishment. One stretch of nearly four years, 1906-10, saw no Sable wrecks at all. This was the longest wreck-free period to date in the history of the Sable Island Establishment.

The marine radio station certainly increased the value of the Establishment as an aid to shipping. It served as a relay station for messages from ships at sea to the mainland and to each other. By passing on distress signals and warnings of ocean hazards, it probably cut down ship losses in general, if not actual Sable wrecks.

Strictly speaking, the radio station was not part of the Sable Establishment. The Canadian Marconi Wireless Telegraph Company ran the station and supplied all its personnel. Because of the station's location and the limitations of the equipment of the time, Sable Island was, after Cape Race, the busiest and most useful station on the Canadian coast. It handled traffic with the luxury liners on the transatlantic run between Europe and the United States. Sable therefore required crack operators who, because of its isolation, had to be capable of maintaining and repairing the equipment as well.

The need for such an operator on one occasion resulted in a happy accident. It led to what may well be the most lasting benefit of the era of wireless telegraphy at Sable Island. The man in charge of all Marconi shore stations in the Maritime Provinces virtually forced a skilled seventeen-year-old operator to accept a posting to Sable. The teenager's name was Tom Raddall. In another life, as it were, he would become the celebrated Canadian author Thomas H. Raddall. The year he spent at Sable Island furnished the experience and eventually the inspiration for what he and many others have called his best novel, *The Nymph and the Lamp*.

For the Sable Establishment, however, the most significant aspect of the wireless telegraph was that it foreshadowed the inventions of the future that would contribute so much toward safety at sea: voice communication ship to ship and ship to shore, radar and sonar aboard ship, radio beacons on land. As the electronic age developed, the Sable Island shipwreck promised to become a thing of the past. By mid-twentieth century, search and rescue at sea had become a high-tech affair of deep-sea cutters, helicopters, and the like.

Gradually Sable Island ceased to be the terror of the North Atlantic. As its threat diminished, so did the need for its lifesaving stations. The Sable Island Humane Establishment shrank steadily and finally ceased to exist. No new Sable disaster struck in the aftermath of its demise.

The age of the Sable Island Establishment has ended, but Sable is still with us. Dare we tempt fate by declaring that we have seen the last of the shipwrecks at Sable Island?

Notes

Chapter One

p.1. Sir Humphrey Gilbert: Brief biography in *Dictionary of Canadian Biography* (Toronto: University of Toronto Press, 1966–), I, 331–36, by David Quinn, the world authority on Gilbert. I have relied heavily on the admirable summary of Gilbert's voyage and background events in this account.

p.3. "Assembled all the knowledge...": *DCB*, I, 333.

p.3. "A man noted of not good happ by sea": *DCB*, I, 333.

p.3. Hakluyt's *Principal Navigations: The Principal Navigations Voiages and Discoveries of the English Nation* (London, 1589). Many editions of this work, often referred to simply as Hakluyt's *Voyages*, exist.

p. 3. Edward Hayes: Brief biog. in *DCB*, I, 362–65. I have used the version of Hayes's account of the voyage in the wonderful collection of documents edited with commentary by David Quinn titled *New American World* (N.Y.: Arno Pr. and Hector Bye Inc., 1979; 6 vols.), IV, Ch. 69, No. 536, 23–42.

p.8. Richard Clarke: Brief biog. in *DCB*, I, 228–30.

p.9. According to Clarke. See Clarke's version of the wreck of the *Delight* and its aftermath in *New American World*, IV, Ch. 69, No. 537, 42–44. In the following account, I have taken Clarke at his word.

p.9. Gilbert's chosen course: Westnorthwest; *DCB* says erroneously northwest.

p.10. Quinn concluded: *DCB*, I, 335.

p.10. Morison was more emphatic: Samuel Eliot Morison, *The European Discovery of America: The Northern Voyages A.D. 500–1600* (N.Y.: Oxford University Press, 1971), 582.

p.11. Banquereau: See *Sailing Directions Nova Scotia (Atlantic Coast)* (Ottawa: Department of Fisheries and Oceans, 1990), Part C, 39.

p.12. An existing document: "Instructions for a Voyage of Reconnaisance to North America in 1582 or 1583," *New American World*, III, Ch. 52, No. 401, 239–45.

p.12. Dee's Map: *New American World*, III, Plate 90, "Map of America, Based on the Arctic; Made by John Dee for Sir Humphrey Gilbert."

p.14. "Having a bad repute for shipwrecks": Johannes de Laet, *Novus Orbis* (*New World*), as quoted in George Patterson, *Sable Island* (Halifax, N.S., 1894), p. 9. Patterson gives the date as 1633, but the earliest edition was the Dutch *Nieuwe Wereldt* published in 1625.

Chapter Two

p.15. Wreck of the Cathrine: *Boston Weekly News–Letter*, No. 1744, 11–18 August 1737.

p.17. Alexander Cosby: Brief biog. in *DCB*, III, 143–44.

p.18. Andrew LeMercier: See "Brief Memoir of Rev. Andrew LeMercier" in *New England Historical and Genealogical Register*, XIII (1859), 315–24; his petition is printed in *Nova Scotia Archives III* (Halifax: Public Archives of Nova Scotia, 1908), 18–19.

p.18. "Enterprising character": Justin Winsor, *Memorial History of Boston* (4 vols.; Boston, 1880–81), II, 258.

p.18. LeMercier's earlier scheme: See Winthrop P. Bell, *The "Foreign Protestants" and the Settlement of Nova Scotia* (Toronto: University of Toronto Press, 1961), 41–43.

p.19. Armstrong's proclamation: *Nova Scotia Archives II* (Halifax: Public Archives of Nova Scotia, 1900), 219–20.

p.19. Ordered Cosby: See *Nova Scotia Archives II*, 119.

p.19. According to Mascarene: C.O.217/39, f. 229, Mascarene to Duke of Newcastle, 15 Nov. 1740; brief biog. of Mascarene in *DCB III*, 435–40.

p.20. "They have sundry Times Stole...": *Boston Evening Post*, 30 January 1744.

p.20. John Gorham: Brief biog. in *DCB*, III, 260–61; for his enterprises elsewhere than Sable Island, see George T. Bates, "John Gorham, 1709–1751: An Outline of His Activities in Nova Scotia, 1744–51" in N.S. Historical Society, *Collections*, XXX (1954), 27–77.

p.21. Gorham's Memorial: See C.O. 218/2, ff. 379–82, Board of Trade to Privy Council, 28 Feb. 1745, and ff. 383–84, Board of Trade to Mascarene, 8 August 1745.

p.21. The partners' recent claims: See *Acts of the Privy Council of England, Colonial Series* (6 vols.; London, 1908–12), VI, 264.

p.21. LeMercier's description of Sable Island: *Boston Weekly News–Letter*, 8 February 1753.

p.22. "One of the greatest upsets...":Bates, 36.

p.23. Duc d'Anville: Brief biog. and summary of his disaster, *DCB*, III, 356.

p.23. Guillimin: For a few details about his Quebec roots and the official record of his shipwreck and its aftermath, see Pierre–Georges Roy, "La famille Guillimin," in *Le Bulletin des recherches historiques*, XXIII (1917), No. 4, 111–16.

p.23. One of the survivors *and* one of their comrades in arms: Guillimin's pilot and an army captain aboard one of the other ships, whose names are unknown.

p.24. According to his shipmates: In a document dated 15 Dec. 1746, signed by Guillimin and 15 others; see Roy, 114–16.

p.25. Pilot's version: See "Journal historique en forme de lettre d'un officier" in *Collection de documents* inédit sur le Canada et l'Amérique, publiés par "Le Canada–français" (3 vols; Québec, 1888–90), I, 75–108.; pilot's story on pp. 93, 95–96.

p.26. Gorham's claims: See Gorham to Jonquière (undated, 1751) in *Collection de manuscrits contenant lettres, mémoires, et autres documents historiques relatifs à la*

Nouvelle–France (4 vols; Québec, 1883–85), III, 507; for brief biog. of Jonquière, see *DCB*, III, 609–12.

p.26. Knowles said: In a letter 10 August 1747; see *Collec. de manuscrits*, III, 383.

p.27. A contemporary history: William Douglass, *A Summary, Historical and Political,...of the British Settlements in North America* (2 vols.; London, 1755), I, 334–35, "Island of Sables."

Chapter Three

p.29. A Boston newspaper: *Boston Weekly News–Letter*, 2 Dec. 1756.

p.29. Council information to Loudon: See *Documentary History of the State of Maine* (Me. Hist. Soc. *Collections*, 2nd. Series) (24 vols.; Portland, Me., 1869–1916), XIII, 62–63, "Letter, John Osborne to Lord Loudon," 12 May 1757.

p.30. The only central authority: *DCB*, III, xxvi.

p.30. Follow–up story: *Boston Weekly News–Letter*, 9 June 1757.

p.30. *Buchanan*: Robert F. Marx, *Shipwrecks in the Americas* (N.Y.: Bonanza Books, 1983), 134, no. 11.

p.32. Sequel: *Boston Weekly News–Letter*, 11 May 1758.

p.33. Robert Elliot: Brief biog. in *DCB*, III, 211–12.

p.34. Elliot's shipwreck and its aftermath: John Knox, *An Historical Journal of the Campaigns in North America*, ed. A.G. Doughty (3 vols.; Toronto: Champlain Society, 1914–16), III, 14–20, Major Elliot of the 43rd Regiment to Gen. Amherst, 24 January 1761; *Annual Register* (London, 1759–   ), V (for 1762), 65–66, "A letter to a nobleman from lieutenant colonel Elliot, who was miraculously preserved, after being shipwrecked on the Island of Sable," 9 May 1761.

p.36. 1762 Memorial: *Massachusetts Archives*, vol. 66, 186–87; the memorialist was actually "Robert Hooper Esquire" on behalf of his fellow citizens.

p.37. Seventy: *Ann. Reg.*, V, 66.

p.37. Authorized £76: On 12 June 1762; *Mass. Ar.* Vol. 66, 187.

p.37. 32 gallons of rum: *Mass Ar.*, vol. 66, 190, "An Account of Charges on a Voyage."

p.38. Thomas Hancock: Brief biog. in *Dict. of American Biog.* (22 vols.; N.Y., 1928–44), VIII, 220–21.

p.38. "20 or 30 horses...": *Boston Weekly News–Letter*, 8 Feb. 1753.

p.38. "An island barren and uninhabited...": *Ann. Reg.*, V, 66.

Chapter Four

p.40. Capt. Cunningham and Sable castaways: *Royal Gazette and Nova Scotia Advertiser*, 30 January 1798.

p.42. Prince Edward: Brief biog. in *DCB*, V, 296–98; he was the future father of Queen Victoria.

p.42. Commission to Millers: PANS, RG 1, vol. 172, 72.

p.44. Fate of transport sealed: Report datelined Halifax, 25 May in London *Times*, 26 June 1800.

p.44. Scambler at Sable: See PAC *Report* (1895), Note B, "Papers Relating to Sable Island 1800–1801," 88–89, Lt. Joseph Scambler to Capt. R. Murray, 17 May 1800.

p.45. Twenty–second of the previous December: PAC *Rep.* (1895) gives date as Dec. 2, but the *Royal Gazette* says Dec. 22, as does Simon D. Macdonald, referring to Scambler's report in "Ships of War Lost on the Coast of Nova Scotia and Sable Island, During the Eighteenth Century," Nova Scotia Historical Society *Collections*, IX (1893–95), 134.

p.45. Pilot's tale: See PAC *Rep.* (1895), 89, paragraph following Scambler's report.

p.45. Newspaper story of wreck: *Royal Gazette*, 3 June 1800.

p.46. John Howe's report: Published in PAC *Rep.* (1895), 86–90, as "Statements of Facts Relating to the Isle of Sable"; included Scambler's and pilot's reports.

p.47. Patterson's addendum: "Supplementary Notes on Sable Island," in Royal Society of Canada, *Transactions*, 2nd. Series, vol. III (1897), section II, 131–38.

p.49. "Even where vessels…": PAC *Rep.* (1895), 89.

p.49. Package to Whitehall: Enclosed in Wentworth to Secretary of State Portland, 21 June 1800; see C.O. 217/74, ff. 56–58.

p.50. Wentworth's Observations: "Observations upon an Establishment proposed to be made on the Isle of Sable, for the relief of the distressed and the preservation of Property"; see PAC *Rep.* (1895), 84–86.

p.50. October dispatch: See Portland to Wentworth, 17 Oct. 1800, C.O. 217/74, ff. 429–30.

p.50. Another wreck report: *Nova Scotia Royal Gazette*, 11 June 1801.

p.52. Vessel dispatched: See Wentworth to Seth Coleman, 11 June 1801, in PAC *Rep.* (1895), 92–93.

p.52. Assembly action: See N.S. House of Assembly *Journals*, 15, 16, & 24 June, 1801; also PAC *Rep.* (1895), 92–93.

p.52. Joint committee: See PANS, RG 1, vol. 214, Executive Council, *Minutes*, 16 July 1801.

p.52. Commissioners explained: PANS, MG 1, vol. 676, no. 6, Report of the Commissioners for Settling Isle Sable to House of Assembly, 10 April 1802.

p.52. James Morris: CO 217/75, ff. 163–64, Commissioners for Sable Island to Lt. Gov. Wentworth, 10 October 1801; for brief biog. of Morris and a summary of the beginnings of the Sable Establishment, see *DCB*, V, 608–609.

Chapter Five

p.53. Wreck *Hannah and Eliza*: My account of the wreck and subsequent events is based on a daily journal kept by Superintendent James Morris during his first tour of duty at Sable Island, plus his remarks and observations that form a supplement to it; see C.O. 217/76: ff. 288-366, Journal, October 1801 to May 1802, and ff. 367-420,

Notes

"Remarks and Observations on the Isle of Sable"; references to the journal will be given simply as dates, and the supplement will be cited as "Remarks."

p.53. Passage of *Hannah and Eliza*: See "Remarks," f. 394.

p.53. Actions of crew: 17 & 19 Dec., "Remarks," f. 395.

p.55. Halfway house: See 8 Dec.

p.55. Patrick King's agreement: C.O. 217/75, f. 175.

p.56. "All cheerfully agreed": 21 Dec.

p.57. Salvaging, including "camboos": 19 Dec.

p.57. "In a miserable grope": 24 Dec.

p.58. Morris decided to build vessel: 28 Dec.

p.58. Morris & Burrows begin boat: 18 January 1802.

p.59. Dimensions of boats: 19 March.

p.60. "Poison the minds": 29 January.

p.60. Seizure of King's cotton: 5 Feb.

p.60. "Moore and Ross, shews bad dispositions": 3 March.

p.60. "I took a copy of their articles...": 5 March.

p.61. Crew of *Hazard*: "Remarks," f. 412.

p.62. "A large codfish...": 10 April.

p.62. Gift from fishermen: 13 April.

p.63. "The wind never ceases to blow...": 14 April.

p.63. Robinson the only good oarsman: 16 April.

p.63. "Excellent venison, and very fat": 20 April.

p.64. "They may eat of it who has a mind...": 21 April.

p.64.. Two halibut heads & four seagulls: 10 May & 21 April.

p.65. "In terms of the warmest gratitude...": PANS, MG 1, Vol. 676, No. 6, (10 April 1802) Report of the Commissioners for Settling Isle Sable.

Chapter Six

p.66. Hodgson family: See PANS MG 100, vol. 38, no. 46, Edward Hodgson 1765–1831, Governor of Sable Island; the unofficial title of Governor may have begun with Hodgson, and it continued through successive Superintendents into the 20th century—see Thomas H. Raddall, *In My Time: A Memoir* (Toronto, McClelland and Stewart,1976), 99.

p.68. Wreck *Adelphi*: C.O. 217/144, 24 Sept. 1825, Edward Hodgson to Michael Wallace, ff. 355–56; 28 Sept. 1825, Capt. Edward Potter to Aide de Camp at Government House, ff. 349–52; *Novascotian*, 5 Oct. 1825.

p.68. Wreck *Union*: Same sources as for *Adelphi*; the newspaper gives the time of the wreck as 4:00 P.M., Hodgson says it was on Saturday, Potter says the morning of the 18th (Sunday); it probably happened overnight, about 4:00 A.M. on the 18th.

p.69. Sir James Kempt: Brief biog. in *DCB*, VIII, 458–65.

p.69. Kempt's Sable report: For copy, see C.O. 217/157, ff. 613–19, Memorandum relative to Sable Island a Dependency of Nova Scotia, 25 June 1825.

p.69. Darby chart: See also Chap. 7.

p.70. Kempt's reminder: C.O. 217/144, 23 Dec. 1825, Kempt to Earl Bathurst, ff. 345–46.

p.71. Wrecks *Brothers* & *Elizabeth*: *Novascotian*, 12 April 1826.

p.72. Hodgson re *Elizabeth*: PANS RG 5, Ser. P, vol. 41, Draft of petition of Edward Hodgson, giving details of his service at Sable Island.

p.73. Bathurst's commitment: See C.O. 217/146, ff. 553–54, Asst. Secretary at Treasury to Under Secretary for War and the Colonies, 25 April 1826.

p.74. Wreck *Traveller*: *Novascotian*, 1 June 1826.

p.74. Wreck *Nassau*: See excerpt of William Hodgson's letter, from "the son of Mr. Hudson," in newspaper story of *Traveller*.

p.75. Wreck *Agamemnon*: C.O. 217/146, 20 June 1826, Kempt to Bathurst, ff. 183–84.

p.75. "That most excellent, but expensive Establishment": N.S. House of Assembly *Journals*, 8 Feb. 1827.

p.75. Kempt's letter of thanks: His dispatch of 20 June.

p.75. Wallace's list of wrecks: C.O. 217/146, f. 187.

Chapter Seven

p.77. "The Rogue" and "A Paranoiac…": Bruce Armstrong, *Sable Island* (Toronto: Doubleday, 1981), 62.

p.77. Darby's Sable career: For his own brief summary, not entirely reliable, see PANS RG 1, vol. 425, Papers relating to the Sable Island Establishment, no. 15, Darby's petition to Lt. Gov. Le Marchant.

p.78. Wreck *Africaine*: C.O. 217/141, James Kempt to Earl Bathurst: 28 May 1822, ff. 87–90 & 18 June 1822, ff. 107–109.

p.78. Thanks to Supt. Hodgson: See PANS RG 5, Ser. P, vol. 41.

p.79. "In a very wretched state": Kempt, C.O. 217/141, f. 88.

p.80-81. Capt. Epron's report & minister's letter: See Hfx. *Times and Courier*, 12 April 1849, "Correspondence."

p.81. "Deeply touched," etc.: My translations.

p.81. Arrival of corvette & ceremony: Beamish Murdoch, *Hist. of Nova Scotia* (3 vols.; Hfx., 1865–67), III, 488.

p.81. *Africaine* & Darby's chart: See *Times and Courier*, 20 March 1849, "Correspondence," Darby to the public.

p.82. "The most efficient crew…": *Times and Courier*, 3 March 1849, "Correspondence," Darby to the public.

p.84. Wreck *Maria*: C.O. 217/176, ff. 219–21; *Times and Courier*, 5 April 1849, "Correspondence: Captain Darby's Certificates."

p.84. Clye's injury & treatment: See PANS RG 31–120, vol. 2, no. 1214, Surgeon Fixotz's receipt, £5 for services.

p.84. Born's testimonial: *Times and Courier*, 5 April 1849 (my translation).

p.85. Minister of Marine's report: C.O. 217/176, ff. 219–21: 11 May 1840, Extract of report to king (my trans.).

p.85. Guizot's comments: C.O. 217–176, ff. 215–17 (my trans).

Chapter Eight

p.89. Wreck *Growler*: PANS MICRO BIOG, McKenna Journals, 17 Dec. 1849; these journals are Supt. McKenna's daily record of Sable events and are the chief source for this chapter; specific references will be given by date only.

p.90. "Simply the man for the place": Patterson, *Sable Island*, 28.

p.90. Figurehead: See James A. Farquhar, *Farquhar's Luck* (Hfx.: Petheric Press, 1980), 20, 22.

p.91. "The wretched hovel": PANS RG 1, vol. 425, no 88, McKenna to Commrs. of Sable Island, 9 Nov. 1850.

p.93. McKenna's investigation & discoveries: 8 Jan. 1850.

p.94. Run–in with another crewman: 8 Feb.

p.95. McKenna recorded problems with captain: 16 Feb.

p.96. "A still tongue showed a wise head": 18 Feb.

p.96. "Going through" the house: 21 Feb.

p.98. "We can never again go through such fatigue…": PANS RG 1, vol. 425, no. 88.

Chapter Nine

p.99. Farquhar's discovery of wreck: *Farquhar's Luck*, 28–29.

p.100. Supt. McKenna's record: McKenna's Journal (see Ch. 8, first note), 16 Dec. 1852; PANS RG 1, 426 1/2, Papers relating to the Sable Island Establishment, no. 4, Letters from McKenna to Hugh Bell: 28 Jan. 1853.

p.101. "I have no doubt…": 426 1/2, no. 4, 28 January.

p.101. Autobiography: *Farquhar's Luck*; for family, see pp. 1–5, 10–11.

p.103. "Dry wearing apparel…": 426 1/2, no. 4, 28 Jan.

p.105. McKenna's distrust: 426 1/2, no. 4, 30 March 1853.

p.105. Follow–up letter: 426 1/2, no. 4, 5 April 1853.

p.107. Dorothea Dix: See Francis Tiffany, *Life of Dorothea Dix* (Boston, 1890): for her early life, Gladys Brooks, *Three Wise Virgins* (N.Y., 1957), pp. 3–80, "Dorothea Lynde Dix."

p.107. Dix's Sable visit: McKenna's Journal, 26–28 July 1853.

p.107. Wreck *Guide*: Hfx. *Novascotian*, 8 Aug. 1853; PANS RG 1, vol. 427, Log Books of the Schooner *Daring*, 28 July 1853.

p.108. D. Dix's Sable project: See Tiffany, 216–20.

p.110. Wreck *Arcadia*: McKenna's Journal, 27–29 Nov. 1854; PANS RG 1, 426 1/2, no. 15, McKenna letters: 6 Dec.1854 (excerpt in Tiffany, 222–23); Farquhar, 33–35.

p.113. Dix's efforts for lifesavers: See Tiffany, 225–27 (includes her letter to McKenna, 1 October 1855).

p.114. Farquhar recalled: p. 32.

Chapter Ten

p.115. S.S. *State of Virginia*: *New York Times*, 18 July 1879; N.R.P. Bonsor, *North Atlantic Seaway: an Illustrated History of the Passenger Services Linking the Old World and the New* (Prescot, G.B.: T. Stephenson and Son, 1955), 281.

p.116. Janet Carnochan: The source for the story of her Sable adventure is her own account, written partly at Sable Island; the most accessible version is Janet Carnochan, *Shipwrecked at Sable Island* (Ed. by John L. Field; St. Catharines, Ont., 1986); it is Pamphlet No. 44 of the Niagara Historical Society, of which she was one of the founding members in 1895 and the first president; will be referenced as Carnochan.

p.117. Wreck *State of Virginia:* Besides Carnochan, see *NYT* and *Halifax Morning Herald*, 18 July 1879.

p.117. "With a message...": Carnochan, 4.

p.119. "Wifeless and childless"*: NYT*, 18 July.

p.119. Marie Moutin: She was eight years old according to *NYT:* the *Morn. Her.* says "Marie Mouton" was "about 14," but it also says Alice "Wilson" was "about 4."

p.122. Lights visible 18 miles: DMF Annual Report 1872/73, xxii–xxiii.

p.123. Address of thanks: Carnochan, 14.

p.124. Second report: *Morn. Her.*, 19 July.

p.125. Burials on Sable Island: Carnochan, 12; *NYT*, 18 July.

p. 125. "I have planted lilies...": Carnochan, 25.

Chapter Eleven

p.127. Wreck *Amsterdam*: *Halifax Morning Herald*, 7 Aug. 1884; *NYT*, 7 & 8 Aug. 1884.

p.129. Ludwig's further comments: *Morn. Her.*, 8 Aug.

Pg.131. "I can account for this...": *NYT*, 18 July 1879.

Pg.132. Farquhar: See Chap. 9.

p.132. "The ship will be buried...": *Morn. Her.*, 8 Aug.

p.133. One observer: The author of an account of the salvage operation published in the newspaper as a letter from Sable Island signed only "D.B." (see PANS MG 9, vol. 25, Thomas Scrapbook, "Sable Island Bar").

p.134. Third version of *Amsterdam* episode: *NYT*, 11 Aug.

p.135. Lost men listed elsewhere: *NYT*, 8 Aug.

p.136. The actual Sable setup: See William Smith, "The Lighthouse System of Canada," pp. 39–54, 120–33 in *Nautical Magazine*, New Ser., vol. 54, pt. I (1885), 46.

p.138. Smith on *Amsterdam* episode: *Naut. Mag.*, 47.

p.140. Policy re Sable horses: See Dept. of Marine and Fisheries Annual Report 1872/73, xxvii; *Naut. Mag.*, 50.

Chapter Twelve

p.141. Boutilier takes charge: The chief sources for this chapter are PANS MG 1, vols. 4–7, R.J. Boutilier, Diaries and Letter Book, 1884–1911; the diaries, like the journals of previous superintendents, are Supt. Boutilier's daily record of Sable events; specific references to the diary will be by date only; the letter book contains copies of the official letters that will be cited in notes.

p.141. Boutilier's first reports: See Boutilier to H.W. Johnston, Agent Marine & Fisheries Dept., 12 Dec. & 16 Dec., 1884. (The Department of Marine was actually separate from the Department of Fisheries at this time and until 1892.)

p.145. Wreck *A.S.H*: 20–22 Dec. 1884; Boutilier to Johnston, 22 Dec.

p.148. Sunday burial: 21 Dec.

p.148. Lone survivor: B. to J., 22 Dec.

p.149. List of awards: DMF Ann. Rep. 1884/85, appendix 39, p. 247.

p.150. Presentation of medals: 25 March 1886.

p.150. Guinan sick: 1 April 1886.

p.151. Death of Guinan: 24 Sept. & 9 Oct. 1886.

p.152. Sable telephone system: 21–23 Sept. 1885.

Chapter Thirteen

p.153. Wreck *Gerda*: (See Chap. 12, first note, re Boutilier's diaries and letter book.) 27–28 July; Boutilier to H.W. Johnston, 4 Aug. 1890.

p.153. Rocket apparatus: See *The Oxford Companion to Ships and the Sea* (Ed. Peter Kemp; London, 1976): 106, Breeches buoy; 208, Costain gun.

p.160. On Wednesday: 30 July.

p.160. Capt. Olsen & crew depart: 9 Aug.

p.160. Boutilier's report: B. to J., 4 Aug. 1890.

p.162. *Grace Darling*: See Chap. 9.

p.162. Mrs. Egan's wreck (*Raffaele D.*): 8–10 July 1896; B. to J., 14 July 1896.

p.163. Eyewitness description: Hfx. *Evening Mail*, 27 July 1896.

p.164. Boutilier issued clothing: 9 July.

p.165. "And she thumped heavily...": *Eve. Mail*, 27 July.

p.165. "It is a matter for congratulations...": B. to J., 14 July.

p.166. Wreck chart: *Known Wrecks on Sable Island* (Hfx., 1882).

p.166. Macdonald declared elsewhere: "Notes on Sable Island," 19 (See next note.).

p.166. Series of articles: "Notes on Sable Island," "Sable Island, cont'd," and "Sable Island, Number 3" in N.S. Institute of Natural Science, *Proceedings and Transactions*, VI, 12–33, 110–19, & 265–80.

p.167. Macdonald's doomsday conclusion: NSINS, *Proc. and Trans.*, VI, 280.

p.170. "The Thanks of a Shipwrecked Crew": *Halifax Herald*, 29 July 1896.

Chapter Fourteen

p.172. "An odd facet...": Thomas E. Appleton, *Usque ad Mare: A History of the Canadian Coast Guard and Marine Services* (Ottawa: Dept. of Transport, 1968), 138.

p.173. Cameron on messenger pigeons: DMF Ann. Rep. 1889/90, appendix No. 21, "Messenger Pigeons," 198–210.

p.173. Downs declared his optimism: See Andrew Downs to H.W. Johnston, 12 Jan. 1891, in DMF Ann. Rep 1889/90, app. 21, p. 197.

p.173. Cameron's report: Cameron to Dep. Min. W. Smith, 2 Sept. 1891, in DMF Ann. Rep. 1890/91, app. 36, pp. 244–50.

p.173. Following Cameron's visit: See DMF Ann. Rep. 1892/93 app. 10, pp. 73–75.

p.174. Mulholland's Sable visit: (See Chap. 12, first note, re Boutilier's diaries & letter book.) 23 Nov. 1893.

p.174. Boutilier's description of storm: Boutilier to Johnston, 23 Jan. 1894.

p.175. Wreck *Robert J. Edwards*: 13–15 Jan. 1894; Boutilier to Johnston, 23 Jan.

p.177. Boutilier's message: See DMF Ann. Rep. 1892/93, cxix; *NYT*, 12 Feb. 1894.

p.178. Capt, Crittenden and pigeon: *NYT*, 12 Feb.

p.178. Capt. Mills's report: DMF Ann. Rep. 1892/93, 74.

p.179. Pigeon flights in summer: DMF Ann. Rep. 1894/95, app. 9, pp. 138–39.

p.179. Pigeon loft at Hazel Hill: DMF Ann. Rep.: 1894/95, 64; 1895–96, app. 7, p. 140; 1896/97, app. 12, p. 87; 1897/98, app. 10. p. 57.

p.179. "You will perhaps pardon me...": DMF Ann. Rep. 1898/99, app. 11, p. 62.

p.180. "This service will be discontinued": DMF Ann. Rep. 1898/99, 21.

p.180. Radio communication: Appleton, 85–86.

p.180. First Sable messages: 27 June 1905.

p.180. Wreck *Heimdal*: DMF Ann. Rep. 1910, app. 18, p. 218; 19–25 June 1910.

p.181. Sable radio station: See Thomas H. Raddall, *In My Time: A Memoir* (Toronto: McClelland and Stewart, 1976), 96–97, 108.

p.182. His best novel: See *In My Time*, 296.

Index

Index